Investigating Culture and Identity

Paul Taylor

▄▄ Collins Educational

An Imprint of HarperCollins*Publishers*

Published by Collins Educational
An imprint of HarperCollins*Publishers*
77–85 Fulham Palace Road
Hammersmith, London W6 8JB

www.**Collins**Education.com
On-line support for schools and colleges

First published in 1997
Reprinted 1998, 2000

ISBN 0–00–329091–3

Commissioned by Emma Dunlop
Cover design by Derek Lee
Typesetting by Derek Lee
Cartoons by Martin Shovel
Project managed by Kay Wright
Production by Emma Lloyd-Jones
Printed and bound by Scotprint

You might also like to visit
www.**fire**and**water**.co.uk
The book lover's website

Contents

Acknowledgements
The author and publisher would like to thank the following individuals and organizations for permission to reproduce material:

AKG London (pp. 15, 17 [left], 21, 103 [top left], 144, 167, 229 [both])
Steve Allen (p. 116)
Australian Tourist Commission (pp. 3, 221 [left])
BBC Picture Library (p. 183)
Brentford Football Club (p. 38 [bottom left])
Martin Brown (pp. 115, 129, 133, 240)
Patricia Briggs (pp. 16, 19 [both], 49 [top left], 55 [left], 78, 170, 215, 217)
British Heart Foundation (p. 223[bottom])
East Berkshire College (p. 112)
Eurostar (U.K.) Ltd Image Library (p. 223 [centre right])
Football Archive (pp. 39 [bottom right], 135)
HarperCollins*Publishers* (pp. 12, 146 [right])
Imperial War Museum (p. 235)
Lady Thatcher's Private Office (p. 63)
Phil Masters (p. 39 [bottom left])
Charlie Mitchell (p. 89 [left])
Modus Publicity (p. 13 [right])
PA News Photo Library (pp. 8, 13 [centre], 17 [right], 18, 38 [top left, bottom right], 49 [left], 59 [both], 66 [mid right, bottom right], 94 [both], 102 [top left], 103 [bottom centre and right], 124, 132, 150 [both], 157, 168, 201, 213, 215, 223 [top left, centre left], 238, 245)
Royal British Legion (p. 39 [top left])
Royal College of Nursing Archives (p. 77)
Telegraph Colour Library (p. 43 [right], 148, 235)
Topham Picturepoint (p. 140)
V & A Picture Library (p. 103 [bottom left])
John Walmsley (pp. 89 [centre, right], 102 [top left, bottom right], 221[right])
Kay Wright (pp. 30, 38 [top right], 39 [top right])

While every effort has been made to contact copyright holders, the publishers would be pleased to hear from any copyright holders who have been overlooked.

Introducing culture and identity

Key ideas	Key thinkers
Culture	E.O. Wilson
Sociobiology	Sigmund Freud
Instincts	Norbert Elias
Id, ego and superego	Robert Redfield
Civilizing process	David Harvey
Folk and urban societies	Stuart Hall
High, low, popular and mass culture	G.H. Mead
Absolutist and relativist approaches to culture	Charles Cooley
Modernity and postmodernity	
The Enlightenment project	
Identity	
Looking-glass self	
'I' and 'me'	

Introduction

This chapter introduces the concepts of culture and identity. It starts by looking at what is meant by culture and examines the sociological view that human behaviour cannot be explained solely in biological or genetic terms – culture provides an important influence on our social behaviour.

We then consider different types of culture, including the difference between the folk culture of traditional societies and the culture of urban industrial societies. We will also consider whether contemporary societies can be seen as characterized by a postmodern culture.

The last part of the chapter focuses on what is meant by identity and considers how our identity is shaped by our membership of society and the roles we play. We conclude by examining the impact of postmodernity on identity, in particular the claim that it has caused a fragmentation and dislocation of identity.

 In a group (or individually) carry out a brainstorming exercise. Take the word 'culture' and give as many definitions and ideas associated with the term as you can. Get one member of the group to write the ideas down as they are contributed. Don't worry about what order ideas occur in, simply record everything that is contributed by the group.

Once you have brainstormed read the section below and then discuss which of

the two types of definition each of your ideas of culture fit in with. If any of them don't fit in with either you may need to invent a third category to include these.

Defining culture

How is it possible for us to understand what other people say when they speak? Why do we share similar interpretations of written words, pictures, music and other symbols with other people? Why do we sometimes find the attitudes and behaviour of people in other societies or ethnic groups strange or difficult to understand? The answer to all these questions lies in understanding the concept of culture.

Unfortunately there is no agreed definition of the term culture. In a critical review of the subject Kroeber and Kluckhohn (1952) found over 200 definitions of the term. Raymond Williams, one of the leading British sociologists of culture, suggests that culture can be defined in two main ways. In everyday speech culture is normally taken to refer to artistic and intellectual activities. For example, art exhibitions, works of literature and music would be cited by most people as examples of culture. Williams points out that this kind of definition is:

> … now much more broadly defined, to include not only the traditional arts and forms of intellectual production but also all the 'signifying practices' – from language through the arts and philosophy to journalism, fashion and advertising – which now constitute this complex and necessarily extended field.
>
> (Williams 1981, p. 13)

Williams points out that most sociologists and social anthropologists use a second much broader definition of culture. For them culture includes the whole 'social order' or way of life of a society. This kind of definition is reflected in the work of the nineteenth-century social anthropologist Edward Tylor. He argued that:

> Culture or Civilisation, taken in its wide ethnographic sense, is that complex whole which includes knowledge, belief, art, morals, law, custom and any other capabilities and habits acquired by man [*sic*] as a member of society.
>
> (Tylor 1958 [1871], p. 1)

Thus for sociologists and social anthropologists culture is far more than art, music and literature, though these are important parts of the culture of a society. Every aspect of human life is influenced by culture since we consciously or unconsciously constantly refer to our society or social group for guidance about how to think and behave.

Cultural diversity

Take, for example, the first hour in your day. You get out of bed, get dressed, eat some breakfast, talk to members of your household and so on. In each of these mundane social activities you would be influenced by the culture of your society.

The fact that you sleep in a bed in a special room called a bedroom is the norm in British society, but a Chinese peasant in Xinkiang would probably sleep on a *kang* or raised platform with other family members in the room that is also used for eating and other everyday activities.

The clothes you dress in will probably be those which are defined as appropriate to your age, sex and social status by British culture. In other cultures norms of dress might differ widely – Australian Aboriginal Bushmen go virtually naked, while women in many Islamic cultures are expected to cover up their faces and bodies entirely when in public places.

For breakfast you might eat toast, breakfast cereal or bacon and egg. It is unlikely that you would eat sago or ants for breakfast, though these might be appealing if you were a member of the Manus tribe in New Guinea or an Australian aborigine.

Finally, you would probably converse over your breakfast in English, though you might equally speak in Welsh, Gujerati or Italian. However, the language you use would reflect the fact that you belong to a particular culture and made use of its language as your normal means of communication.

As the examples above suggest, human cultures are enormously diverse. What is considered normal in one culture may be considered deviant or offensive in another culture. However, the examples also illustrate how every aspect of social life can be seen as cultural. Our culture provides us with guidelines and rules which help us to accomplish everyday activities and relate socially to other people.

Interpretation and application activity
Think of examples of ways in which other cultures have alternative ideas of what is normal and acceptable to those of your own culture.

Biology and culture

Culture is often contrasted by sociologists with nature or biology. Things that are cultural are human creations; they involve the transformation or controlling of natural elements. The term culture originally denoted growing or cultivation. Thus a gardener or a farmer cultivates plants in a controlled way, and unwanted wild plants are eliminated as weeds. Nature is tamed and controlled to produce food for human consumption. Sociologists argue that all forms of culture are in a sense similar to this.

They involve humans developing shared ways of doing things which enable them to live together cooperatively and survive in their physical environment.

Sociobiology

Some social scientists have concluded that ultimately all social behaviour is therefore directed by natural instincts or biological drives. This argument has been most clearly developed by sociobiologists like E.O. Wilson. Wilson (1975) argues that human beings like all species are the result of a process of evolution. Humans, like all plants and animals, are the product of a process of natural selection whereby traits or characteristics which are likely to assist in survival will tend to be passed on to future generations. Over many generations these traits, for example higher intelligence or physical strength, will become spread through more of the population of the species as those who possess them are likely to be more successful in surviving, reproducing and passing on their genes to future generations.

Sociobiologists see human social behaviour as controlled by basic human drives, in particular the drives to survive and reproduce. Wilson, for example, explains differences in male and female sexuality in terms of the different reproductive roles of the sexes. A human female has to invest a lot of time and energy to rear one child. During her lifetime she has only a limited number of chances to reproduce. A male by contrast can potentially father thousands of children by different mothers. This implies that females have a vested interest in a stable relationship with one partner since, with his assistance, she is more likely to ensure that her limited number of offspring survive and pass on her genes. Males, however, have a vested interest in promiscuity. The more females a male can impregnate in order to pass on his genes, the more successful he will be reproductively. Males, it would seem, have little to gain in reproductive terms by remaining faithful to one partner.

Case Study　Genes and identity

Stephen Mobley, armed robber and murderer, is a very bad man. But he should escape the electric chair, his lawyers argue, because he was born that way. They say that generations of crooks, robbers, rapists and killers in his family gave him no real choice – his genes predestined him to a life of violent crime. Today the Georgia Supreme Court is expected to rule whether it will allow 28-year-old Stephen (also known as Tony) to undergo genetic testing and appeal against the death sentence on the results.

Violence, aggression and behavioural disorder run through four generations of the Mobley family. But so does business acumen. Stephen's father, Charles, made millions selling training shoes. There is a fine line, as one attorney put it, between aggressive success and violent outrage in the family tree.

Tony was sent to a series of institutions, ending up in Annewakee, a residential therapeutic centre which he left aged 18. His psychologist, Dr Stephen Ziegler, wrote in a 1982 report: 'Tony is unable to delay gratification … he goes from wishes to fulfilment, without intervening prac-tice, work or decision, thought or struggle … and sees everything as an attack upon himself. For some reason Tony has never internalized a true value system, only that which has direct effect on himself is important. He does not seem to have loyalty to anyone, including parents.'

In February 1991, Tony, then 24, walked into a Domino's Pizza store, cleaned out the cash register and shot the manager twice in the back of the neck. He had already committed six other armed robberies.

The argument that Mobley was predestined to murder is brought into question by the success of his father, a self-made millionaire who used what aggressive genes he had to build up his Sportshoe chain of shops. The boundaries between the criminal and the entrepreneur have always been thin. Most geneticists argue that genes provide the blueprint only for your potential, not exactly who and what you are. Environment plays a large part.

Source: adapted from Sarah Boseley,
'Genes in the dock', *Guardian*,
11 March 1995

Evaluation activity

1 *Using the extract above and any other evidence, assess the arguments for and against the view that the kind of people we are is determined by our genes.*

2 *If scientists were able to pinpoint a gene for criminal or anti-social behaviour, what implications might this have?*

Sociobiology and the problem of culture

Most sociologists have been very critical of sociobiology precisely because it explains culture in purely biological terms. Sociobiology tends to emphasize the way in which all human beings respond to the same universal biological drives. This argument comes up against some difficulties in explaining the enormous diversity of human cultures. In relation to sexual and reproductive behaviour, how do we explain the fact that in some societies men are indeed polygynous, that is, are permitted multiple wives and concubines, while in other cultures monogamy (one husband to one wife) is strictly enforced? In a few cultures (for example the Todas of South India) polyandry is permitted and a woman may have several husbands – often brothers. Sociobiology also has some difficulty in explaining why some humans apparently refuse to give in to their biological drives, for example why some individuals choose to remain celibate.

For most sociologists, the answer to these questions lies in the existence of culture. Human societies establish patterns of behaviour which govern the conduct of their members to such an extent that in many instances individuals are prepared to suppress their biological drives because they believe it is what their culture expects. For example, monks and nuns will abstain from sex because of their religious beliefs and soldiers will die for their country because of patriotism.

Instincts and biological needs

Whether human beings have instincts at all is questioned by many sociologists and biologists. One strict definition of an instinct is 'a *complex* pattern of behaviour that is genetically determined' (Giddens 1993, p. 36). The patterns of behaviour of most animal species are instinctive. For example, it has been shown that weaver birds can build complex nests identical to those of others in their species even when they have been reared separately from other birds. The ability to build a nest is therefore genetically transmitted and does not need to be learned from other birds. However, human beings must learn their behaviour from other humans. The American anthropologist Clifford Geertz summed this up when he wrote:

> … there is no such thing as a human nature independent of culture. Men [*sic*] without culture would not be the clever savages of Golding's *Lord of the Flies* thrown back upon the cruel wisdom of their animal instincts; nor would they be the nature's noblemen of Enlightenment primitivism or even, as classical anthropological theory would imply, intrinsically talented apes who somehow failed to find themselves. They would be unworkable monstrosities with very few useful instincts, fewer recognisable sentiments, and no intellect: mental basket cases.
>
> (Geertz 1965, pp. 112–13)

This is not to say that biology plays no part in human behaviour. However, what are often seen as instinctive forms of behaviour are more properly termed *reflex acts*. Thus when a person touches something hot and withdraws their hand quickly or blinks when something threatens to strike them in the face, they are responding to a reflex. As this is not a complex form of behaviour it is not strictly instinctive.

Human beings also have *biological* needs which are often expressed as drives. For example, the needs for food, sex and warmth are expressed in physical feelings of hunger, sexual desire and feeling cold. However, it is the culture of a society which influences how these feelings are satisfied. In most cultures certain foods are taboo or forbidden and people will not eat these foods even if hungry. Jews and Muslims, for example, will not eat pork, and vegetarians will not eat any meat. The extract below illustrates the importance of cultural taboos about food.

Case Study / Cannibalism

A plane carrying a group of Argentinian rugby players crashed in the Andes mountains. The survivors had run out of food and there was no sign of rescue.

'It's not going to be easy getting out of here,' said Canessa.

'But if we aren't rescued, we'll have to walk out,' said Fito.

'We'd never make it,' said Canessa. 'Look how weak we've become without food.'

'Do you know what Nando said to me?' Carlitos said to Fito. 'He said that if we weren't rescued, he'd eat one of the pilots to get out of here.' There was a pause; then Carlitos added, 'That hit on the head must have made him slightly mad.' 'I don't know,' said Fito, his honest and serious features quite composed. 'It might be the only way to survive.'

Inside there was silence. The boys cowered in the plane. Canessa told them that the meat was there on the roof, drying in the sun, and that those who wished to do

so should come out and eat it. No one came, and again Canessa took it upon himself to prove his resolution. He prayed to God to help him do what he knew to be right and then took a piece of meat in his hand. He hesitated. Even with his mind so firmly made up, the horror of the act paralysed him. His hand would neither rise to his mouth nor fall to his side while the revulsion which possessed him struggled with his stubborn will. The will prevailed. The hand rose and pushed the meat into his mouth. He swallowed it.

He felt triumphant. His conscience had overcome a primitive, irrational taboo. He was going to survive.

Source: from Piers Paul Read, *Alive*

Discussion question

Using the extract above and any other examples discuss the view that culture is such a powerful influence on human behaviour that it can often override biological drives.

Psychoanalytic theory and culture

It is not only sociologists who have questioned the view that human behaviour can be explained in purely biological terms. Sigmund Freud (1856–1939), the founder of psychoanalysis, saw human behaviour as the result of a constant conflict between biological drives and cultural constraints. Freud argued that the human personality or 'psychic apparatus' was made up of three elements, the id, the ego and the superego.

The id

The id is the part of the personality that responds directly to biological drives in the body, for example demands for food, warmth or sex. The id is the most basic part of the human personality since it is present from birth and does not require socialization. The id is governed by the **pleasure principle** – it is concerned with seeking pleasure and avoiding pain. Thus a small baby will cry for food in response to the biological drive of hunger. However, even as adults we may give in to the impulses of the id when we behave selfishly or impulsively rather than obeying social restraints on our biological drives.

The ego

The ego is described by some psychologists as the executive of the personality; it is concerned with thinking, planning and decision making. It is the ego which enables us to distinguish between a wish and reality, subjective from objective and so on. The ego is governed by the **reality principle** – it enables the selfish demands of the id to be reconciled with the reality of the world surrounding the individual. Thus the child moves from being a baby whose demands are entirely centred on itself to a person who has come to terms with the reality that a demand for food may not be met if it is not the appropriate time for a meal.

The superego

The superego is the moral part of the personality concerned with right and wrong behaviour. Its formation involves the internalization of the moral values of a person's culture so that they become an integral part of how they think and behave. The superego operates through both the **conscience**, which punishes with guilt the individual who offends morals, and the **ego-ideal**, which rewards good behaviour with self-esteem and pride.

Sources of personal conflict

For Freud the human personality is inevitably subject to tensions and conflicts because of the conflicting demands of the id and superego. The id demands that biological drives are satisfied but the superego often conflicts with this, demanding conformity with social norms. Freud thus recognizes the tension between biology and culture in human behaviour. For example, the libido or urge for sexual gratification is a powerful biological drive; however, a variety of social norms restrict how, when and with whom it is socially acceptable to find sexual gratification.

For Freud culture as represented by the superego was necessary in order to keep the selfish biological drives of the id in check. However, excessive self-control could also be unhealthy, leading to repression. Thus Freud suggested that a healthy individual was one whose ego was able to compromise between the demands of the id and the superego. (Freud's theories about sexual development are discussed on pp. 84–5.)

 Application and evaluation activity
Discuss, using examples, how far Freud's concepts of id, ego and superego are useful in explaining human behaviour.
You might consider situations in which your desire for immediate pleasure was contradicted by what your conscience or cultural norms were telling you. How did you – in the form of your ego – resolve this conflict?

Evaluation of Freud

Freud's ideas have had an enormous influence on the social sciences including sociology. The American sociologist Talcott Parsons (see pp. 44–8 and 85–6), for example, developed his theories to explain how the social system served to constrain individualistic behaviour and harness biological drives to socially useful ends. However, many sociologists feel that Freud's work fails to take into consideration the importance of cultural differences. His ideas were largely based on his analysis of wealthy Viennese patients, but he assumed that the theories derived from these observations were universally applicable to all societies. However, the kind of neurotic symptoms from which many of Freud's patients suffered may have reflected the formal and sexually repressive nature of their society at that time. Some social anthropologists, such as Bronislaw Malinowski (1929), have suggested that the psychological development of individuals in other cultures can be very different where there is less sexual repression or where boys are less subject to authoritarian control by their fathers.

Freud was not a sociologist, thus his work fails to consider fully how aspects of culture such as norms and values come into existence. While Freud gave some consideration to this in his later work, his work focused mainly on the workings of the individual psyche rather than how people living together in societies create and recreate their own cultures.

Norbert Elias: the civilizing process

The German sociologist Norbert Elias (1978) developed Freud's view that culture and civilization involved the imposition of social constraints on human biological impulses. Elias saw this as something which had developed in modern times with the rise of nation states. In the Middle Ages, for example, the centralized state was relatively weak and consequently its ability to control individuals' behaviour was limited. Constraints on sexual and aggressive urges were relatively weak and there was little to stop those with power using violence or coercion from getting their own way.

Elias argued that as a centralized state exerted increasing control, a **civilizing process** occurred. This involved the imposition of increasing restraint on personal behaviour. Greater refinement in manners and higher standards of personal behaviour spread from royal courts down to ordinary people. In the Middle Ages it was common for strangers to share a bed in an inn, for people to eat with their fingers from common bowls and for both men and women to go to the toilet in public. By the late Middle Ages textbooks on etiquette were advising the nobility that activities such as burping, breaking wind, spitting and picking one's nose in public were

Do contemporary concerns about violence in society support or refute Elias's theory?

considered uncouth and bad mannered. By the nineteenth century such behaviour was increasingly seen as unacceptable in all but the lowest classes.

For Elias the kind of personality found in modern societies is entirely different from earlier societies, involving a need for far greater standards of personal control. Moreover, in modern societies one of the main factors distinguishing the higher social classes from the lower classes in cultural terms is the higher degree of refinement in manners and restraint in personal behaviour.

Critics of Elias have pointed out that events such as the Holocaust, in which six million Jews were murdered by the Nazis, cast some doubt on his theory. However, Elias was himself a Jewish refugee from Nazi Germany and believed that the civilizing process is not an even one. Civilization moves backwards (as with the Holocaust) as well as advancing.

Application and evaluation activity
Think of your own examples of ways in which modern societies impose higher standards of personal control on individuals than those of the past.

Culture and society

While sociologists contrast culture with the biological aspects of human behaviour, culture is not the same as society. Bill Sugrue and Calvin Taylor argue that culture 'is located in society as a unique mediating apparatus between the individual on the one hand, and the system of structural interrelationships (e.g. made up of social institutions such as marriage and the family) on the other' (1996, p. 11). For example, all societies have some form of kinship structure but these kinship structures are patterned by the culture of society. Thus in a culture where polygyny is permitted different kinds of kinship structures will be found from a culture which values monogamy.

Figure 1.1 illustrates how culture helps to provide a link between the individual and the structures of his or her society.

Figure 1.1 Where does culture fit?

Source: adapted from Sugrue and Taylor (1996)

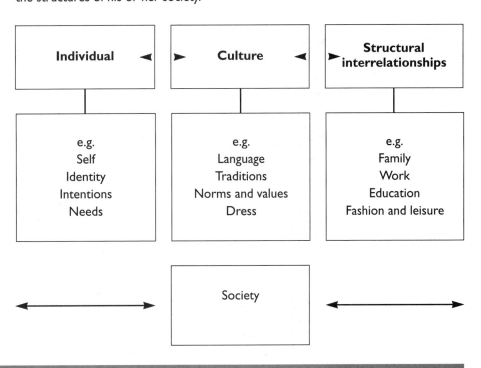

Interpretation and application activity

Take one area of social life other than family life, for example work, education, fashion or leisure, and discuss the following:

1 How social behaviour can be seen as organized into structural relationships, i.e. where the behaviour of groups of people is patterned by society.

2 How the culture of society helps to provide guidelines for individuals in this area of social life, for example norms or rules of behaviour.

Folk and urban societies

In simple societies such as tribal societies there is little social differentiation. In other words, most people share a common way of life, do similar work and are often bound together by ties of kinship. The social anthropologist Robert Redfield (1947) described such societies as **folk societies** and contrasted them with **urban societies** – large-scale, industrial societies where most of the population live in towns and cities. Redfield was not suggesting that all societies fitted into one or the other of these categories; he saw them as at either end of a continuum, with many societies sharing some of the characteristics of both types. For example, Redfield's own research in Mexico was based on a tribal settlement, a peasant village, a town and a city which he saw as representing successive stages moving from the folk to the urban end of the continuum. The main characteristics of each type of society are summarized in Table 1.1.

Table 1.1 Characteristics of folk and urban societies

Folk	**Urban**
small	large
sacred	secular
spontaneous	restrained
intimate	impersonal
ascribed status	achieved status
traditional	rational
family centred	'mass society'
cohesive	individualistic
homogeneous	heterogeneous
low mobility	high mobility

Source: adapted from Redfield (1947)

Interpretation and application activity

Discuss what is meant by the terms in Table 1.1 and check that you understand them.

Give an example of one society which could be described as a folk society and one which could be described as an urban society. Consider how far each has the characteristics of its type listed above.

Social solidarity in folk cultures

It would be an oversimplification to classify all small-scale pre-industrial societies as being in some way culturally similar; however, Redfield's classification of folk society may have some validity. Such societies often share a high degree of cultural homogeneity, in other words, their members share common norms and values. Emile Durkheim (see p. 35) described this as a system of mechanical solidarity, where members of society are bound together by shared experience and commitment to common beliefs and cultural symbols. Folk cultures are also often characterized by a high degree of respect for tradition, as in the example below.

> A native American chief describes his upbringing as a member of the Blackfoot tribe:
>
> Blackfoot mothers spent long hours telling their children the legends of the tribe. Long Lance recalls that, 'We had a legend for everything that was good, and the more we youngsters lived up to the legends which our mother told us the more highly respected we were in the tribe.' Children were told stories about the 'great shame' befalling those who told lies and the prestige which results from courage and brave deeds. Long Lance states, 'We had no Bible as the white boys have; so our mothers trained us to live right by telling us legends of how all the good things started to be good.'
>
> Source: from Long Lance (1956)

Interpretation and application activity

1   *In what ways might myths and legends help to reinforce social solidarity in folk societies?*
2   *Why are most urban industrial societies less respectful of tradition than folk societies?*

The urban way of life and mass culture

Redfield's theory has been criticized for oversimplifying the differences between different societies. However, his approach does highlight the existence of important differences between the culture of societies which are small scale, rural and pre-industrial and those which are large scale, urban and industrial. Some sociologists, notably Georg Simmel (1950) and Louis Wirth (1938), have argued that urban societies have a distinctive **urban way of life** characterized by anonymity of the individual, superficial social relationships and a competitive and calculating approach to life.

This type of approach subsequently led to the development of mass society theories which argued that the erosion of ties of kinship, neighbourhood and community was leading to a society of isolated and atomized individuals where people increasingly relied on the mass media as a means of communication. Some theorists, such as the Frankfurt School (see pp. 64–5), saw this as leading to a **mass culture** where differences of class and locality were being obliterated by a common culture disseminated by the mass media.

More recently this kind of approach has been criticized for failing to take into account the cultural diversity of urban industrial societies. Elsewhere in this book you will find numerous examples of research illustrating the way in which differences of class, gender, ethnicity, age and many other factors create cultural diversity and a range of identities in contemporary urban societies.

High culture and low culture

One source of cultural difference noted by many writers is the distinction between high and low culture. In large-scale developed societies the culture of the elite or higher social classes is often distinct from the culture of the masses or the lower classes. For example, in Britain aspects of culture such as opera, the theatre, fine art, literature and intellectual films can be seen as examples of high culture. These aspects of culture are seen as having some artistic merit but also as requiring a degree of sensibility and education on the part of the audience in order to appreciate them as cultural forms. By contrast the culture of the masses or low culture is often portrayed as an inferior form of culture. Table 1.2 gives some examples of this contrast between high and low culture.

Table 1.2 Some examples of the contrast between high and low culture

High culture	Low culture
Classical music	Pop music
Shakespeare plays	West End musicals
Intellectual foreign films	Hollywood popular films
Arts documentaries	Soap operas
The Times/Guardian	*The Sun/Daily Mirror*
Booker Prize-winning novels	Popular romances/thrillers

Interpretation and application activity
Think of some examples of your own to illustrate the distinction between high culture and low culture.

Some writers have seen high culture as inherently superior to the culture of the masses. The literary critic F.R. Leavis feared that high culture was being eroded by the spread of a mass culture purveyed by the mass media. He believed that there was a risk that media, such as television, would lower the cultural standards of the population and turn people away from more intellectually demanding cultural forms such as English literature. A similar concern can be seen in recent revisions of the National Curriculum for schools where, at the insistence of government ministers, a list of approved texts for English was introduced and Shakespeare was made a compulsory part of the curriculum.

Evaluation question
Should the government decide what aspects of culture are worthy of study in the school curriculum? If not, who should decide and on what basis should the selection be made?

Low culture or popular culture?

Many sociologists and cultural theorists reject the notions of high culture and low culture, arguing that it is not possible to claim that one culture is intrinsically superior to another. The French writer Pierre Bourdieu, for example, argues that the culture of the dominant class is only regarded as superior because it holds power in society and is able to claim that its cultural forms are better than those of the working class. Bourdieu claims that middle-class children succeed in the education system not because they are more intelligent but because of their familiarity with the culture of the dominant class, which is required in order to achieve success in examinations and other measures of educational success. (Bourdieu's ideas are discussed in more detail on pp. 67–70.)

Other writers have argued that the culture of ordinary people is just as much a matter for academic research as high cultural forms such as art or literature. These writers prefer to use the term **popular culture** rather than low culture. For example, the Centre for Contemporary Cultural Studies (CCCS) has carried out research into cultural forms such as television, advertising, youth subcultures, fashion and teenage magazines. The CCCS argues that what might appear on the surface to be mundane and simple aspects of culture, such as a teenage fashion, often carry deeper meanings that can be analysed in the same way as a work of art.
(See pp. 151–5 for a discussion of the CCCS's work on youth subcultures and pp.165–9 for a discussion of semiotic analysis of popular culture.)

Evaluation activity
Using the pictures above and examples of your own discuss the questions below with other students in a group.

1 *Is high culture necessarily superior to popular culture?*
2 *What are the arguments for and against studying popular culture in the same way as high culture?*

Absolute and relative approaches to culture

The debate about high and low culture is part of wider debate between two opposing views of culture: absolute approaches to culture, which see some cultures as inherently superior to others, and relative approaches, which argue that it is impossible to judge cultures by any objective measure.

Absolutist approaches

Absolute views of culture argue that some cultures or cultural forms can be seen as absolutely better than others. Thus someone who takes an absolute view of culture might argue that the work of Shakespeare is an inherently superior form of literature to a romantic novel by Barbara Cartland. This view is also taken by many members of particular cultures who view their own culture as essentially superior to others. Thus Muslims or Christians may believe that their religions are based on some ultimate truth. While members of each faith may be tolerant of those who have other beliefs, they will still be forced to the conclusion that other beliefs are ultimately false since they contradict those of their own faith.

Relativist approaches

Most sociologists, to varying degrees, approach culture from a more relativist standpoint. This approach implies that it is not possible to judge one culture as objectively superior to another. A culture can only be judged as good or bad by employing the morality of another culture; how do we then judge the rightness of the culture we are taking as our own moral standpoint? For example, if as a Christian I judge Muslims to be mistaken in their beliefs, I am judging them by the standards of Christianity, but how do I judge objectively whether Christianity is correct?

Taken to its extreme this viewpoint implies that there is no such thing as truth and falsity, only different cultures' versions of the truth. Thus the Christian belief that life on earth was created by God and the scientific theory of evolution are simply different truths; we should not attempt to judge one as superior to the other. This extreme version of relativism clearly creates problems for sociologists, who aim to make objective statements about the nature of the social world. How are we to establish that the sociologists' version of events is any better than anyone else's? Moreover, this approach implies that the Nazis' view that the killing of 6 million Jews in the Holocaust was politically acceptable is equally valid to the view of those who would condemn it as an act of mass murder.

Soft relativism

Many sociologists take an intermediate position between absolutism and relativism, what has been described as 'soft relativism'. Thus most sociologists accept that we need to be cautious about judging other cultures by our own standards while at the same time insisting that some claims about truth rest on more scientific evidence than others. For example, some native American peoples such as the Moki of Arizona engage in rain dances to encourage rain when there is a drought. Western scientists might argue that this is based on a misplaced faith in the efficacy of the rain dance. However, anthropologists who have studied such rituals point out that they play an important role in binding members of a community together in an expression of shared beliefs, something for which western societies arguably provide few opportunities.

While sociologists are reluctant to condemn cultural beliefs as false or mistaken, many sociologists use the concept of **ideology** to imply that certain beliefs involve a distortion or concealment of the truth. Feminists, for example, refer to the concept of patriarchal ideology. This implies that the culture of society is male-dominated and provides a view of the world that is favourable to men, one in which women and their experience of the world is ignored or denied any importance. The concept of ideology thus implies that sociology can play a role in unmasking certain beliefs and showing that they are one-sided or primarily serve the interests of one section of society at the expense of another. We return to this argument in Chapter 3.

Modernity and culture

Many sociologists see the distinction between high culture and popular culture as something that emerged with modernity. It is only in modern times that the higher social classes have become literate and received the formal education that allowed them to develop the tastes and sensibilities necessary to appreciate high cultural forms such as literature or classical music. In most traditional or folk societies there was little differentiation between the culture of dominant groups and that of ordinary people.

Modern societies are seen by sociologists and historians as emerging in Europe around the sixteenth century with the decline of feudalism and the challenges to traditional beliefs provided by the Renaissance and the Reformation. The Renaissance encouraged artists and philosophers to re-examine the cultures of ancient Greece and Rome and this led to a questioning of many of the established ideas of the Middle Ages. This was followed by the Reformation, when the Protestant churches broke away from the supremacy of the Roman Catholic Church. Again, the established religious ideas of the Middle Ages were questioned and members of many European societies were offered a choice of alternative religious beliefs.

The French Revolution was based on the belief that it was possible to create a better society based on 'liberty, equality and fraternity'.

The Enlightenment

Probably the most important development in producing a modern outlook on life was the Enlightenment of the eighteenth century. The Enlightenment is a term used to describe the new ways of thinking associated with science and rationality which challenged belief systems based on religion and superstition. The Enlightenment led to the increasing application of scientific thought, both in understanding and exploiting the natural world and in attempting to understand human societies.

The Enlightenment was also associated with new social and political ideas. Enlightenment thinkers believed that society should be governed by 'reason', in other words, on rational principles. This led to a questioning of the view that traditional political systems necessarily served the interests of the majority of citizens. This could most clearly be seen in the French and American Revolutions, which challenged the traditional rule of monarchs and aristocrats and led to the emergence of modern concepts such as democracy, citizenship rights and personal freedom.

Finally, the Enlightenment paved the way for a new kind of economic system, capitalism. The breaking down of restrictions on economic activity, for example on free trade and borrowing money, led to the emergence of a free-market trading system. Combined with new technologies, facilitated by scientific discoveries, this led to rapid industrialization, first in western societies and eventually worldwide, leading to the emergence of a global economy.

Modernity and globalization

The Enlightenment transformed the culture of western societies and in the long run this had an impact on the cultures of all societies. Colonial expansion in the eighteenth and nineteenth centuries followed by the emergence of a fully-fledged global economy in the twentieth century have led to a process of globalization (see p. 128). Even the most isolated societies are now touched by these developments. This makes it increasingly difficult to see the world as made up of distinct cultures. While there are of course important cultural differences between societies, each culture is increasingly influenced by other cultures, particularly by the dominant cultures of western capitalist societies.

Even the most isolated cultures can now be seen as part of a global society.

The Enlightenment project and identity

One of the most important consequences of the Enlightenment for people's identity was the emergence of a belief in progress. The belief systems of most traditional societies were religious and often emphasized the importance of preserving the status quo. The existing social system might be seen as divinely ordained. In Western Europe, for example, Christians believed in Providence – the view that things were as they were because God had provided for them. Similarly in the Hindu religion of India, events are seen as the result of *karma* – the consequences of actions in past lives which continually influence events in a cycle of birth, death and rebirth.

These sorts of beliefs were challenged by Enlightenment philosophers. They believed that human beings were in control of their own destinies and that in order to control

Auguste Comte (*left*) is often regarded as the founder of sociology. He believed sociological knowledge could be used to understand, predict and control human behaviour in order to establish a better and more rational society.

Karl Marx (*right*) was the founder of communism. Marx believed that the course of history was determined by economic laws. By understanding these he hoped to bring about a workers' revolution in order to create a classless society.

events it was necessary for them to understand them in a rational way. What sociologists often term the 'Enlightenment project' involved a belief in human progress and the capacity of people to create a better world for themselves. Many of the social and political philosophies of the modern era have been based on this kind of assumption. For example, liberalism espoused the freedom of the individual to accumulate wealth and the right to democratic political representation. Socialism, on the other hand, is usually seen as opposed to liberalism, arguing that the unrestrained pursuit of personal wealth leads to injustice and exploitation of the poor by the rich. However, both liberals and socialists in different ways are concerned with pursuing their differing visions of a better society based on personal freedom.

From modernity to postmodernity

Some sociologists believe that in the late twentieth century we are moving into a new and radically different type of society, what is often referred to as postmodernity. Postmodernism can be seen to be characterized by a loss of faith or disenchantment with the Enlightenment project. Some sociologists feel that in the latter part of the twentieth century we have lost confidence in our ability to control the world scientifically or to understand rationally what is going on in society.

Postmodernism in architecture

The loss of faith in progress can be seen in the emergence of postmodernism in the field of architecture. Modernism in architecture developed most fully in the 1920s. Modernists rejected all previous forms of architecture on the grounds that they were more concerned with outward form rather than function. Modernists advocated a style that emphasized rational principles and the design of buildings purely for the function for which they were intended. Modernist architects such as Le Corbusier opposed the use of decoration or symbolism in their buildings and argued that architects should become more like engineers than artists. By the 1950s modernist ideas had resulted in the international style of architecture based on large, mostly rectangular buildings constructed from materials such as steel, concrete and glass.

Modern high-rise housing was seen as a solution to slum living in the post-war period, but large numbers of such buildings have been demolished in recent years as they failed to live up to their designers' expectations.

By the 1970s, however, the faith of the modernists that their new style of building would provide the basis for a better living environment was proving to be misplaced. Large, impersonal and soulless buildings such as high-rise office blocks and apartments came under increasing criticism. The American architect Charles Jencks argues that 'Modern architecture died in St Louis, Missouri on July 15, 1972 at 3.32 pm' (1977, p. 9). This was the moment that the Pruitt-Ighoe housing project was dynamited. The project was an ambitious public housing scheme designed to eradicate poverty and provide better living conditions. However, the project suffered recurrent vandalism at the hands of its unimpressed inhabitants and swallowed up millions of dollars in attempts to renovate it. For Jencks, the destruction of this housing project symbolizes the whole loss of faith in modern architecture's ability to improve people's lives and by implication the whole Enlightenment project.

Postmodern architects reject the grand ambitions of modernists and have embraced more playful and divergent styles. Postmodern buildings typically draw on a wide range of architectural styles and may combine these in a random and eclectic fashion. The styles of Las Vegas are often seen as typical of postmodern architecture since they reject any distinction between high art and popular culture. For example, Caesar's Palace has a Roman theme but looks more like a Hollywood film set than a real ancient Roman building. Another Las Vegas casino is shaped like a huge pyramid, harking back to ancient Egypt, but with modern overtones of blue glass windows and a powerful searchlight shining up vertically from the pyramid's apex. Many of these characteristics of postmodern architecture can be seen in the styles of other postmodern cultural forms such as music, films, television and advertising (see also pp. 216–17).

Postmodern culture

Sociologists, like David Harvey (1990), believe that we are witnessing the emergence of a postmodern culture. Harvey argues that the kind of change seen in the field of architecture is now apparent in all cultural forms, including music, television, films, advertising and fashion.

In all these areas the distinction between high culture and popular culture is increasingly blurred. For example, television has popularized classic novels such as

The Pompidou centre, Paris (*left*), an example of a modern building.

The pyramid at the entrance of the Louvre in Paris (*right*) is a postmodern building.

Jane Austen's *Pride and Prejudice*, Verdi opera has been used as a theme tune for World Cup football and advertisers have used images based on famous paintings such as the *Mona Lisa* to sell their products.

Postmodern cultural forms are also seen as more concerned with surface image and style rather than content or a serious message. Just as postmodern buildings contain playful allusions to other cultural forms (the AT&T building in New York has a roofline like the top of an eighteenth-century Chippendale chair), so other cultural forms mix and match styles and genres. A good example of this is the development of 'world music', where artists from one musical tradition draw on elements of other cultures, for example Paul Simon's use of South African musical styles or the development of bhangra (a cross between western rock and traditional Indian music) by British Asian musicians.

Globalization and culture

A number of sociologists have linked the emergence of postmodern culture to the process of globalization. **Globalization** describes the process whereby what happens in one society is increasingly interconnected with events in other parts of the world. This implies that cultures can no longer be seen as separate from one another (if they ever were). Thus even in remote parts of relatively underdeveloped societies people can be found drinking Coca-Cola, wearing baseball caps and watching western television programmes dubbed into their own languages. This all has the effect of further encouraging the mixing and mingling of different cultures or elements of cultures which is seen as a characteristic of postmodernism.

Application activity
Suggest other examples of how globalization might be breaking down the barriers between different cultures.

Postmodernity or higher modernity?

Not all sociologists agree that the emergence of these new cultural forms necessarily mean that we are moving into a postmodern society. Some sociologists argue that we are simply moving into a higher stage of modernity. Writers such as Anthony Giddens (1990) argue that the breaking down of barriers between cultures has been a feature of all modern societies. Since the beginning of modern times there has been a **compression of time and space** as faster travel and better communications have made distances between places seem shorter. Developments in the twentieth century such as computer technology, telecommunications and air travel have simply accelerated this process.

Moreover, one of the dominant features of modern cultures has been that cultural forms have become **commodified**. In other words, songs, stories or visual images become things to be bought and sold at a profit. In contemporary societies new, supposedly postmodern cultural styles may have emerged. However, many of these are still linked to huge global cultural industries such as advertising, broadcasting, music and publishing which seek to exploit new styles for commercial profit.

We will return to debates about modernity and postmodernity throughout this book and review them in detail in the final chapter. We now turn to the issue of personal identity and its relationship to culture.

Identity: who am I?

The concept of culture suggests that members of social groups share common norms, values and ways of interpreting the world around them. This suggests that how we see ourselves – our **identity** – can only be understood in relation to our culture.

Seventeenth-century poet John Donne's famous statement, 'No man is an island', neatly sums up what sociologists have to say about culture and identity (though most sociologists would include 'woman' as well!). In other words, our identity or image of ourselves is formed through our interaction with other people. Cases of individuals who have been isolated from contact with other human beings reveal the importance of socialization or the learning and acquisition of culture in the formation of social identity (see the case of Isabelle on p. 29).

> *Interpretation and application activity*
> *Take a sheet of paper and head it 'I am …'. Underneath complete the sentence in ten different ways.*
>
> *In small groups discuss your ten statements beginning 'I am …' with other students. In particular compare similarities and differences between your statements about your personal identity and those of others.*
>
> *Finally, discuss in your group how many of the statements about your personal identity in some way identify you as part of a group or in a relationship to other people. What is the significance of this?*

Society and identity

Identity is a concept used by sociologists to describe the way we see ourselves in relation to other people. If you completed the activity above you may well have written down statements such as 'I am a man/woman', 'I am a father/mother/son/daughter', 'I am overweight/shy/fun to be with', 'I am studying sociology' and so on. Most of these statements will probably say something about how you see yourself and more importantly about your relationship to others. Identifying as a man or woman is what sociologists call a gender identity. We also develop identities in families or other groups as fathers, daughters, students, workers and so on. Finally, we come to see ourselves as having certain characteristics such as being 'a good friend' or 'a tough boss', often because we are described or treated as such by other people.

For sociologists, the identity of the individual is inseparable from his or her place in society and how the individual is defined by the culture of that society. In the process of socialization we acquire a social identity and develop roles for ourselves in our relations with other people. For example, a disabled person may consider their disability to be an important part of their identity because in our society people who are disabled are treated as different and, unfortunately, in some cases as inferior. Disabled people have some choice in how to deal with this. Some may passively accept being treated as inferior, so this becomes part of their identity. Others may reject the way they are labelled by society and fight back by emphasizing their abilities rather than their disability. However, it is difficult in either case for the individual to ignore entirely the way society has categorized them.

Alternative conceptions of identity

Stuart Hall distinguishes three different conceptions of identity which he describes as: 'those of the (a) Enlightenment subject; (b) sociological subject; and (c) postmodern subject' (1992, p. 275). We will now examine these in turn.

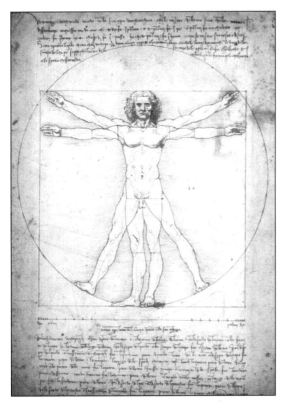

The Enlightenment subject

We have already encountered the view of society which emerged with the Enlightenment. It emphasized the possibility of human progress and rational understanding of both the natural and social worlds. The subject or individual human being was seen as a unified individual endowed with capacities of reason. People were seen as having an inner core or self which remained more or less fixed throughout life. This was the person's identity or sense of self. Moreover, this identity was seen as internally consistent – there was no sense of one part of a person's personality or identity being in conflict or contradiction with another. The Enlightenment view of identity was very individualist; each person was seen as unique and fully in control of their own consciousness and actions. Identity was also seen very much in male terms by Enlightenment thinkers; women were not seen as being as well endowed with the capacity for reason as men.

The sociological subject

The sociological conception of identity corresponds to the kind of view outlined above in the section on 'Society and identity'. While Enlightenment thinkers saw individuals as autonomous and self-sufficient, sociologists have emphasized the way in which we form a sense of ourselves only through our interaction with others. This idea was first fully developed by the American social psychologist George Herbert Mead (1863–1931).

The self and others

Mead taught at the University of Chicago in the 1920s and 1930s and was influenced by Charles Cooley's (1902) concept of the **looking-glass self**. Cooley suggested that each individual constantly monitors how his or her self is reflected in the reaction of other people. For example, if other people laugh at us we may react with embarrassment because the self we would like to project is not the one perceived by others. If others praise us this may make us proud and increase our self-esteem. Thus Cooley suggests our self-image and self-esteem reflect how others react to us.

Mead: the I and the me

Mead (1934) argues that the self has two aspects, the **I** and the **me**. The I is the thinking and acting part of the self, similar to Freud's ego. It is the 'I' which makes sense of events going on around the individual and also considers the 'me' in present, past and future situations. The 'me' is the self on which the 'I' reflects; it corresponds to Cooley's looking-glass self. For example, if I remember a past event with embarrassment because I made a fool of myself, it is the 'I' which feels embarrassed because the 'me' has been made to look stupid in front of others. I might feel the same sense of embarrassment if a person other than myself made a fool of him/herself. Mead thus suggests that one part of the self – the 'I' – monitors and makes judgements about the other part – the 'me' – almost as another person.

Mead argues that socialization involves developing the 'I' so the individual is able to engage in **role taking**. This involves the ability to be able to take on the role of others and thus to be able to see oneself as others do. Mead points out that many children's games, for example playing 'mummies and daddies' or 'doctors and nurses', involve role taking and thus help children to see the world from the viewpoint of others. These alternative viewpoints help children to start evaluating their own behaviour from the viewpoint of others – the 'I' begins to evaluate the 'me'.

Interpretation and application activity
Give one or more examples of Mead's concept of role taking from your own experience, i.e. a situation where you examined your own behaviour as other people might see you. If possible compare your examples with those of other students.

Mead argued that the self reaches its most advanced stage of development when it is able to take the role of **generalized other**. This means that the self starts to reflect the views of the society surrounding the individual and in this way a person starts to evaluate their own behaviour in the same way as the majority of people in society. Thus a child who steals something may feel guilt or shame because he or she is able to imagine what significant others such as parents or friends would think if they knew about the theft. In time the child ceases to consider these as specific individuals but their attitudes become part of the self.

Mead's work was fundamental to the development of the sociological perspective known as symbolic interactionism, which is discussed further in Chapter 8.

Case Study ⟩ A changed identity

Guthrie (1938) told the story of a female student, a dull and unattractive girl. Some of her classmates decided to play a trick on her by pretending she was the most desirable girl in the college and drawing lots to decide who would take her out first, second and so on. By the fifth or sixth date, she was no longer regarded as dull and unattractive – by being treated as attractive she had, in a sense, *become* attractive (perhaps by wearing different clothes and smiling more, etc.) and her self-image had clearly changed; for the boys who dated her, it was no longer a chore! Before the year was over, she had developed an easy manner and a confident assumption that she was popular.

Source: adapted from Gross (1992)

Interpretation and application activity

1 *What support is given to Cooley's and Mead's theories of the self by the extract above?*
2 *Discuss other examples of situations where an individual's self-concept could be changed by the way he or she is treated by other people.*

Culture and identity

Stuart Hall points out that the sociological conception of identity developed by Mead sees identity as a bridge 'between the "inside" and the "outside" – between the personal and the public worlds' (1992, p. 276). In other words, our identity provides a link between our inner sense of self and the place we occupy in the wider social and cultural world, for example our roles within families, schools, workplaces, leisure and friendship groups and so on. As Hall puts it:

> Identity thus stitches ... the subject into the structure. It stabilizes both subjects and the cultural worlds they inhabit, making both reciprocally more unified and predictable.

(Hall 1992, p. 276)

The postmodern subject

We have already encountered the argument that the culture of contemporary societies is being transformed by a shift from modernity to postmodernity. Those sociologists who support this argument also suggest that this has important implications for our sense of identity. According to Hall, the postmodern subject is seen 'as having no fixed, essential or permanent identity … The subject assumes different identities at different times, identities which are not unified around a coherent "self"'.

Fragmented identities

Postmodern theorists argue that globalization and the rapid pace of change in postmodern societies means that people increasingly feel a sense of dislocation and fragmentation in their identities. In the past individuals were more likely to live their lives in a particular community. Their place in that community was likely to be clearly defined in terms of social status, for example, wealth, occupation, gender or age. People who lived together were likely to speak the same language, share the same religious beliefs and have a common understanding of the world around them.

Today this sense of stable identities has been disrupted by the rapidity of social change and by the breakdown of traditional cultural boundaries and social distinctions. Societies like Britain are increasingly multicultural because of the coexistence of many religious and ethnic groups. Other distinctions such as those of gender and class seem to have been eroded. Even people's sense of time and space has been distorted because modern communications mean people can move from place to place more rapidly and can be in touch with what is going on virtually all over the world.

Postmodernity: liberation or disorientation?

Commentators such as Hall see these changes as leading to a **decentring** of subjects. In other words, it is increasingly difficult to have a stable and consistent sense of self. Instead people are likely to feel a sense of having many identities, some of which may be contradictory. This decentring can be potentially liberating or lead to a sense of disorientation. Those who celebrate postmodernity argue that it allows people more freedom to experiment with different identities, for example men and women are not so tied down by traditional gender stereotypes in terms of how they develop their identities. Similarly young people from different ethnic groups are seen to be mixing and matching elements of diverse cultures. For example, some young Whites have drawn on Black Caribbean and American culture for inspiration in fashion and music, while young British Asians may draw on elements of both their parents' traditional culture and aspects of western European culture.

The retreat to fundamentalism

While postmodernity may lead to a sense of liberation for some, for others it may encourage a retreat into traditional certainties. A number of sociologists have noted the spread of 'fundamentalist' social movements. These include religious sects which emphasize adherence to traditional religious teachings, for example evangelical Christianity in the United States and traditionalist sects of Islam. The spread of nationalist political movements can be seen as a similar reaction where groups appeal to an 'imaginary community' of the past and seek to resurrect it as a new nation state, for example the splintering of a country such as Bosnia into smaller ethnic states following the civil war in former Yugoslavia.

Both religious fundamentalist and nationalist groups reject the uncertainty created by the decentring of identity by replacing it with a belief in fundamental truths. Postmodernity has brought about a 'relativization' of truth – this implies that there is no ultimate truth or certainty, merely many different versions of reality or 'the truth'. For those who find this unacceptable, fundamentalist beliefs provide reassuring certainties: the Koran is the word of Allah, God did create the world in seven days, the British are superior to all other nations, Muslims will always be the enemies of Serbs, and so on.

What next?

In the next chapter we will explore the traditional sociological view that societies rely on a shared culture to unite and integrate their members. In subsequent chapters we will consider a variety of cultural divisions in society based on class, gender, sexuality, race, ethnicity and age. We will examine the sociological conception of identity further and how our own sense of identity is shaped by all these social characteristics.

We will also examine the postmodern conception of identity further by considering evidence that fixed identities in terms of class, gender and so on are breaking down. For example, feminism has traditionally focused on women's identity as women, in particular the way they are oppressed and exploited because of their gender. However, contemporary feminists, influenced by postmodern theory, have been interested in how women are affected by their identities in terms of class, ethnicity, nationality, age, sexuality, disability and many other factors.

References and further reading

Bowlby, J. (1951) *Maternal Care and Mental Health*, Geneva: World Health Organization.

Cooley C.H. (1902) *Human Nature and the Social Order*, New York: Charles Scribner's Sons.

Davis, K. (1948) *Human Society*, New York: Macmillan.

Elias, N. (1978) *The Civilizing Process*, Oxford: Blackwell Publishers.

Freud, S. (1984 [1923]) *The Ego and the Id*, Pelican Freud Library (11), Harmondsworth: Penguin.

Geertz, C. (1965) 'The impact of the concept of culture on the concept of man', in J. Platt (ed.), *New Views of the Nature of Man*, Chicago: University of Chicago Press.

Giddens, A. (1990) *The Consequences of Modernity*, Cambridge: Polity Press.

Giddens, A. (1993) *Sociology*, Cambridge: Polity Press.

Gross, R.D. (1992) *Psychology*, London: Hodder and Stoughton.

Guthrie, E.R. (1938) *Psychology of Human Conflict*, New York: Harper.

Hall S. (1992) 'The Question of Identity' in S. Hall et al (eds) *Modernity and Its Futures,* Cambridge: Polity.

Harvey, D. (1990) *The Condition of Postmodernity*, Oxford: Blackwell Publishers.

Jencks, C. (1977) *The Language of Post-Modern Architecture*, New York: Rizzoli.

Kroeber, A.L. and Kluckholm, C. (1963[1952]) *Culture: a review of concepts and definitions*, New York: Random.

Long Lance, Chief Buffalo Child (1956) *Long Lance*, London: Corgi Books.

Malinowski, B. (1929) *The Sexual Life of Savages in North-Western Melanesia*, London: Routledge and Kegan Paul.

Mead, G.H. (1934) *Mind, Self and Society*, Chicago: University of Chicago Press.

Redfield, R. (1947) 'The folk society', *American Journal of Sociology*, vol. 52, no. 3.

Read, P.P. (1993[1974]) *Alive: Story of the Andes Survivors*, Ormskirk: Causeway.

Simmel, G. (1950 [1903]) 'The metropolis and mental life', in K. Wolff (ed.), *The Sociology of Georg Simmel*, Glencoe: Free Press.

Sugrue, B. and Taylor, C. (1996) 'Cultures and identities', *Sociology Review*, vol. 5, no. 3, pp. 10–13.

Tylor, E.B. (1958 [1871]) *Primitive Culture: Researches into the Development of Mythology, Philosophy, Religion, Art and Custom*, Gloucester, MA: Smith.

Williams, R. (1981) *Culture*, London: Fontana.

Wilson, E.O. (1975) *Sociobiology: The New Synthesis*, Cambridge, MA: Harvard University Press.

Wirth, L. (1938) 'Urbanism as a way of life', *American Journal of Sociology*, vol. 44, no. 1.

2 Consensus, socialization and social solidarity

Key ideas	Key thinkers
Norms and values	Emile Durkheim
Socialization	Robert Merton
Social facts	Bronislaw Malinowski
Collective consciousness	Talcott Parsons
Value consensus	
Anomie	
Mechanical and organic solidarity	
Roles and institutions	
Pattern variables	

Introduction

The previous chapter introduced the idea that sociologists see culture as more than simply art, music, literature and so on. For sociologists culture is the whole way of life of a society. Sociologists argue that everyday social life would be impossible without culture since it provides us with guidelines about how to behave in almost every social situation and with the means to make sense of what happens to us in everyday life.

This view is emphasized by those sociologists who take a functionalist perspective. This approach argues that social life is based on consensus or agreement. The culture of a society therefore represents shared ideas and understandings about the social world which are handed down and modified from generation to generation. For functionalists the individual is inseparable from society, since it is society that gives us a place in relation to other people and guidelines about how to behave towards them. Thus individual identities are always social identities, and an individual's understanding of themselves is always linked to what they have learnt from their culture and their relationships with other people.

This chapter starts by examining the concept of socialization: the way in which we learn the ways of thinking and behaving accepted by our culture. We then move on to consider some of the main ideas of functionalist sociology, in particular the influence of two key theorists, Durkheim and Parsons. The chapter concludes by examining the view that the culture of western industrial societies represents the future for all societies worldwide.

Social norms

Sociologists see social norms as an important part of the way in which cultures guide the behaviour of individuals. Norms are guidelines or social expectations about how someone will behave in a specific situation. Social norms are important in every area of social life; the way we dress, how we behave towards other people, the meaning of words in our language and how we drive our cars on the road are all governed by norms of behaviour.

Norms are often specific to a particular situation or particular groups of people. Social status affects norms of behaviour; different norms of dress are seen as appropriate for women and men or for a doctor and someone working on a building site. Similarly, what might be regarded as normal leisure activities for a teenage girl and a 70-year-old grandmother would differ considerably.

Cultural variations in norms

Norms also vary between societies or between different social groups in the same society. In the 1950s a famous book by Nancy Mitford distinguished between U and non-U language and behaviour. U stood for Upper Class and U people used words like 'napkin' rather than 'serviette' or 'lavatory' rather than 'toilet'. The upper class was thus distinguished by norms about language. Norms about choice of words are a good illustration of how in different cultures what is acceptable varies.

Application activity
In English-speaking countries a wide range of words are used instead of 'toilet'. Make a list of examples of these terms and against each one note in which social groups or social situations it would be most likely to be used.

Try to think of other examples where different social groups use different words to mean the same thing.

Values

Social norms reflect the values of the culture of a social group. Values are ideas about what is important or what is good and bad in a society. For example, in western societies a high value is placed on the sanctity of human life. This is reflected in laws against murder and other violent acts which seek to protect human life. However, it also underlies many other norms in British society. For example, doctors and other medical professionals see it as their duty to help preserve life. Employers are expected to preserve their workers and customers from accidents that might endanger their health and safety. Complex regulations govern the sale of food, drugs, cars, electrical goods and many other products in order to ensure that consumers are not put at risk by faulty or contaminated merchandise.

Each of these rules, regulations or professional ethics represents a norm dealing with a specific aspect of social behaviour. However, they all reflect the more general value placed on human life in our culture.

Application and evaluation activity

The following might be seen as important values in British society:

1   equality of opportunity;
2   monogamy;
3   private property;
4   democracy.

In each case give examples of social norms that are influenced by this value and explain how they reflect the value in question.

When you have done this, discuss how far these values are contradicted or opposed by alternative values.

Socialization

In many animal species the newly born can walk, feed themselves and survive in their environment. This is less so in the case of mammals, which are more closely related to humans in evolutionary terms. Young mammals must be fed on their mothers' milk and often need to learn skills from adults such as distinguishing edible food or hunting. Because human behaviour is directed by norms and values, human beings have more to learn than any other species and thus there is a long period of learning and mental development from birth to adult maturity.

Sociologists describe the process by which a child learns the ways of his or her culture and becomes a skilled and competent member of society as **socialization**. Socialization involves learning the norms and values of a culture to the extent that the ways of thinking, behaving and perceiving things which are accepted by that culture come to appear normal, natural and inevitable.

Parents and socialization

Parents and other family members play a key role in socialization, since a child's parents are usually the most significant social influence on his or her early social development. Most children learn to walk, talk, go to the toilet, eat food for themselves and so on from parents. Normally children acquire these basic social skills in the first few years of life. This stage is described by some sociologists as **primary socialization**.

Some psychologists regard this stage in a child's development as having a crucial influence on his or her adult personality and later development. John Bowlby (1951) claimed that young children who were deprived of a close and loving relationship with their mothers because of death or separation would suffer from **maternal deprivation** leading to emotional disturbance and possibly deviant behaviour. However, there is considerable evidence to suggest that as long as some substitute for the biological mother takes her place children need not suffer emotional disturbance because they are not socialized by her.

Socialization in the kibbutz

The psychologist Bruno Bettelheim (1969) studied the childrearing methods in Israeli kibbutzim, where children are reared separately from their parents in special children's houses. Responsibility for socialization rests with the community as a whole, not with biological parents alone. Children are cared for by specially trained educators called metaplets; however, much of the socialization takes place through a child's peer group. Children live with a group of other children of roughly the same age and the group encourages its members to conform to group norms. Bettelheim acknowledges that kibbutz life produces a different type of personality from that found in a conventional family. However, he points out there is less risk of a child suffering child abuse and other forms of 'bad' parenting and kibbutz children seem more rather than less likely to grow into emotionally stable adults.

Case Study   Isabelle: an unsocialized child

Isabelle was an illegitimate child who was only discovered by the authorities when she was approximately six and a half years old. Her mother was a deaf mute and it appears that she and Isabelle spent most of their time together in a dark room. As a result Isabelle had no chance to develop speech; when she communicated with her mother it was by means of gestures. Lack of sunshine and inadequacy of diet meant that she suffered from a disease called rickets. Her legs in particular were affected; they were so bowed that as she stood erect the soles of her shoes came nearly flat together, and she got about with a skittering gait. Her behaviour towards strangers, especially men, was almost that of a wild animal, manifesting much fear and hostility. In lieu of speech she made only a strange croaking sound. In many ways she acted like an infant. She was apparently unaware of relationships of any kind. When presented with a ball for the first time, she held it in the palm of her hand, then reached out and stroked the donor's face with it. Such behaviour is comparable to that of a child of six months. At first it was even hard to tell whether or not she could hear, so unused were her senses. Many of her actions resembled those of deaf children.

Once it was established that she could hear, specialists who worked with her pronounced her feeble-minded.

Even on non-verbal tests her performance was so low as to promise little for the future. The general impression was that she was wholly uneducable and that any attempt to teach her to speak, after so long a period of silence, would meet with failure. Yet the individuals in charge of her launched a systematic and skilful programme of training. The task seemed hopeless at first, but gradually she began to respond. After the first few hurdles had at last been overcome, a curious thing happened. She went through the usual stages of learning characteristic of the years from one to six not only in proper succession, but far more rapidly than normal. In a little over two months after her first vocalization she was putting sentences together. Nine months after that she could identify words and sentences on the printed page, could write well, could add to ten and could retell a story after hearing it. Seven months beyond this point she had a vocabulary of 1,500–2,000 words and was asking complicated questions. Starting from an educational level of between one and three years, she had reached a normal level by the time she was eight and a half years old. In short, she had covered in two years the stages of learning that ordinarily required six. She eventually entered school where she participated in all school activities as normally as other children.

Source: adapted from Davis (1948)

Interpretation and application activity
1   What social skills normally expected in a six-year-old did Isabelle lack when she was found?

2 *What was unusual about the way Isabelle developed after she was put through a programme of training?*

3 *How does Isabelle's case illustrate the importance of socialization in human development?*

Other agencies of socialization

Families provide most people with the main agency of primary socialization. However, sociologists argue that a wide range of other social institutions and groups also play a part in socialization. These are sometimes referred to as agencies of **secondary socialization**. Secondary socialization is seen by many sociologists as building on what has been learnt in primary socialization and preparing a child to take its place in adult society. The following are seen as some of the main agencies of secondary socialization.

Schools

In many societies formal schooling does not exist. Children are prepared for adult occupational roles by learning skills from family members or other adults. In Western Europe up until the eighteenth century it was common for children of aristocratic families to go and live in other families to complete their training as adults. Working-class children were often apprenticed to a master craftsman for seven years, living in his household and learning a trade.

Formal education in schools did not become widespread in Britain until the 1870 Education Act. Since then schools and other educational institutions have taken an increasingly significant role in preparing children and young people for adult life. Schools are important not only in teaching pupils knowledge and skills needed in adult life, but also in transmitting culture. In subjects such as history, religious studies, English literature and art, aspects of the culture of the wider society are passed on to children. Even apparently culturally neutral subjects such as science involve looking at the world from the viewpoint of western scientific rationality. Schools also have a **hidden curriculum** in which values and norms of behaviour are transmitted. For example, wearing a school uniform, keeping to a set timetable and showing deference to teachers all encourage standards of behaviour which could be seen as producing disciplined future workers.

Since 1944 a daily religious assembly has been a legal requirement for all state schools in England and Wales. The 1988 Education Reform Act reinforced the principle, enshrining 'collective worship ... wholly or mainly of a broadly Christian character'.

Interpretation and evaluation activity

This extract comes from a study of a first-year secondary school humanities lesson in Manchester. The authors use it to illustrate the way in which teachers and pupils handle initial classroom encounters, in particular the way in which teachers are concerned with 'getting pupils down to work' in the first lesson.

Teacher: OK, we'll do that then. In future, when you come into this lesson, you come in, you put your bag on the floor by your place and then quickly go and get your booklet yourself, and you'll find that it works. You might think that there'll be sixty kids all charging over there at the same time, but it doesn't happen. You'll find that you'll be able to come in, walk quietly over to the trolley, get the booklet that you need, go back to your place, and you'll be ready to start work … Are you listening?

Pupil: [*Nods*]

Teacher: What are we going to do with your books?

Pupil: Sir, you'll put them down on the trolley.

Teacher: Right. You'll find your books on the trolley. [*Further elaboration and repetition of instructions.*] And we'll see if that works. You'll be able to come in, get your book, go and collect your booklet, sit down and get down to work. In that way, we don't have to spend ten minutes while you have to wait for everything to be done – while you have to wait for us to start you off. You'll be able to get yourself going all on your own.

The following lesson.

Teacher: Well, I'd like to compliment some people who came in and worked very well. Some people came in straight away, they remembered what they had to do. They saw the books and they saw the tray of booklets and they came in and got on with it and sorted themselves out … If you come in and see the books out like that, and if Mr – doesn't give you any instructions, what should you do? … What's the routine when you come in, what should you do?

Pupil: Sir, you get out your books and start work. [*Starting work is then elaborated again by one of the teachers.*]

Source: adapted from Tony Edwards and John Furlong, *The Language of Teaching* (1978), quoted in Burgess (1985), pp. 119–20

1   *In what way do the teachers in this extract attempt to socialize their pupils?*
2   *Drawing on your own experience of schooling, think of other examples of ways in which schools act as agencies of socialization.*
3   *Assess the importance of schools in transmitting the culture of society from one generation to the next.*

Peer groups

Peers are people of a similar social status to ourselves with whom we associate on a regular basis. They may be friends, workmates or other members of a group to which we look for approval and guidance on how to behave. For young people in particular friends of the same age may be a more powerful influence than parents and teachers. Numerous studies of education have demonstrated how certain groups of pupils reject the norms and values of their school and create what has been described as an **anti-school subculture** (see, for example, discussion of Willis's study *Learning to Labour* on pp. 207–9).

Even in adult life peer groups are important in defining norms of behaviour. In professional occupations this may be formalized through professional associations, which train their members and set standards of entry. Most professions also have ethical codes and professionals who violate these rules may be disbarred from practising. For example, doctors are governed by rules about how to behave towards patients.

In most occupations peer group control is more informal. A famous study of an electrical factory by Roethlisberger and Dickson (1939) described how groups of workers imposed an informal limit on how much work could be done in a shift. Workers who attempted to exceed this quota in order to achieve a pay bonus would be called names and even threatened with physical violence in order to encourage conformity to the group norm on output.

Research activity

Observe a group of people in a social situation, for example students in a classroom or canteen, people in a pub or colleagues at your workplace. Note down any informal norms of behaviour which are accepted by the group being studied. You may have to think hard as some of these norms may not be obvious if you are part of the group yourself! To complete the exercise, note down how you think members of the group studied are socialized into these norms. If possible, compare your findings with those of other students.

Religion and magic

In traditional societies religious beliefs often form a central part of the culture of society. Peter Berger and Thomas Luckmann (1969) describe religion as providing a **universe of meaning**. Religious beliefs provide an explanation and justification for everything experienced by people in the world around them.

The anthropologist Edward Evans-Pritchard (1937) studied the Azande tribe in the Sudan. The Azande use their belief in witchcraft to explain mysterious or unfortunate events. For example, if someone falls ill it may be blamed on witchcraft, whereas a British person might blame stress or a virus. In these circumstances one of the Azande would consult the 'poison oracle' rather than a doctor. The oracle would feed a potion to a chicken and ask the chicken questions. The answers depend on whether or not the chicken dies from the poison in the potion. In this way it is possible to establish who is responsible for causing the witchcraft and call on them to stop it.

Belief systems such as that of the Azande make perfect sense to the people who accept them and enable them to make sense of events in the world around them. Because everyone has been socialized into the same set of beliefs, this creates a sense of unity and enables everyone to interpret reality in the same way. However, Berger and Luckmann argue that it is becoming more difficult for religion to perform this function in modern industrial societies. Because there is no longer a single religious belief system but rather a multiplicity of competing faiths, religion is less convincing as an all-embracing explanation. Religion is further undermined by scientific thought, which provides another set of explanations often competing with religion. (The role of religion in society is discussed further on pp. 39–42.)

Evaluation activity

Discuss how far religious beliefs are significant in the culture of contemporary British society. You could start off by making a list of ways in which religious beliefs are significant and another list of ways in which religion is challenged by more secular norms and values.

Mass media

Many sociologists believe that the mass media, especially television and the press, are increasingly important in modern industrial societies in helping people to make sense of events in the world around them. Most people have little direct experience of the places, people and events portrayed in the mass media, thus the images and representations they see or read about are likely to be quite influential on their view of the world.

Television and newspapers provide not only an enormous amount of information but also frameworks for interpreting and making sense of this information. In this sense they have perhaps taken over something of the role of religion and traditional belief systems. When disaster befalls the Azande they turn to their belief in witchcraft and oracles to explain why this misfortune has occurred. In western societies we are likely to hear about such events through the mass media, together with commentary and expert opinion that may seek to provide a rational explanation or apportion blame. Sociologists thus see the mass media as a significant influence on social attitudes and behaviour and as an agency of socialization. (The importance of the mass media in contemporary societies is discussed in a number of places later in this book, notably pp. 178–84.)

Research activity

Watch, or if possible video, a TV news programme. Take one item in the programme and analyse its content. First, list any factual information in the item. Next, list those elements in the report that could be described as opinion, interpretation or comment. Using the information from your analysis, discuss how far it suggests that the mass media transmit cultural values as well as information.

Resocialization

The functionalist approach to socialization tends to portray it as a process of preparation for adult life, as something which is completed once a child takes on his or her adult role. However, many sociologists recognize that socialization continues throughout a person's life. Every time we encounter a new social situation, meet new people or take on a new role, we are resocialized. This concept is particularly emphasized by the symbolic interactionist approach in sociology, which suggests that life can be seen as a **career** in which individuals move from one role or status to another. At each stage in this career the individual negotiates a role for themselves with other people.

Postparental socialization

Irwin Deutscher (1962) gives an example of this in a study entitled 'Socialization for postparental life'. He argues that parents gradually adjust to the idea of children leaving home. When children go on holiday without their parents or leave home to go to university, this gives parents a chance to practise their new role of post-parenthood. In this process parents are socializing themselves for a new role. In due course the children who have left home may have to socialize themselves into the role of parents, while their parents are socialized into the grandparent role.

Resocialization and anomie

Resocialization is not always such a gradual process. In some situations individuals have to adjust very rapidly to new or changing circumstances. In these situations some individuals may not be able to cope with a situation where the norms and values with which they are familiar are no longer relevant; these people suffer from what Emile Durkheim called anomie, or normlessness (see p. 35). For example, there have been a number of cases of people who have won the National Lottery or football pools who have found it difficult to cope with sudden wealth.

Resocialization in total institutions

In other situations, individuals may be rapidly resocialized into an entirely new identity in a process that strips away their former self and replaces it with a new role based on a set of norms defined by an organization. This usually occurs in what Erving Goffman (1968) (see also pp. 194–7) calls **total institutions**, for example prisons, mental hospitals, boarding schools, monasteries and military training camps. On joining such institutions there occurs a **mortification of the self** – the old self is destroyed and replaced with a new identity. Thus in army training a new recruit is transformed from a civilian into a soldier. The recruit is given a haircut, a uniform and a rank and number, and is taught to march, salute, obey orders and so on. In this process a group of individuals socialized into different norms and roles outside the army are taught to live by the rules of the military organization they have joined. The use of uniforms and numbers or surnames means the recruit ceases to have a separate identity as an individual and becomes part of a unit.

Application activity

In pairs or small groups, take it in turns to recount a period in your life when you have taken on a new role or new responsibilities or joined a new group of people. Explain to your group what new norms or expectations this new role entailed and how you were socialized to cope with this. Compare your experiences of resocialization with those of others in your group.

Durkheim: culture and collective consciousness

The French writer Emile Durkheim (1858–1917) is commonly regarded as one of the founders of sociology. Durkheim rejected the doctrine of liberalism which was dominant in the nineteenth century. It argued that individuals are inevitably self-interested and compete with one another. More recently, this was famously expressed in a statement by former Prime Minister Margaret Thatcher: 'There is no such thing as society, only individuals and families'. Durkheim argued against this view; he claimed that societies are more than an aggregate of the individuals that comprise them. All societies require collective ideas, values and sentiments to bind them together. According to Durkheim, a society based entirely on individualism would not last long but would fall apart because of a lack of common moral principles to hold its members together.

Social facts

Durkheim described the institutions of society that cannot be explained in individualistic terms as **social facts**. These social facts exist as phenomena which are external to individuals. For example, in Britain most people speak English as the main language. Individuals do not choose to speak English but accept it as the language that is generally used for communication. The social fact that an English person speaks English cannot be explained in terms of an individual choice. The individual could of course choose to speak a different language, but most people in England would not understand them, so in practical terms we are constrained by society to speak the language of that society. In Durkheim's terms language is a social fact.

Application activity
Think of other examples of what Durkheim would call a social fact, i.e. forms of thought or behaviour which cannot be explained simply in individual terms but which originate in the shared ideas of a group or society.

The collective consciousness

Durkheim argued that it is not only language but every aspect of social behaviour which operates on individuals in this way. Individuals learn norms, values and an entire set of cultural perceptions from their society which enable them to share the ways of thinking and behaving of the rest of their society. Durkheim described these shared ways of thinking as the *conscience collective*, or **collective consciousness** of society. Durkheim went on to argue that individuals **internalize** this collective consciousness so that it becomes part of their whole way of thinking and behaving. Thus most English people do not stop to question whether they should speak English or another language; they take it for granted that this is the language that is naturally spoken in England.

Durkheim believed that individuals need society to provide them with a moral framework of norms and values. For Durkheim society was necessarily based on a moral **consensus** – agreement about what is right and wrong. In simple societies like tribal societies this is relatively unproblematical. These societies are small in scale and have little social differentiation. Individuals share a common way of life and there is little specialization in the work people do. As a result common norms of behaviour are applicable to everyone.

The division of labour and anomie

As societies become more complex, Durkheim (1984) argued that they become more differentiated. This means that different groups in society specialize in different activities – there is in Durkheim's terms a more complex **division of labour**. In peasant societies, for example, virtually everyone – with the exception of a few specialists – would be a peasant; in an industrial society there are thousands of specialized occupations. As a result it becomes harder to bind society together with a set of norms of behaviour which are common to all. For example, the ethics that direct a doctor's behaviour towards a patient would make little sense for a waitress in a fast-food restaurant.

For Durkheim this specialization of individuals that resulted from industrialization tended to weaken the collective consciousness and threatened to undermine the consensus on which society depended. Individuals would increasingly pursue their own individualistic aims without being bound by a moral code provided by society. For Durkheim the result would be a state of **anomie** – literally translated as normlessness. Anomie results from individuals not knowing what is expected of them by society and having no clear ideas of what is the right or wrong way to behave in a situation.

Durkheim argued that anomie is particularly acute at times of rapid social change, when traditional norms of behaviour appear increasingly irrelevant to a new and changing situation. Ironically, war, which would normally be seen as a cataclysmic social change, strengthens the collective consciousness according to Durkheim. The feelings of patriotism and common purpose created by war actually bind people together and provide a defence against anomie.

Merton: anomie and deviance

The concept of anomie has been used by other sociologists, most notably the American writer Robert Merton (1968). He argued that the concept of anomie could help to explain deviant behaviour. He suggested that in American culture there is a strong emphasis on achievement in material terms. Success is defined as having a highly paid job, a big house, an expensive car and so on. Unfortunately, not everyone can achieve these success goals through the conventional means provided by society – for example, by achieving educational qualifications and getting a good job. Individuals who fail to achieve success will feel a sense of anomie. Society pressurizes them to achieve success but fails to provide them with an opportunity to do so. These individuals become uncertain about how to proceed and will tend to respond in a variety of deviant ways. Merton distinguishes four main deviant responses, summarized in Table 2.1.

Table 2.1 Merton's classification of responses to anomie

Conformity	Acceptance of society's goals and adoption of legitimate methods of achieving them.	Individual achieves educational success and gets a well-paid job or sets up successful business.
Innovation	Attempt to achieve material success by illegitimate methods.	Individual turns to crime to achieve economic success, e.g. bank robber, fraudster.
Ritualism	Adoption of scaled-down goals which are easier to achieve but outwardly conformist lifestyle.	Individual 'goes through the motions' of conformity but in reality is deviant because he/she has given up goal of success, e.g. petty official.
Retreatism	Abandonment of both culturally accepted goals and norms of behaviour.	Individual drops out of society, e.g. tramps and drug addicts.
Rebellion	Rejection of society's goals and norms of behaviour in favour of an alternative belief system.	Individual is regarded as deviant by wider society but sees him/herself as conforming to an alternative set of values, e.g. religious sect members, terrorists.

Evaluation of Merton

In the 1940s and 1950s Merton's theory was highly influential in explaining deviant behaviour, especially crime. His concept of innovation in particular seemed to explain why so much crime in the United States was property crime – innovators seek to achieve economic success but by using deviant methods. A drug dealer, for example, has the same goals as a legitimate business – to provide goods which are in demand to customers at a price they are prepared to pay, and to make a profit – although, unfortunately, the commodity being sold is illegal.

Merton's theory was also criticized for a number of reasons. For example, it was not very effective at explaining crimes that had no apparent economic motive, such as violence and vandalism, or crimes perpetrated by the wealthy, such as frauds committed by top business people. More importantly, some critics have questioned Merton's assumption that everyone in society shares the same goals. It could be argued that not everyone seeks material success; whether those who seek alternative goals are necessarily regarded as deviants is questionable.

Nevertheless, many sociologists and criminologists have seen a link between social deprivation and criminal behaviour. Like Durkheim and Merton, they believe that social stability rests on the need for the majority of society to feel that the existing system is fair and just. Where significant sections of society feel the system is unjust and deprives them of opportunities available to others, they may become disillusioned with the norms and values of the wider society; in Durkheim's terms they may become anomic. The extract below from criminologist Jock Young illustrates this argument. Although Young does not use the concept of anomie in his work, his argument reflects some aspects of Merton's theory.

Evaluation activity: social deprivation and riots

Two youths stole a police motorbike in Hartcliffe, Bristol, on Thursday night; in the subsequent police chase they crashed, and were killed. Trouble ensued: crowds of young people, white and black, set fire to the local library and community centre, and looted shops. The following night there were more riots. It is a familiar pattern, repeating what has occurred in depressed estates from Teeside to Salford.

Riots are the politics of despair, the collective bargaining of the dispossessed. Whether in Brixton or Los Angeles, whenever a part of the community is economically marginalized and feels politically impotent, riots occur.

But history never repeats itself, and the causes of riots today are specific to the modern recessions. First there is a notion of consumer citizenship. With political and social rights, the affluent societies of the West have fostered new expectations. Advertising and the rules of an economy based on mass consumption teach us that if we are truly to belong to our society we must possess its glittering prizes. Hunger no longer propels the riots: in its place is the video-recorder, the BMW and the mountain bike. Kids may be robbed not for their pocket money, but for their trainer shoes or designer clothes.

It is riots and crime which have confronted the 'haves' with the despair and hopelessness of the 'have nots'. No society can permanently exclude so many people from the rewards and prospects which the majority take for granted, without bearing these consequences.

(Adapted from Jock Young, 'Riotous rage of the have-nots', *Observer*, 19 July 1992)

1 *In what ways does Young suggest that a lack of social solidarity has led to riots and an increase in crime?*

2 *Assess the usefulness of Durkheim's concept of anomie in relation to social problems in contemporary Britain. Make use of the extract above and any other evidence.*

Mechanical and organic solidarity

For Durkheim the solution to anomie was to create a new type of social solidarity in industrial societies. Simple societies were based on **mechanical solidarity**. This meant that individuals were bound together by common experiences and shared norms of behaviour. Although many tribal societies are differentiated by kinship – for example, into clans and family groups – common roles, practices and beliefs are found in each section of society. The specialization of industrial society means this is no longer possible; the doctor and the waitress in the example above have different experiences of life, and the norms that govern how they do their jobs are necessarily different.

Durkheim argued that if industrial societies were to avoid the problem of anomie they must develop a system of **organic solidarity**. This would emphasize the interdependence of different occupational groups in industrial society. Diversity could still be a source of unity if individuals recognized that they needed one another. The waitress could recognize that she needed the doctor when she fell ill and the doctor could recognize that she needed the waitress when she wanted a hamburger. In a system of organic solidarity each group would develop its own occupationally specific norms. Thus, just as doctors have medical ethics to guide them, even waiters and waitresses might have a code of conduct about how to serve customers.

Social groups and social solidarity.

Interpretation and application activity

Make a list of social groups or organizations to which you belong. In each case consider what creates social solidarity in the group. If you can't think of many examples of groups to which you belong, you could use the examples illustrated above. Examining the following questions may help in this:

1 What norms and beliefs are shared by the group?

2 How does the group deal with people within it who question some of its beliefs or break its rules?

3 What activities does the group engage in together, and how might this strengthen members' sense of belonging and commitment to the group's values?

Religion and social solidarity

Durkheim developed his ideas about social solidarity in *Elementary Forms of Religious Life* (1915). For Durkheim religion is associated with what he called the **sacred**. Things that are sacred are in some sense set apart or treated with reverence and are distinguished from ordinary or mundane aspects of the life which Durkheim termed the **profane**. Things associated with religion are sacred; for example, it is regarded as irreverent to shout or swear in a church. But even secular symbols may have a sacred quality; for example, it would be regarded as shocking for someone to burn their own country's flag. For some pop fans pictures of their idols may have a sacred quality.

Totemism

Durkheim believed that religious beliefs were one of the most effective means of creating social solidarity. To illustrate this he examined the religious beliefs of the Arunta, one of the aboriginal tribes of Australia. Australian aborigines traditionally live in small bands which travel and hunt together. However, each band is part of a larger clan which traces its descent from a common ancestor. Each clan has a **totem** or symbol; the totem may take the form of a plant or animal and is used like a flag or coat of arms as a symbol of the clan as a social group. For aborigines their totem is a sacred object and acts as a means of expressing their feelings of allegiance to their society. According to Durkheim, the totem represents not only their god but also their society. In worshipping the totem individuals also worship society as something on which they depend for life itself.

Application and interpretation activity
What sacred symbols are important to people in contemporary British society?
Consider the examples on the previous page and any other examples of your own.
In what ways do such symbols or totems strengthen social solidarity?

Rituals and collective consciousness

In participating in religious ceremonies, individuals' religious beliefs and loyalty to their tribe are strengthened. Sharing in religious rituals strengthens the collective consciousness. In collective events members of society express, communicate and understand the moral bonds that unite them. Durkheim argued that the role of religion can be seen most clearly in a small-scale simple society like the Australian aborigines. However, even in larger and more complex societies individuals need rituals and ceremonies to unite them and strengthen the collective consciousness. Durkheim argued that in complex industrial societies religion could perform the function of promoting social solidarity in a similar way to simple societies like the Australian aborigines. Durkheim believed that one means of developing organic solidarity was through national events that would bring people together in a feeling of shared beliefs and common purpose.

Civil religion in Britain and America

Civil religion is a form of religion that promotes national unity and social cohesion. There has been considerable research into what is called civil religion in American society. For example, Robert Bellah (1965) points out how in all major religions in the United States (Protestants, Catholics and Jews) there is an emphasis on loyalty to the nation state and a concern with underpinning American secular values. In this sense, religious beliefs help to support a consensus on what it means to be a good American. M.B. McGuire (1981) also observes how secular values in American society have religious overtones. Events such as Memorial Day and the Fourth of July, national monuments such as the Lincoln Memorial, and national heroes such as George Washington or Davey Crockett have a 'sacred' quality and are treated in a similar way to religious festivals, shrines or saints. In Britain there has been less research into civil religion; however, the following two contrasting views of the 1953 Coronation provide a good example.

Case Study — Two views of the Coronation

According to our interpretation of the Coronation of Queen Elizabeth in 1953, it was a ceremonial occasion for the affirmation of moral values by which the society lives. It was an act of national communion. Like Independence Day, Thanksgiving Day, May Day or any other great communal ritual, the Coronation is exactly the kind of ceremonial in which the society reaffirms the moral values which constitute it as a society, and renews its devotion to those values by an act of communion.

Just as the Coronation service in Westminster Abbey was a religious ceremony in the conventional sense, so then popular participation in the service throughout the country had many of the properties of the enactment of a religious ritual. The Coronation was throughout a collective not an individual experience. The fact that the experience was communal means that one of society's values, the virtue of social unity or solidarity, was acknowledged and strengthened in the very act of communion.

Source: adapted from E. Shils and M. Young (1953), 'The meaning of the Coronation', *Sociological Review*, vol. 1, no, 2

The very absence of shared values in Great Britain accounts for some of the attention paid to the Coronation. The Coronation provided, for some sections of the populace, some measure of respite from that condition of conflict which is more or less permanent for complex societies of the capitalist type.

From this viewpoint, the role of the press in stirring up popular enthusiasm for the Coronation is understandable. In response to the class interests it generally represents, the press continually seeks to minimize awareness of the real conflicts characteristic of British society. In this context, the personality of the Queen and her family functioned as the objects of various fantasies and identifications in a way not much more 'sacred' than the cult of adulation built up around certain film stars.

Source: adapted from N. Birnbaum (1955), 'Monarchs and sociologists: a reply to Professor Shils and Mr Young', *Sociological Review*, July

Interpretation and evaluation activity

1 What similarities are there between Shils's and Young's analysis of the Coronation and Durkheim's analysis of the role of totemism for Australian aborigines?
2 Compare the views of the two extracts above and highlight the differences between them. Which argument do you agree with and why?
3 Take any other national ritual or ceremonial event and evaluate how far it performs the function of promoting social solidarity in British society.

Alternative views of civil religion

The functionalist approach to civil religion offered by Durkheim emphasizes the way in which religious and/or quasi-religious beliefs can have a functional value for society as a whole by promoting social solidarity. There is an implicit assumption here that unity and consensus in society is for the benefit of everyone. This view is challenged by Marxists, like Birnbaum above (see also Chapter 3). They argue that religious beliefs and events that promote national unity represent an attempt to divert the attention of the populace away from real conflicts and divisions in society. From this viewpoint civil religion is seen as promoting 'false class consciousness' in the working class.

Marxism and civil religion

Marxists agree in one sense with functionalists like Durkheim since they both see religion as a unifying force. For functionalists, religion is functional because social solidarity is necessary in order to ensure social stability and avoid anomie. In this sense, common values and beliefs are beneficial to everyone. For Marxists, an apparent consensus in society is of benefit only to the ruling class, those who have wealth and power in society. They see capitalist societies as essentially exploitative and based on class conflict. Religious beliefs simply divert the working class from seeing their exploited state and trying to change society for the better. Marx summed this up in his famous description of religion as the 'opium of the people', likening it to a drug that gave people a false sense of well-being.

Brian Turner and civil religion

Some sociologists reject the view that religion is particularly significant in uniting society (whether this is desirable or undesirable). Brian Turner (1983) argues that the concept of civil religion has been extended to so many different beliefs and activities that it has become meaningless. Turner argues that there is an assumption that because civic rituals such as the Coronation, royal weddings or Trooping the Colour exist, they must have the function of integrating individuals into society. Turner argues that in a trivial sense individuals involved in these events may feel a sense of pride in their country, but he argues that this does not necessarily prove the case for the argument advanced by both functionalists and Marxists that communal rituals are functionally necessary to maintain the stability of capitalist society. (The ideas of Turner and his colleagues are discussed further on pp. 72–3.)

Social anthropology and culture

The kind of functionalist analysis developed by Durkheim was developed further by social anthropologists like Bronislaw Malinowski (1884–1942) who were interested in studying pre-industrial societies. Malinowski saw society and the culture associated with it as the way in which human beings ensure that basic needs such as food, shelter, protection and sexual satisfaction are met. In setting up social institutions to serve these needs – for example, an economic system to provide food or customs of marriage to regulate sexual behaviour – other secondary needs are created, for example the need to communicate, to control conflict and so on. Thus aspects of culture such as language, norms of behaviour and political institutions all develop in order to enable human beings to meet their needs more effectively. Like Durkheim, Malinowski emphasizes the way in which human culture is functional, enabling people to live together and fulfil their needs as human beings. This perspective emphasizes the **consensual** nature of culture; in other words, culture is based on agreed ways of doing things which are beneficial to everyone in society.

Malinowski and the Kula

Some aspects of culture seem strange or even bizarre to members of other societies. However, social anthropologists argue that these beliefs or activities may well be functional for the society concerned. Malinowski lived in the Trobriand Islands in the Pacific between 1915 and 1918 and published several books based on his research, including *Argonauts of the Western Pacific* (1922).

One aspect of the culture of the Trobriands described by Malinowski is the institution of the Kula. The Kula is a form of ritual trade. Only two types of articles are traded – *soulava* (long necklaces made of red shell) and *mwali* (bracelets of white shell). The Kula takes the form of a circle of islands round which these articles are traded. The *soulava* travel round the circle in one direction and the *mwali* in the opposite direction. Only certain men are allowed to take part in the Kula and each man has partners on either side of him in the circle with whom he trades. Men may not hang on to objects received in the Kula; there is an obligation to exchange an object for one of the other type within a fairly short space of time. The objects in the Kula have no practical use – their role is purely symbolic.

Thorstein Veblen coined the term **conspicuous consumption** to describe the way in which rich people in western societies gain status by consuming expensive commodities like champagne, caviar, Rolls Royces or sailing yachts. However, in the Trobriands status comes not from consuming or keeping things but from giving them away; generosity is valued far more highly than the acquisition of wealth.

Functions of the Kula

For the individual Trobriander, the Kula is a means of gaining social prestige by giving gifts and acquiring a reputation for generosity. However, Malinowski argues that the Kula has a deeper function in that it helps to unify scattered islands both politically and economically. By participating in the Kula, islands which might not otherwise trade with one another are encouraged to do so. Trobrianders will often undertake long and hazardous voyages to trade with other islands and, as well as trading Kula objects, other more practical goods are usually exchanged.

The Kula thus brings together the Trobriands and other islands in the Western Pacific in a network of mutual dependence, combining a number of tribes in a loosely linked social unit. Like many functionalist writers, Malinowski argues that aspects of culture may have **latent functions** – functions that are hidden and often not apparent even to members of that society. Thus the unifying role of the Kula might not be apparent to those who participate in it, just as the latent functions of totemism might not be apparent to Australian aborigines.

Mauss and gift giving

Some writers have criticized the concept of latent function, arguing that social scientists may be reading functions into social life which those involved are not aware of and which may not exist. Nevertheless, Malinowski's work on the Kula was developed by anthropologist Marcel Mauss in his book *The Gift* (1966). Mauss argues that gift giving is characteristic of all human societies and that it is always based on the principle of **reciprocity** – that the receiver returns the gift with an equivalent or larger gift. Like Malinowski, Mauss saw gift giving as a means of binding members of society together in social relationships and therefore functional for society.

Interpretation and evaluation activity
The pictures above show just two examples of gift giving, but there are, of course, many others. Drawing on as many examples as you can think of, discuss the following questions:

1   Is gift giving functional for society? Give reasons for your answer.

2   Is there always an obligation to reciprocate a gift? If so, why? If not, under what circumstances would a gift not need to be returned?

Parsons: social action and social structure

Durkheim argued that the behaviour of individuals can only be understood in the context of society. The culture of society provides the individual with an identity and makes him or her feel part of a larger social unit. These ideas were developed by the American sociologist Talcott Parsons (1902–79). Parsons became one of the leading figures in American sociology from the 1940s to the 1960s and his theories had enormous influence on the development of sociology.

Parsons believed that it was necessary for sociologists to understand the meaning which social actions had for individuals. However, like Durkheim, he argued that individuals' actions always take place within a social context – actions are not random but socially structured. Also like Durkheim, Parsons emphasized the idea that society is based on common values or consensus. Thus individuals tend to follow the patterns of behaviour which are generally agreed to be normal or appropriate to situations in their society. To illustrate this Parsons uses the example of a doctor dealing with a patient. The doctor has a degree of choice about how to behave towards the patient. However, the doctor's actions will also be structured by factors such as the way the surgery is organized, his or her own training and the patient's expectations of how a doctor should behave. In practice most doctors behave in similar ways and there is a consensus among doctors and patients about what this role involves.

 Application activity

Give three examples from your own experience where your actions towards other people are structured by their expectations of you.

Socialization

Parsons developed these ideas in *The Structure of Social Action* (1937) and in his major work *The Social System* (1951). The concept of socialization is central to Parsons's theory because he argues that it is through the process of socialization that individuals internalize the norms and values of their society. As a result of this, what Parsons calls the 'commitments' or inclinations of the individual come to be identified with those of society. For example, small children are taught that stealing is dishonest, and this reflects the value of private property in western societies. If successfully socialized, the child internalizes this value and grows up believing stealing is wrong. Thus stealing is controlled, not only by the fear of punishment if caught but by the fact that the members of society agree (there is a consensus) that stealing is wrong, as a result of which a thief might well feel guilty even if not caught and punished. Parsons uses this to explain how social order is possible, in other words, why most people most of the time appear to conform. Parsons's argument was that people conform because they have been socialized to believe it is the right thing to do. Individuals come to identify their own interests with those of society as a whole.

Roles and norms

According to Parsons, socialization involves the learning of **roles**. Roles are made up of a set of norms or expectations about how an individual will behave in a certain situation. For example, the roles of student and teacher are defined by other people's expectations of the person performing that role. Teachers are expected to know their subject, to be able to control a class, to be competent at facilitating learning and so on. Students are expected to show some interest in the subject, pay attention in class, complete work set and so on. Roles are also defined in relation to other roles.

Thus a teacher's role only makes sense in relation to students, a shop assistant's role is defined in terms of behaviour towards customers.

Parsons saw roles as one of the fundamental building blocks of society. Roles form part of larger structures or **institutions**. For example, teachers and students are part of a larger institution such as a school or college. Within this structure there are many other roles such as headteacher/principal, caretaker, canteen assistant and laboratory technician, each with different norms governing how they are expected to behave.

Interpretation and application activity

Make a list of the social groupings to which you belong (for example, family, school/college, workplace, friendship groups, clubs/leisure organizations). In each case consider the following:

1 your role in the group and what social norms define how you are expected to behave;

2 the roles of other individuals in the group with whom you interact and how you are expected to behave in relation to them;

3 how you were socialized into the role you play in each group.

Social institutions

Parsons argued that there are two main types of institutions in society – regulative and cultural institutions.

Regulative institutions are concerned with regulating social behaviour. Their main function is to limit individual self-interest for the good of society as a whole. For example, businesses need to be regulated otherwise there would be no restriction on how they operated. Firms could sell heroin or other dangerous drugs, they could adulterate food products and they could force their workers to work long hours or in unhealthy conditions. All these areas of economic activity are regulated by laws. While this may limit the ability of individual businesses to make a profit, it is seen as serving the collective interests of society as a whole.

Cultural institutions are less concerned with regulating social behaviour; their function is to support important values in society. For example, Christian religious morality underpins many important values in western societies such as the value of human life, respect for others' property and the sanctity of marriage. Similarly, scientific beliefs underpin much of the way we think about the world. For example, a patient given a drug by a doctor has faith that it will work because it has been scientifically proved to be effective.

Instrumental and expressive action

Parsons went on to analyse the different ways in which individuals behave towards one another in their social roles. He identified two main types of social action, which he termed instrumental and expressive action.

Instrumental actions are actions that are oriented towards a particular goal. For example, traditional economic theories emphasize instrumentality in economic behaviour since it is concerned with maximizing benefits and minimizing costs to an individual. Instrumental behaviour therefore involves weighing up which actions will achieve a goal with the minimum cost.

Expressive action is by contrast less calculating and is oriented towards an immediate end rather than being a means to an end. Emotion rather than reason usually underlies expressive forms of behaviour.

In some areas of social life instrumental actions are more dominant, while in others expressive actions are more important. For example, in work and economic life instrumental action is dominant. People go to work primarily to earn money and employers run businesses to earn a profit. In domestic and personal life expressive actions are more important. People show affection for partners and children because they love them rather than as a means to an end.

Interpretation activity

Take the following social actions and in each case try to classify them as either expressive or instrumental forms of action. In some cases you may feel an activity could fall into either category; if so, explain why.

Supporting a football team
Investing money in a building society account
Giving Christmas presents
Kissing someone you love
Choosing a course at university
Getting married
Doing a part-time job
Playing a musical instrument

Pattern variables

Social norms provide guidelines for an individual's behaviour in specific social situations and roles are defined by norms. However, Parsons argued that norms reflect more general ideals about what is good or desirable in society – what he called **values**. Parsons believed that values could be classified into a number of types or **pattern variables**. Each pattern variable represents two opposing types of values which can be seen to underlie norms of behaviour in all societies. In each pattern variable one alternative represents an instrumental and the other an expressive value. These are summarized in Table 2.2.

Table 2.2 Parsons's pattern variables

Instrumental	**Expressive**
Affective neutrality	Affectivity
Self-orientation	Collectivity orientation
Universalism	Particularism
Achievement	Ascription
Specificity	Diffuseness

Source: Parsons (1951), p. 67

Affectivity versus affective neutrality refers to the presence or absence of emotion in an individuals' actions. An example of affectivity is a parent showing affection to a child. The opposite is affective neutrality, where emotion is suppressed; for example, a judge is expected to treat all defendants the same and not allow personal feelings to influence the case.

Self-orientation versus collectivity orientation indicates whether individuals are primarily concerned with their own interests or those of a wider social group. A worker competing with colleagues for promotion is self-oriented, while a group of workers in a trade union striking for a pay rise are collectively oriented.

Universalism versus particularism defines how others are judged. Universalistic values emphasize that everyone should be judged by the same standards. For example, at a job interview we might expect an employer to judge applicants by the same standards and not to favour a candidate because of gender, race or personal relationship. However, parents would judge their own child by particularistic standards. Even if the child was not as clever or beautiful as other children it would still be loved more than others by the parents.

Achievement versus ascription defines how others are categorized. In the case of achievement we view other people according to their achievements; for example, a Black female lawyer would be judged by her competence as a lawyer. In the case of ascription some intrinsic quality in the individual is the basis for evaluating them; thus the lawyer would be evaluated as 'Black' or 'a woman' rather than by ability and qualifications.

Specificity versus diffuseness is concerned with the functional scope of an actor's interest. If a person is interested in another person only in a very restricted area of social life then specific values influence how they interact. For example, a customer is probably only interested in a shop assistant while he or she is paying for a purchase. Diffuseness is characteristic of relationships where actors are concerned about one another in a range of contexts. For example, a husband and wife will probably share a range of interests and be concerned with most aspects of each other's lives.

Norms and values

A single value may be linked to a wide range of social norms. For example, Parsons argues that universalism is a dominant value in American society. Thus a teacher is expected to mark all students' work according to the same standards, courts are expected to judge all defendants by the same legal standards and employers are expected to select staff on the basis of stated qualifications or experience. These are all norms relating to specific areas of social life which reflect the general value of universalism.

Interpretation and application activity
Take the occupational role of a doctor and relate it to Parsons's five pattern variables. With each pattern variable consider which of the two alternative values is dominant in defining the doctor's role. In some cases you may feel the doctor's role also has some elements of the opposing value in the pattern variable. If so, consider why there is this ambiguity in how the doctor's role is defined.

Industrialization and changing values

Parsons believed that the process of industrialization led to a change in emphasis in the values of societies. He argued that pre-industrial societies were dominated by more expressive pattern variables, especially those of particularism and ascription. In many traditional societies individuals are allocated to positions on the basis of birth or social background. Parsons sees industrial societies as becoming increasingly based on the instrumentally oriented values of universalism and achievement. For this reason Parsons sees formal education as much more important in industrial societies. Young people are encouraged to achieve a social position on their own merits and are judged by universal values, thus class, gender, ethnicity and kinship connections become less significant in securing privileged positions than merit and ability.

Parsons acknowledged that the transition from pre-industrial to industrial society is not always smooth, pointing to societies such as Germany in the 1930s and 1940s where fascism based on traditional nationalistic values developed as a reaction against aspects of modernization. Nevertheless, like Durkheim, Parsons saw the complex division of labour necessitated by industrialization as requiring a new set of values to provide social stability. He believed that the values of achievement and ascription that were characteristic of liberal democracies like the United States would eventually become dominant in all industrial societies.

> *Interpretation and evaluation activity*
> *Do you agree that universalism and achievement have become dominant values in western industrial societies? Is there any evidence that people are still treated according to values of ascription and particularism? If so, in what circumstances?*

Convergence theories

Parsons's view that industrial societies would evolve towards a similar set of values is reflected in the work of a number of other sociologists. While writing from rather different perspectives, these theorists all argue that contemporary societies are converging or becoming in some ways culturally similar.

Clark Kerr et al.: the logic of industrialism

In the 1960s **convergence theorists** such as Clark Kerr and his colleagues (1960) argued that industrial societies were converging towards a common type of political and social system. They argued that there was a logic to industrialism whereby both capitalist and communist industrial societies would be forced to adopt similar forms of social organization. For example, capitalist societies would be forced to provide equality of opportunity and common rights to all citizens, moving them closer to the egalitarianism of communism. Communist societies in turn would be forced to create differentials of pay between workers, reflecting differences in skill, thus becoming more unequal like capitalist societies.

Daniel Bell: post-industrial society

A similar argument was reflected in Daniel Bell's (1974) theory of **post-industrial society**. Bell argued that the United States was the first post-industrial society, since for the first time the proportion of workers providing services exceeded the proportion engaged in extractive (agriculture, mining, fishing, forestry) and manufacturing industries. Bell argued that in such a society professionals, scientists, engineers and other workers who had specialist knowledge would exercise power rather than capitalists or owners of wealth. The post-industrial society would be one dominated by knowledge and information. Bell argued that this type of society would spread from the United States to other industrial societies as new technologies freed more and more of the workforce from being actually involved in producing raw materials or processing them into actual products.

Francis Fukayama: the end of history

The most recent version of this type of theory has been advanced by the American philosopher Francis Fukayama (1989). While Fukayama cannot be described as a functionalist, he suggests that western liberal democracy is becoming the dominant set of political and economic values in the world today. Fukayama argues that with the collapse of communism in Eastern Europe there is no real alternative to liberal capitalism. Alternative value systems based on religious fundamentalism and nationalism are in his view peripheral since they are found mainly in underdeveloped societies.

Fukayama thus proclaims that we have reached the 'end of history' in the sense that there will be no more major ideological conflicts. The question of how human societies should be organized in the future has, in his view, been settled in favour of liberal capitalism since it offers the maximum political and economic freedom to individuals. Individuals' energies in the future will be channelled into economic competition rather than into political conflicts and wars.

Evaluation of convergence theories

The view that societies across the world are converging or becoming culturally more similar has been given added force by recent sociological interest in the process of globalization. This would imply that we are living more and more in a 'global village', where barriers between nations and cultures are being broken down by modern communications. However, the type of theories outlined above have been heavily criticized for a number of reasons.

Their work gives little consideration to some of the disadvantages of capitalism. Critics argue that capitalism is based on exploitation and domination; for example, feminists point out that women are still oppressed and dominated in a system which is largely male oriented. Ecological perspectives point to the damage done to the environment by unrestrained capitalism and argue that an alternative to our current economic system is essential if the planet is to survive.

The view that world societies are gradually converging towards western liberal democracy ignores the rich cultural diversity of human societies despite the cultural dominance of western industrial societies like the United States. For example, the influence of Islam in parts of the Middle East and Africa and of traditional Asian values in Japan and parts of South-East Asia has meant that many non-western societies have remained culturally distinct despite the onset of industrialization and globalization.

Evaluation exercise

With reference to the pictures above and any other evidence, write a short evaluation of the argument that the values of western liberal capitalism are increasingly the values of all industrial societies.

Structural functionalism: a summary

The work of Durkheim and especially Parsons is seen by sociologists as the basis for the structural functionalist approach to studying society. This approach was dominant in sociology from the 1940s to the early 1960s. It assumes that human societies are based on value consensus – a common culture with shared norms and values is necessary to ensure social solidarity and equilibrium. Structural functionalists are concerned with the way in which the patterns of behaviour laid down by norms and values become institutionalized into regular and persistent patterns or structures, what Durkheim called 'social facts'. This approach is also concerned to examine the functions of social institutions and behaviour for society. Durkheim's work on religion illustrates the way in which one aspect of culture can be seen to be functional for the well-being of society as a whole. Parsons's work represents an attempt to analyse the relationship between social structures and their functions and to refine them into a grand and abstract theory.

Evaluation

By the 1960s the structural functionalist approach to sociology was coming under attack from a number of quarters as new perspectives such as Marxism, feminism and symbolic interactionism gained influence. Some of the main points of criticism are summarized below.

Society and the individual

Functionalism explains social behaviour in terms of its functions for society or the social system. In this analysis individuals are treated as unimportant; they are seen as simply following the norms and values laid down by their culture. Dennis Wrong (1967) describes this as 'the oversocialized concept of man'. Critics point out that society consists of human beings, and that norms, values and culture are the product of human thought. By treating society as something greater than the individuals who comprise it, there is a risk that society is 'reified' or treated as a thing which has needs of its own separate from the individuals who comprise it.

Freedom of choice versus social constraint

Critics argue that in emphasizing that human beings are a product of socialization, functionalism ignores the freedom of choice enjoyed by individuals. Individuals are not simply actors reading from the script provided by the culture of their society; rather, they choose how to react to social situations in the light of their own interpretations. These arguments were developed by interactionist and phenomenological sociologists who explored how people as individuals create their own reality and give meaning to one another's behaviour (see Chapter 6 for further discussion).

Social change

Functionalist theories tend to explain social change in evolutionary terms. Societies are seen as adapting and evolving to their environment in a constant attempt to establish equilibrium or balance. Critics argue that this is an inadequate explanation of social change. After all, functionalism implies that existing social arrangements are in some way functional for society's well-being; if this is the case it is not clear why societies change. Conflict theories argue that societies change because they do not in fact benefit all their members equally. This creates contradictions and conflicts which are the basis for social movements that change society. Feminism and nationalism are two examples of such movements; these are discussed in Chapters 4 and 5.

Power and conflict

Functionalists have little to say about power or the ability of some to influence events at the expense of others. For Parsons, power is a resource which is used for the benefit of society as a whole. Conflict theorists reject this view and argue that power is unequally distributed. Chapter 3, for example, considers how Marxists have emphasized the way in which the culture of society reflects how power is distributed through the economic system. Those who have wealth have more influence in defining what are the dominant norms, values and beliefs in society. From this perspective there may be an apparent consensus in society, but this is in reality created either through coercion or manipulation by those with power.

Conclusion

In the 1970s and 1980s it was fashionable for sociology textbooks to be highly critical of functionalism and it was often contrasted unfavourably with theories such as Marxism and interactionism. Much of the criticism faced by functionalism was perhaps merited in view of the arguments above. However, writers like Durkheim and Parsons have provided basic concepts which are still widely used in the sociological analysis of culture. For example, the concepts of norms, values and roles, with their assumption that social life depends on shared ideas and assumptions about normal behaviour, remain widely used by sociologists. Moreover, the idea that beneath the surface of a society's culture there are deeper structures or patterns has been explored by other perspectives in both sociology and cultural studies (some of these are examined in Chapter 8).

Functionalism has been perhaps rightly condemned as a conservative sociological perspective because of its emphasis on consensus and the functional nature of social institutions, and its failure to address aspects of society that involve inequality of power and exploitation. Nevertheless, the concept of culture does imply a sharing of norms and beliefs and a common understanding of the meaning of symbols and social actions. In this sense, all societies do depend on some kind of consensus, since without it there would be no culture and no social order.

Coursework suggestion

Functionalists are interested in how culture helps to bind together and integrate individuals in a social group. This offers a starting point for research in a variety of social settings. You could, for example, study integrative mechanisms in groups such as a religious group (e.g. church, mosque or temple), a workplace, a leisure group (e.g. a sports club, local pub or group with a shared hobby) or an educational institution. You might consider what norms and values are shared by members of the group, how new members are socialized into these norms and values, and how a sense of group identity is maintained (e.g. through shared rituals or other integrative experiences). You might also consider the roles played by different members of the group and how they contribute to the smooth functioning of the whole. This area also offers opportunities to use a number of research methods, for example participant observation and in-depth interviews, as well as secondary sources such as literature produced by organizations.

DATA RESPONSE QUESTION
Item A

Societies are characterized ... by complex, more or less definite (though not of course unchanging) networks of relationships, institutions, groups and practices, but there are also important shared cultural **norms** and **values** and symbols interwoven into those social arrangements and into the consciousness of individual members. Thus, people work out their lives individually and collectively by drawing on shared ideas about what is desirable and undesirable, appropriate and inappropriate, good and bad, right and wrong.

Indeed, we cannot and should not ignore the strength and shaping capacity of societal norms and values for the individual's behaviour and their own sense of self. A whole series of everyday ordinary social practices in which we engage and which may be regarded as making up our identities are outcomes of our interactions and relationships with others and are rooted in socially generated norms and values.

(Bilton et al. 1996, pp. 10–11)

Item B

Children are born with abundant potentialities but begin their lives undeveloped. The newborn child previously knew no distinction between himself and his warm nourishing environment. Despite the birth trauma, he still considers himself the centre of the universe. He is not aware that other people exist separately. Only gradually and painfully does the 'Copernican revolution' dawn. First he discovers that his mother is not part of himself, then he discovers that his father is distinguishable from his mother. Later he discovers they have needs of their own and other roles apart from mothering and fathering him. Finally, he learns that his role is not simply to receive but to give, and that he must temper his impulses to meet the needs of others. Only then is he fully human.

This humanization is socially significant because the child graduates from the family into the outside world. If he has been properly humanized, society will not have to defend itself from his aggressive impulses and can depend on him to conform to social norms. The fabric of society would soon crumble were more than a few of its new recruits unsocialized. The machinery of justice can cope with a few criminals, but society relies on the inner controls of the vast majority.

(Blood Jnr 1969, p. 457)

Item C

Following Durkheim, Parsons considers the value system of a society to be one of its essential characteristics. For both thinkers, common agreement on certain fundamental values among the members of society is an element of the definition of a society. Without such agreements there would be no society.

(Cuff et al. 1984, p. 45)

1 *Briefly define and give an example of the following concepts referred to in Item A: (i) norm; [2 marks] (ii) value. [2 marks]*

2 *Identify and explain two ways in which our identities are 'rooted in socially generated norms and values' (Item A, line 14). [4 marks]*

3 What is the term used by sociologists for the process described in Item B? [1 mark]

4 With reference to Item B and any other evidence, assess the view that the family is the most important social institution in encouraging social conformity. [8 marks]

5 Evaluate the view set out in Item C. [8 marks]

References and further reading

Bell, D. (1974) *The Coming of Post-industrial Society*, London: Heinemann.

Bellah, R.N. (1965) 'Religious evolution', in W.A. Lessa and E.Z. Vogt (eds), *Reader in Comparative Religion: An Anthropological Approach*, New York: Harper and Row.

Berger, P. and Luckmann, T. (1969) 'Sociology of religion and sociology of knowledge', in R. Robertson (ed.), *Sociology of Religion*, Harmondsworth: Penguin.

Bettelheim, B. (1969) *The Children of the Dream*, London: Thames and Hudson.

Bilton, T. *et al* (1996) *Introductory Sociology*, Houndmills: Macmillan

Birnbaum, N. (1955) 'Monarchs and sociologists: a reply to Professor Shils and Mr Young', *Sociological Review*, July.

Blood, R.O. Jnr. (1969) *Marriage*, New York: Collier Macmillan

Bowlby, J. (1951) *Maternal Care and Mental Health*, Geneva: World Health Organization.

Burgess, R.G. (1985) *Education, Schools and Schooling*, Basingstoke: Macmillan Education.

Cuff, E.C. *et al* (1984) *Perspectives in Sociology*, London: George Allen and Unwin

Davis, K. (1948) *Human Society*, New York: Macmillan.

Deutscher, I. (1962) 'Socialization for postparental life', in A.M. Rose (ed.), *Human Behaviour and Social Process*, London: Routledge and Kegan Paul.

Durkheim, E. (1915 [1912]) *Elementary Forms of Religious Life*, London: George Allen and Unwin.

Durkheim, E. (1984 [1893]) *The Division of Labour in Society*, London: Macmillan.

Evans-Pritchard, E. (1937) *Witchcraft, Oracles and Magic among the Azande*, Oxford: Clarendon Press.

Fukayama F. (1989) 'The End of History?' *The National Interest, Vol* 16, Summer.

Fukayama, F. (1992) *The End of History and the Last Man*, New York: The Free Press.

Goffman, E. (1968) *Asylums*, Harmondsworth: Penguin.

Kerr, C., Dunlop, J.T., Harbison, F. and Myers, C.A. (1960) *Industrialism and Industrial Man: The Problems of Labour and the Management of Economic Growth*, Cambridge, MA: Harvard University Press.

McGuire, M.B. (1981) *Religion: The Social Context*, California: Wadsworth.

Malinowski, B. (1922) *Argonauts of the Western Pacific*, London: Routledge and Kegan Paul.

Mauss, M. (1966 [1925]) *The Gift*, London: Routledge and Kegan Paul.

Merton, R.K. (1968) 'Social structure and anomie', in R. Merton, *Social Theory and Social Structure*, New York: The Free Press.

Parsons, T. (1937) *The Structure of Social Action*, New York: McGraw-Hill.

Parsons, T. (1951) *The Social System*, New York: The Free Press.

Parsons, T. (1966) *Societies: Evolutionary and Comparative Perspectives*, Englewood Cliffs, NJ: Prentice-Hall.

Roethlisberger, F.J. and Dickson, W.J. (1939) *Management and the Worker*, Cambridge, MA: Harvard University Press.

Shils, E. and Young, M. (1953) 'The meaning of the Coronation', *Sociological Review*, vol. 1, no. 2.

Turner, B.S. (1983) *Religion and Social Theory*, London: Heinemann Educational.

Wrong D. (1967) 'The Oversocialized Concept of Man in Modern Sociology' in L. Coser and B. Rosenberg (eds) *Sociological Theory: a Book of Readings,* New York: Collier Macmillan.

Young, J. (1992) 'Riotous rage of the have-nots', *Observer*, 19 July.

3 Class, power and ideology

<table>
<tr><td>Key ideas</td><td>Key thinkers</td></tr>
<tr><td>Ideology</td><td>Karl Marx</td></tr>
<tr><td>Infrastructure and superstructure</td><td>Antonio Gramsci</td></tr>
<tr><td>Commodification of culture</td><td>Herbert Marcuse</td></tr>
<tr><td>Social reproduction</td><td>Pierre Bourdieu</td></tr>
<tr><td>Hegemony</td><td>Max Weber</td></tr>
<tr><td>Cultural capital</td><td>Nicholas Abercrombie, Stephen Hill</td></tr>
<tr><td>Rationalization</td><td>and Brian Turner</td></tr>
<tr><td>Consumption</td><td>Michel Foucault</td></tr>
<tr><td>Discourse</td><td></td></tr>
<tr><td>Disciplinary power</td><td></td></tr>
</table>

Introduction

The previous chapter examined culture and the process of socialization as seen by consensus theories such as structural functionalism. From this type of perspective the culture of a society in seen as reflecting shared norms, values and beliefs.

This chapter moves on to examine how conflict theories approach culture and identity. These theories reject the view that society is based on consensus or agreement. They argue that where there are inequalities of wealth, power or status the dominant norms and values of society will reflect the views of the most powerful group or groups. Less powerful groups may be encouraged or forced to accept rules of behaviour which have been created to serve the interests of the dominant group. Subordinate groups may also develop their own culture and way of life as a form of resistance to the dominant culture.

This chapter focuses on the significance of class inequalities in relation to culture and identity, though subsequent chapters will examine other forms of inequality including gender, ethnicity and age. The first part of the chapter examines the ideas of Karl Marx, in particular his view that cultural institutions are ultimately shaped by the economic system and class relations of society. We will also consider the work of a number of neo-Marxist writers who have developed and modified Marx's work.

The next part of the chapter examines the work of Max Weber, who explored how cultural ideas, notably religion, can influence economic development. We also consider some of the debates over how far class remains important as a source of identity in modern Britain.

In the last part of the chapter we look at the ideas of Michel Foucault, whose work has been a major influence on sociologists' ideas about how forms of knowledge are closely linked to power relations in society.

Karl Marx: ideology and culture

The nineteenth-century thinker Karl Marx (1818–83) developed a materialist theory of society. Marx argued that all human societies are organized around their **mode of production** – that is, the way in which society is organized to provide for its members' material needs, for example food, clothing and shelter. For Marx the culture and realm of ideas of any society were simply a reflection of the kind of economic system that provided for these material needs.

Infrastructure and superstructure

Marx made a distinction between the **infrastructure**, or economic base of society, and the **superstructure**, or social and cultural institutions. For instance, in a capitalist society such as contemporary Britain Marx would describe the system of investment in businesses by capitalists – for example, by financiers and shareholders – as the basis of the infrastructure. Another important element would be the relationship between employers and workers, whereby employers pay workers wages to produce goods and services which can be sold at a profit.

The process of capital investment and wage labour enables goods and services to be provided for consumers. It also means that workers are able to earn money to buy the goods that they have produced. In this way people's material needs are satisfied by our economic system. In other societies very different economic arrangements may apply. For example, in hunting and gathering societies such as the Inuit (Eskimos) of Northern Canada and Greenland, people are largely self-sufficient and obtain what they need directly from their environment.

Interpretation and application activity
Compare the two pictures above and discuss how differences in the economic systems of Inuit and British society might create differences in their cultures and way of life.

Economy and culture

For Marx it was how a society organized itself to provide for these material needs that shaped its culture and other forms of social organization – what he describes as the superstructure. Marx sums this up as follows:

> The mode of production of material life conditions the general processes of social, political and intellectual life. It is not the consciousness of men that determines their existence, but their social existence that determines their consciousness.
>
> (Marx 1982, p. 37)

By this Marx implies that people do not develop a particular economic system because of their cultural beliefs and values, rather that it is the economic structures of society that produce a particular kind of culture. Thus the kind of legal and political system, education system, mass media, family life, religious beliefs, art, literature and so on that are found in a society are all a reflection of its material basis – the kind of economic system on which these superstructural elements are based.

Evaluation activity
Discuss how far aspects of the culture of British society are influenced by the existence of a capitalist free enterprise economic system. You could, for example, consider the content of what is taught to children in the education system or the organization and content of the mass media.

Figure 3.1 Marx's model of infrastructure and superstructure

Elements of the superstructure are shaped ultimately by the requirements of the mode of production of economic infrastructure

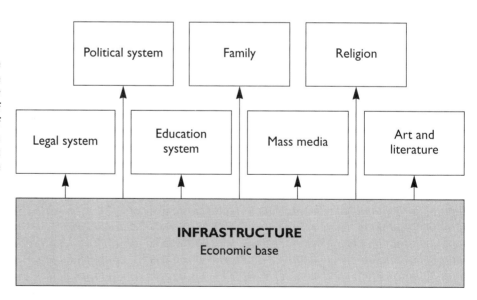

Class relations

According to Marx the economic systems of all past societies (with the exception of very simple or 'primitive communist' societies) have given rise to class relationships. This is because in most societies one class of people has taken control of the way in which the economy is organized and exploited the remainder of society to produce food and other necessary goods and services. This creates an inevitable conflict of interest between those who produce – the **subject class** – and those who live off the surplus created by the work of the producers – the **ruling class**. For example, in medieval feudal societies food was produced by serfs or peasants, who were obliged to hand over part of their produce to their feudal lords, who used it to feed themselves and their retainers.

Marx believed that modern capitalist societies are just as exploitative. In this case workers are employed to produce goods and services which are sold by their employers at a profit. However, although these profits are the result of the labour of workers, only a small proportion of the profits ends up in the pockets of the workers as wages; the remainder is appropriated by the employer or capitalist.

Evaluation activity

Do you agree with Marx's view that a capitalist economic system is unjust and exploitative? If you disagree, justify your answer. If you agree, how would you explain the fact that most people seem to accept the prevailing economic system?

Ideology

Marx argued that because economic relationships in class societies are based on exploitation, conflict is inevitable. In the long run the tensions and contradictions created by these conflicts mean that one type of economic system is inevitably overthrown and replaced by another. However, Marx explained the ability of apparently unjust and exploitative societies to survive for long periods by the concept of **ideology**.

According to Marx, members of a subordinate class are controlled not simply by coercion and fear but also by persuasion and the influence of the ideas of the ruling class. It is these ideas that help to legitimate and justify the existing economic system and social relations which Marx described as ideology. In a famous phrase Marx and Engels stated:

> The ideas of the ruling class are in every epoch the ruling ideas, i.e. the class which is the ruling *material* force in society, is at one and the same time the ruling *intellectual* force.

> (Marx and Engels 1970, p. 64, original italics)

An example of ruling-class ideology under capitalism is its emphasis on personal freedom. Workers are in theory free to work for any employer, unlike feudalism, where serfs were tied by custom to working for a feudal lord for life. However, Marx argues that this freedom is illusory since in reality workers are forced by economic necessity to work for someone and employers are forced to pay as low wages as possible in order to compete with other capitalists. The ideology of personal economic freedom thus helps to conceal the way in which both workers and employers are constrained by the requirements of the economic system.

Commodification of culture

Another aspect of Marx's work which relates to the study of culture is his concept of **commodification**. Marx argued that in capitalist societies products increasingly become commodities – things that can be bought and sold – and have an exchange value – a monetary price relative to other commodities. In precapitalist societies most products were created by people for their own use, but under capitalism people increasingly buy goods and services that have been produced by someone else. An increasing number of products become commodified, i.e. treated as commodities, including many cultural products.

The mass media and advertising play an important part in this. Advertising convinces people that they need more and more things produced by capitalism. This creates **false needs**, according to Marx, and helps to divert attention away from the contradictions and exploitation inherent in capitalism. The mass media also enables new products to be developed. Modern Marxists have pointed to products such as pop music, films and television as significant cultural products of the twentieth century. While in the past people would have made their own entertainment, today leisure has become simply another capitalist industry.

Commodity fetishism

Marx argued that because products under capitalism are turned into commodities that can be bought and sold, they acquire a value that is unrelated to their use value. For example, a painting may be sold for millions of pounds not because it is any more use as a picture to hang on your wall than any other painting, but because it is an exclusive commodity which has acquired value because of its rarity.

Marx uses the term **fetishism** to describe the attitude towards commodities in capitalist societies to highlight the similarities between the worship of fetishes or objects of religious veneration in traditional societies and the worship of consumer commodities under capitalism. Thus young people may pay a lot of extra money to acquire clothes or shoes with exactly the right designer label. Armani, Boss, Nike and Reebok become like fetishes to be worshipped.

Footwear or status symbol?

Interpretation and application activity
Young people have been mugged and even killed for desirable sportswear. In Detroit in 1985 Shawn Jones, 13, was shot for his Fila trainers. At least four other killings for sports shoes were recorded in the United States in 1988–90.

How might Marx's concept of commodity fetishism be relevant in understanding these events?

Evaluation of Marx

Marx's ideas have been extensively debated and criticized since his death. Here we will examine three significant issues.

Economic determinism

Some critics feel that Marx placed too much emphasis on the role of economic structures in shaping other aspects of society such as ideas and beliefs. Later in this chapter we shall examine Max Weber's work, which suggests that cultural ideas in the form of new religious beliefs can change the economic system; they are not simply a reflection of the existing economic order.

Class consciousness

More recently some sociologists have argued that Marx placed too much emphasis on class as a source of identity. For Marx, capitalist society would eventually devolve into two antagonistic classes as the class struggle intensified. The proletariat or working class would become more aware of its oppressed and exploited state and would see through the ideology of capitalism and rise up and overthrow capitalism in favour of communism. Marx's critics point out that there is little sign of the working class developing this kind of revolutionary consciousness in capitalist societies. In fact, many people seem to have little awareness of class as a significant source of identity at all.

Non-class identities

Class certainly played an important role in the political and economic changes of early industrial society. Trade unions and political parties such as the Labour Party were significant in improving the lot of working-class people. However, many commentators point to the emergence of what have been called **new social movements**. These are often based on alternative sources of identity. For example, the feminist movement is concerned with women's rights rather than class interests, while the environmental movement cuts across class boundaries. Many sociologists feel that these types of social movement represent the most likely source of challenge to the status quo in the future and see little prospect of the kind of class struggle envisaged by Marx developing.

Application and evaluation activity
To what extent do new social movements such as those illustrated above suggest that class is becoming less important as a basis for political identities and organizations? Draw on any other examples and evidence to support your answer.

Bowles and Gintis: the correspondence between education and the economy

Marx's view that the nature of the economic system shapes cultural aspects of social life has been influential on Marxist sociologists. To illustrate this we shall examine the work of Samuel Bowles and Herbert Gintis on the American education system.

Like other Marxist sociologists, Bowles and Gintis (1976) see the education system as part of the superstructure of society. They argue that the education system in capitalist societies serves to shape the consciousness of future workers. Pupils are prepared for work because there is a close correspondence between many aspects of the organization of schools and the organization of work.

The correspondence between school and work

Bowles and Gintis point out that schools are organized on hierarchical lines much like workplaces. In schools headteachers exert authority over teachers, who in turn control the activities of students, just as in a factory a works manager might give orders to line managers or supervisors who would in turn control the activities of ordinary workers.

Similarly, in schools work is fragmented into a variety of specialized activities; for example, pupils study English, maths, history or science as separate subjects, just as in a car factory different departments might be concerned with assembling the engine, spraying the paintwork and fitting the trim.

School pupils also experience what Marxists refer to as **alienation** – work is seen as a means to an end rather than as something which is fulfilling in its own right. Just as factory workers might accept a boring and unsatisfying job in order to earn a wage at the end of the week, so students are prepared to learn about things in which they have little interest simply to avoid getting into trouble or to pass an exam.

Bowles and Gintis argue that by socializing young people into the attitudes and behaviour pattern required to be obedient and efficient workers, the education system serves the needs of the wider capitalist system. They suggest that as part of the superstructure of society the nature of schooling is ultimately determined by the requirements of the infrastructure or economic base. Bowles and Gintis's view of socialization in the education system is very different from that of the functionalists considered in the previous chapter. Functionalists view socialization as a beneficial process which helps new members to adapt and integrate to their society. However, Bowles and Gintis see it as a process largely geared up to the requirements of capitalist business owners, since it is designed to produce a docile and submissive workforce.

Evaluation activity

Do you agree with Bowles and Gintis's view that education in capitalist societies is organized primarily in the interests of employers rather than students? What arguments and evidence can you think of both for and against this view?

Evaluation of Bowles and Gintis

Critics of Bowles and Gintis point out that it is not entirely clear that the content and organization of education does reflect the requirements of capitalist employers. In Britain, for example, many employers have been critical of the education system for failing to concentrate on basic skills needed for employment and being too concerned with irrelevant academic knowledge. Some subjects – notably sociology – have even been criticized for their left-wing bias in portraying the capitalist system as unjust and exploitative.

Marxists have responded to these sorts of criticisms by arguing that the education system must have a degree of relative autonomy or independence from the economic system in order to appear to reflect a range of interests and retain its credibility. Moreover, many studies of education in Britain point to the emergence of a 'new vocationalism' since 1979, which has attempted to strengthen the links between what pupils learn and the world of work. For example, the National Curriculum introduced in 1988 emphasizes core subjects such as English, maths, science and technology, which are seen as particularly relevant to work, while subjects seen as less vocationally relevant such as music, art and sociology have been relegated to a marginal status in the school curriculum.

Interpretation and application activity

Examine the curriculum you studied during your schooling. What kinds of knowledge were emphasized and what kinds of knowledge were given less prominence or omitted entirely? Discuss with other students why some kinds of knowledge are considered more important for school pupils to acquire than others.

Gramsci and humanist Marxism

Marx and many of his followers believed that ultimately the culture of society is shaped by its economic structure. From this point of view changing society must involve changing its economic institutions. Only then can other aspects of society change to reflect this.

The Italian communist leader Antonio Gramsci (1892–1937) questioned the extent to which economic institutions determine culture and beliefs. Gramsci argued that while ideas and beliefs are influenced by the economic system, they can also help to change it. Gramsci was particularly interested in how the working class could develop its own counter-culture in opposition to the ideology of the ruling class as a means of encouraging workers to question the desirability and inevitability of capitalism.

Political society and civil society

For Gramsci, the role of the state under capitalism is to run the system in the interests of the ruling class. He argued that this is achieved through a combination of coercion and consent. Gramsci makes a distinction between **political society**, which comprises the parts of the state that are predominantly coercive, for example the police, army and prisons, and **civil society**, which includes organizations concerned with winning the consent of the working class, such as the Church, schools and the mass media. Gramsci suggested that capitalism operates most effectively when it makes use of persuasion rather than force in order to win the consent of the working class to its subordinate status in society.

Hegemony

An important concept in Gramsci's work is that of **hegemony**. He defines this as 'intellectual and moral leadership'. Thus the bourgeoisie or ruling class in capitalist societies exercises hegemony because its ideas and values are dominant and through them it is able to persuade other groups to consent to its rule. Gramsci saw the Catholic Church as particularly important in helping to maintain ruling-class hegemony in Italy. In the nineteenth century the Church moved to support the liberal and modern ideas associated with both capitalism and Italian nationalism; the peasant class, who were traditionally loyal to the Church, followed its lead. The newly emerging Italian working class was unable to develop an alternative ideology that could attract sufficient followers, so a form of nationalism that was pro-capitalist rather than socialist was what led to the unification of modern Italy.

Gramsci emphasizes that hegemony develops in different ways in different societies. Many modern sociologists and cultural theorists influenced by Gramsci place more emphasis on institutions such as the mass media rather than the Church as key agencies in the maintenance of ruling-class hegemony in societies such as contemporary Britain.

Interpretation activity

Why might contemporary Marxists see the mass media as more important than the Church in maintaining ruling-class hegemony?

Hegemony or false consciousness?

Marxists often use the concept of **false consciousness** to express the way in which the working class is seen as taken in by the false ideology of the ruling class. Gramsci saw hegemony as much more than simply false consciousness. Hegemony is successfully maintained precisely because it appeals to ideas and interests in individuals which are real and not false. Thus Italian peasants supported nationalism because it in some sense appealed to their interests; it was seen as throwing off the yoke of feudalism and imperial domination.

Challenging hegemony

For Gramsci, the overthrow of capitalism can only come about when working-class political organizations develop their own culture in opposition to the hegemonic culture of the ruling class. This counter-culture must appeal to the hearts and minds of the working class to win it away from support for the existing system. This type of approach was pursued for many years by the Italian Communist Party, which organized its own festivals, theatre and art exhibitions in an attempt to provide an alternative to religious festivals and 'bourgeois culture' for the working class.

Gramsci saw the overthrow of capitalism and the establishment of a truly socialist society as a real possibility. However, he believed this would not come about as an historical inevitability but would require hard work by the leaders of working-class political movements. Not all neo-Marxist writers have been so optimistic.

Evaluation of Gramsci

Critics of Gramsci have argued that he places too much emphasis on the significance of hegemony and culture in explaining the failure of the working class to overthrow capitalism. He thus ignores the importance of the material and coercive basis for ruling-class power. Workers, for example, depend on employers for wages and may be reluctant to challenge the existing system simply for fear of losing their jobs. Ultimately, challenging the status quo could result in imprisonment or even death. In these circumstances even those who are critical of the capitalist system may feel there is little alternative but to accept it.

Interpretation activity

Studies of working-class attitudes and behaviour in Britain suggest that while many working-class people are critical of aspects of the existing economic and political system, there seems to be little evidence of a revolutionary class consciousness that could present a serious threat to the status quo. How could this be explained sociologically?

Hall and Jacques: Thatcherism as hegemony

Marxists influenced by Gramsci have used his theories to explain the electoral success of the Conservative Party in Britain between 1979 and 1992. Stuart Hall and Martin Jacques (1983) argued that Margaret Thatcher's success as Conservative leader was due to her success in creating a new Conservative hegemony. The Conservatives appealed not only to their traditional supporters in the middle class but also to significant sections of the working class and the self-employed petty bourgeoisie. In this way Conservative rule was based on what Gramsci called a **power bloc**, an alliance between the dominant capitalist class and other social groups.

Authoritarian populism

Hall and Jacques argue that in the 1970s Britain experienced a severe economic crisis accompanied by growing working-class militancy. The success of Thatcherism lay in persuading people that the post-war consensus politics pursued by both Labour and former Conservative governments was responsible for Britain's decline. Thatcherism was based on what they call 'authoritarian populism'. It appealed to the interests of ordinary people (populism), for example by offering the sale of council houses to tenants and lower rates of income tax. But it was also authoritarian in that it advocated strong law and order policies, more spending on defence and less on welfare services, and tougher policies to weaken trade unions and prevent strikes.

Hall and Jacques argue that Thatcherism's success lay not in deceiving people but in striking chords in the minds of certain sections of the population by appealing to a range of fears and concerns that already existed and by offering attractive and simple solutions. For example, in the 1970s strikes and poor industrial relations were a persistent problem in Britain and Thatcherism blamed this on the irresponsibility of trade unions' wage demands, seeing them as leading to excessive inflation and economic inefficiency. Mrs Thatcher advocated controls on trade unions through tough legislation to curb their powers. Hall and Jacques suggest that such policies appealed to a significant number of people, including even some workers in trade unions, who were concerned about Britain's economic decline. Similarly, concerns about Britain's 'moral decline' may have encouraged support for Thatcherism's hostile stance towards groups such as single parents, gay people, working mothers and advocates of sexual permissiveness.

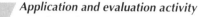

Application and evaluation activity

1 *What relevance does Gramsci's concept of hegemony have for our understanding of the success of Thatcherism in the 1980s?*

2 *Hall and Jacques argue that working-class support for the Conservatives under Mrs Thatcher was not simply a matter of 'false consciousness'; rather, Thatcherism's success lay in its appeal to real concerns of some working-class people. What elements in Thatcherism do you think would be most likely to attract working-class support and why?*

The Frankfurt School

The Frankfurt School was an important group of cultural critics who flourished in Germany in the 1930s under the leadership of Max Horkheimer. They later fled the Nazis and settled in the United States, though some returned to Frankfurt in the 1950s. Although the Frankfurt School was strongly influenced by Marxism, many of its theorists were pessimistic about the overthrow of capitalism. The work of the Frankfurt School is often referred to as **critical theory** because it is critical of both the nature of modern societies and of other social scientific theories that seek to understand them.

Mass society

The Frankfurt School was influential in the development of theories of **mass society**. These theories suggested that a mass culture was emerging in which there was little differentiation by class or locality. The mass media were seen as playing an important role in this, encouraging more and more of the population to consume the same mass-produced cultural messages. A good example of this type of approach can be seen in the work of one of the leading figures to emerge from the Frankfurt School, Herbert Marcuse.

Herbert Marcuse and one-dimensional society

Marcuse was a strong critic of capitalism and the whole modern way of life, but believed that capitalism had become so powerful that it was difficult to see how it could be overthrown. In *One Dimensional Man* (1964), Marcuse argues that alternative ways of thinking and seeing have disappeared and that society has become one dimensional – individuals are unable to imagine any alternative to the status quo.

Disciplines such as art and philosophy which once provided social criticism have become part of the system, according to Marcuse. For example, creative artists increasingly work in advertising, using their talents to sell the products of capitalism rather than presenting alternative and critical views of society. Even artists who appear to present a challenge to the status quo, for example progressive musicians, are quickly incorporated into the system by record companies more concerned with making a profit than with any political message contained in their work.

The end of the class struggle?

Marcuse was pessimistic about the working class as an agent of the overthrow of capitalism. He suggested that most of the working class has been seduced into accepting capitalism by higher living standards and the appeal of mass consumption. Working conditions have become less harsh in advanced capitalist societies and the welfare state has relieved the worst excesses of poverty and other forms of deprivation. Marcuse portrays modern men and women as 'happy robots' chasing false needs. He writes:

> The people recognize themselves in their commodities; they find their soul in their automobile, hi-fi set, split level home, kitchen equipment. The very mechanism which ties the individual to society has changed; and social control is anchored in the new needs which it has produced.
>
> (Marcuse 1964, p. 9)

Evaluation of the Frankfurt School

The work of Marcuse and other theorists of the Frankfurt School has received considerable criticism. Some critics have pointed out that their analysis is based on limited historical evidence. For example, was life really any better in societies of the past? Critical theorists also tend to base their view of society on middle-class intellectuals rather than ordinary working-class 'men or women in the street'.

Mainstream Marxists also point out that there is no real analysis of class in Marcuse's work. The Frankfurt School has been described as 'Marxism without the proletariat'. Although the Frankfurt School sees modern society as a mass society where class differences have ceased to be significant, important cultural as well as economic differences based on class are still apparent. Finally, many strands of critical theory, including Marcuse's, seem very pessimistic; they offer little hope of change in the system and perhaps over-emphasize the power of the system to crush or neutralize opposition.

Despite this, Marcuse's ideas were popular with radical groups such as the student movement and hippies in the 1960s. Marcuse himself believed that groups such as these could provide some opposition to the status quo. However, he saw most such movements as too disorganized and fragmented to present any real threat.

Sagging chin? Work it off in the Chin Gym™

Double chins are a lot easier to acquire than to get rid of – help is at hand with the advent of the remarkable Chin Gym™ from the USA. This patented isometric facial weightlifting system is purpose-designed to trim, strengthen, tone and firm the three muscle groups that directly contribute to a flabby double chin: namely, the masseter, mylohyoid and platysma muscles. You simply hold the mouthpiece between your teeth for around 15 minutes daily – the five chromed steel weights can be combined to allow 19 small increments, achieving a gradual progression of weight over a period of months. Once you have reached your goal of a more youthful-looking chin, you can reduce the daily regime to a twice-weekly 'workout'. (NB: Chin Gym can be highly effective used with the complementary Facial Flex, featured opposite.)

Chin Gym™ £39.95 33407

Masseter

BY PHONE (24 HR) **0990 80 70 60**

Unrivalled quality · Supreme performance

Built-in.

Explore our range of unique built-in appliances and enjoy the ultimate cooking experience.

Take our Tepan, for example. When cold it lies completely flat, then dips to form a well for cooking when hot. For healthy stirfries it's ideal, but it's also versatile enough to cope easily with anything from crispy duck to crêpes suzettes, or flambéd steaks to a traditional English breakfast.

Our unique built-in steam oven is the perfect complement for our range of single multifunction ovens in 60cm, 70cm or 90cm widths. Double and twin ovens are available for those requiring extra capacity – all available in a choice

of stunning finishes, including stainless steel.

Add a streamlined hob, the crowning glory of an elegant cooker hood and you have all the elements of a tailormade kitchen. Plan in Miele laundry, refrigeration and dishwashing products, all of which are designed to last 15 to 20 years, and you have the guarantee of the highest quality and exceptionally long life. Built in.

For details of local Miele Stockists
call (during office hours): (01235) 554465
Brochure line (24hrs): (01235) 554488

Miele
Anything else is a compromise

Evaluation activity

With reference to the pictures above and any other evidence, critically evaluate the following aspects of Marcuse's theory:

1 *The role of the mass media in contemporary societies is to encourage people to chase false needs and sell capitalist commodities; it does little to encourage critical awareness and alternative political views.*

2 *There is no real or effective opposition to a capitalist society based on a high level of technology and ever-increasing levels of consumption.*

Pierre Bourdieu: class and culture

The theories of culture discussed so far in this chapter have all in different ways focused on the notion of culture as ideology. They have explored how the norms and values of the dominant class help to justify the existing system and win the consent of the subject class. The work of the French cultural theorist Pierre Bourdieu moves away from this concern and instead focuses on how the culture of the ruling class helps it to preserve its elite status and differentiates it from other social classes.

Class and taste

Bourdieu shows how people's cultural tastes are influenced by class. Members of the upper class are most likely to enjoy what he calls legitimate taste or 'high-brow' art and literature, for example baroque music, intellectual films and modern art. Members of the middle class are more likely to prefer 'middle-brow' taste, for example more popular classics such as Gershwin's *Rhapsody in Blue* and more popular paintings by Constable and Van Gogh. The working class (and less intellectual members of the higher classes) will prefer popular taste, for example popular classics such as *The Blue Danube* or pop music and mainstream Hollywood films.

Research activity

Try to find information from the mass media section of your library on research into class and media consumption, for example the class distribution of readers of newspapers or television programmes. Use this information to evaluate Bourdieu's claim that there is a link between class and cultural tastes.

Cultural capital

Bourdieu not only observes that people's cultural tastes are influenced by class, he also points out the role that culture plays in reproducing class relations in society. Bourdieu argues that individuals can improve their social class position by possessing not only **economic capital** (wealth), but also what he calls **cultural capital**.

Bourdieu's concept of cultural capital refers to a set of cultural competencies and dispositions, including knowledge, language, tastes and lifestyle. While economic capital is transmitted from one generation to the next through inheritance, the transmission of cultural capital is more complex. A key concept in this process is what Bourdieu calls the **habitus** – 'a matrix of perceptions, appreciations and actions' (Bourdieu and Passeron 1977). The habitus involves a distinction between good and bad taste, between high-brow and low-brow culture and so on. Children from the dominant class learn to appreciate the culture of their class and to view the popular culture of the working class as inferior. For example, middle-class parents tend to encourage their children to read 'good' books and watch the 'right' television programmes. Middle-class children are more likely to be taken on visits to theatres, art galleries and historical sites.

Cultural capital and education

All this means that when middle-class children start school they are equipped with considerable cultural capital. Schools reflect the culture of the dominant class and children from a middle-class background are equipped with the cultural knowledge and tastes to benefit from what the education system offers. Working-class children are more likely to experience a clash of cultures between the home and the school. Their dress, manners and tastes are more likely to be defined as inferior by the school. As a result middle-class children are more likely to excel in the educational system and acquire further cultural capital in the form of educational capital or formal qualifications. In the long run these are an important passport to economic capital since those with the best qualifications tend to get the best-paid jobs.

Working-class children, by contrast, quickly get the message that they have not got the qualities required by the education system and the majority either drop out or are forced out by an examination system that favours those with cultural capital. Of course there are some individuals who succeed on economic capital alone, for example the self-made man or woman who leaves school with few qualifications and who succeeds in business. However, such individuals are often despised by other members of the dominant class as *nouveaux riches* precisely because they often still have working-class cultural tastes. Such individuals are often keen to have their own children privately educated so that they can acquire the cultural capital which their parents never possessed.

Evaluation of Bourdieu

Bourdieu's work is important in demonstrating the links between economic capital and cultural capital as sources of power in society. However, Bourdieu himself points out that some groups may possess more of one than the other, for example a teacher will probably have more cultural capital while a small business owner will tend to have more economic capital. Bourdieu's work has had considerable influence on the sociology of education in helping to explain the 'underachievement' of working-class children.

Garnham and Williams (1980) suggest that Bourdieu's work leaves little room for creative human responses. For example, there is considerable evidence that many working-class children do not passively accept being defined as culturally inferior but develop an anti-school subculture that attempts to subvert the academic culture of the school (see, for example, discussion of Willis's work on pp. 207–9).

A second problem is that Bourdieu perhaps puts too much emphasis on cultural capital as the source of educational success for middle-class children. Anthony Halsey et al. (1980) found that material factors were far more significant than cultural ones in working-class educational failure. Factors such as poor housing, lack of money for books and equipment, and the problems of working-class parents maintaining children after the minimum leaving age without grants were more important than cultural differences, in Halsey's view.

Cultural capital quiz

A lighthearted quiz loosely based on Bourdieu's work.

Answer the questions below and work out how much cultural capital you have got!

1 *If you were buying a tape or CD, which of the following would come closest to the type of classical music you like?*
   ☐ *(a) The All Time Top Twenty Classical Tracks.*
   ☐ *(b) Monteverdi's Vespers of 1610.*
   ☐ *(c) Beethoven's Fifth Symphony.*
   ☐ *(d) Never listen to classical music.*

2 *If you were choosing a holiday abroad, which would you prefer?*
   ☐ *(a) A villa in Tuscany within easy reach of the galleries of Florence.*
   ☐ *(b) A tour of the pyramids and ancient sites of Egypt.*
   ☐ *(c) Two weeks in Benidorm with all the lager you can drink.*
   ☐ *(d) A trip to Disneyland in Florida.*

3 *If you were going out for a meal, which would you choose?*
   ☐ *(a) Steak and chips followed by Black Forest gateau at the local pub.*
   ☐ *(b) An authentic sushi at a Japanese restaurant.*
   ☐ *(c) A really hot vindaloo at the local Indian restaurant.*
   ☐ *(d) A Big Mac at McDonalds.*

4 *If you were buying a picture for your bedroom, which of the following would you select?*
   ☐ *(a) A picture of your favourite film/rock star.*
   ☐ *(b) A print of a Van Gogh painting.*
   ☐ *(c) An original watercolour by a local artist.*
   ☐ *(d) A poster for a modern art exhibition at the Tate Gallery.*

5 *If you wanted to buy a good bottle of wine to take to a friend's house for dinner, which would you choose?*
   ☐ *(a) French estate-bottled Bordeaux.*
   ☐ *(b) German Liebfraumilch.*
   ☐ *(c) Australian vintage Chardonnay.*
   ☐ *(d) Italian Lambrusco.*

6 *If you were choosing a book from a news stand to read on a train journey, which type would you choose?*
   ☐ *(a) A nineteenth-century classic.*
   ☐ *(b) A Mills and Boon-type romance.*
   ☐ *(c) The winner of last year's Booker prize.*
   ☐ *(d) A spy thriller.*

7 *What Sunday newspaper would you read by choice?*
   ☐ *(a) Sunday Sport*
   ☐ *(b) The Observer*
   ☐ *(c) Sunday Mirror*
   ☐ *(d) Sunday Express*

Now score your answers from the points below.

1 *(a) 2 (b) 3 (c) 1 (d) 0*
2 *(a) 3 (b) 3 (c) 0 (d) 1*
3 *(a) 1 (b) 3 (c) 2 (d) 0*
4 *(a) 0 (b) 2 (c) 3 (d) 3*
5 *(a) 3 (b) 1 (c) 2 (d) 0*
6 *(a) 2 (b) 0 (c) 3 (d) 1*
7 *(a) 0 (b) 3 (c) 1 (d) 2*

18–21   *Congratulations! You have either got a lot of cultural capital or else you have been cheating. Either way, you know what is supposed to be good taste even if you don't really always go for it.*

13–17   *You try hard but don't quite make it into the upper crust. Your tastes are middle-brow but not really intellectual.*

8–12   *You are fairly proletarian in your tastes and rather unsure about what is culturally correct.*

0–7   *You are unashamedly culture free. Carry on reading that* Sunday Sport *and swilling that lager!*

Weber: the Protestant ethic

All the theories considered so far have been explicitly Marxist or have been influenced by Marx. We now turn to Max Weber (1864–1920), who developed one of the major alternative perspectives on modern capitalist society. Marx saw the rise of capitalist society as the result of changes in the economic system, which in turn were the result of a class struggle between the old land-owning ruling class and the newly emergent bourgeoisie or capitalist class. For Marx, the cultural changes that accompanied this economic transformation were simply a reflection of material changes in the economic base. Weber, by contrast, tried to show how new ideas actually helped to bring about an economic change in society and led to the rise of capitalism.

This view is developed in one of Weber's major works, *The Protestant Ethic and the Spirit of Capitalism* (1976). Weber argues that it was no coincidence that capitalism developed most rapidly in the European countries such as Great Britain and Germany, where the Protestant religion was strongest, as opposed to Catholic countries such as France, Spain and Italy, or indeed countries where Islam, Hinduism and other religions were predominant. For Weber, it was the beliefs of Protestantism, especially of ascetic Protestant sects such as Calvinism, that were associated with the rise of capitalism.

Weber suggested that the beliefs of most major religions were not conducive to capitalistic behaviour because these religions were 'other worldly'. Catholicism, for example, is concerned with personal salvation, and individuals such as monks who renounce the world are held up as models for those who wish to achieve salvation.

By contrast, Calvinism preaches that individuals cannot achieve salvation through good works or living a pure life. God has already chosen the 'elect' – those who are to be saved; everyone else is predestined for damnation and can do nothing to escape this fate. This might suggest that there is no point in living a good and virtuous life. However, Weber points out that Calvinists believed that the elect could be identified by certain social characteristics, including working hard at one's job or 'calling' and renunciation of worldly pleasures in favour of a simple and frugal lifestyle. In order to convince themselves that they were among the elect, Calvinists were keen to exhibit these traits rather than those of the damned, such as idleness, gluttony, drunkenness and promiscuity.

Protestantism and capitalism

Weber goes on to argue that there is an affinity between the ideals of the Calvinists – what he calls the Protestant ethic – and the spirit of capitalism. For example, the commitment to hard work and investment of profits in one's business was not only characteristic of Calvinism but was the basis of good capitalist business practice. Calvinists tended to be successful business people because they worked hard and had a reputation for honesty. They were also rational and methodical in their approach to work and experimented with new ways of organizing production and more efficient methods of keeping accounts such as double entry book-keeping. As a result, many Calvinists became very rich, but as enjoying wealth was regarded as a sign of damnation, they reinvested this wealth to build up their businesses. Weber contrasts this with the business speculators of former societies who tended to spend what they had made on frivolous luxuries and conspicuous consumption.

Weber sees the Protestant ethic as only an initial cause of capitalism. Once established, capitalism no longer needed Calvinism to justify it but was sustained by its own success. Many who had no belief in Protestantism became successful capitalists while unconsciously adopting the business practices pioneered by the early Calvinists.

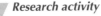

Research activity

Find out more information about the beliefs of Calvinists and the role they played in the Reformation. What evidence is there that the beliefs of Calvinists and other Protestant sects were an important influence on early capitalists? If possible, investigate the beliefs of one other major religion and consider how far it encourages or discourages capitalist economic behaviour.

Gordon Marshall's 'The Protestant ethic' (Sociology Review, September 1991) is a useful introduction, but books on early modern history and the sociology of religion would also be helpful.

Rationalization

In the long run Weber saw the rise of capitalism as a threat to all forms of religious or mystical belief. For Weber, capitalism has resulted in a process of **rationalization** of social action. Individuals increasingly consider the costs and benefits to themselves of their actions and pursue those actions which are most likely to achieve specific ends. Our understanding of the world is based more and more on rational–scientific explanations. This means there is less room for behaviour or beliefs that are based on emotion or tradition, including religious beliefs. Some neo-Weberians such as Brian Wilson (1966) argue that the result of this has been a **secularization** of western societies, whereby religious beliefs, practices and organizations lose social significance.

The Protestant ethic today

Weber's notion of the 'Protestant work ethic' would seem to have little relevance in contemporary industrial societies, where leisure and consumption appear to have become the main life interests of many people. However, Marsha Jones (1996) argues that there is plenty of evidence that many people still see work as something they must do out of a sense of duty. She quotes research by Pahl (1996), which reveals that over 70 per cent of British workers who work more than 40 hours a week w to work less but many feel self-compelled to continue to work long hours. Jone points out that even in apparently pleasurable activities, like sex, many individ a need to perform. Magazines urge readers not simply to have sex but to ha sex' and readers are made to feel guilty if their performance does not match this ideal. Jones suggests that elements of the Protestant ethic, with its feelings of guilt for those who fail to live up to society's ideals, still persist in our culture.

 Application and evaluation activity
Find examples of your own to support the argument that the Protestant ethic continues to influence our culture today.
   Can you think of any evidence to criticize or contradict this argument?

Evaluation of Weber

Weber's theory of the Protestant ethic has received a range of criticisms. First, the relationship between Calvinism and the development of capitalism is not clear. In some countries where Calvinism was particularly strong, such as Scotland and Switzerland, capitalism was relatively late in developing. However, Weber himself points out that religious beliefs were only one causal factor in capitalist development and these countries may have lacked other necessary conditions, for example skilled labour or capital for investment.

A second line of criticism comes from Marxists such as Kautsky (1953). They argue that, far from Calvinism being the cause of capitalism, capitalism actually predated the Reformation. Capitalism was already established in medieval towns and cities and the support that Calvinism gave to capitalistic behaviour provided an ideological justification for the rising bourgeoisie, who readily embraced Calvinism as a religion suited to their economic behaviour rather than vice versa.

Despite these criticisms, Weber's work does highlight the way in which developments at a cultural level may influence changes at an economic level. Weber's analysis of capitalism is essentially a pessimistic one. He sees modern society as an 'iron cage' based on rationality and bureaucracy, where individuals' lives will be increasingly standardized and rule-governed.

However, Weber is also concerned to show how individuals themselves are important in shaping society. Both Parsons and Marx have been accused of presenting an 'oversocialized' concept of humanity by suggesting that individuals simply behave according to the dictates of their socialization and their social role. Weber attempted to show how individuals are creative social actors interpreting one another's actions and responding to situations according to the meanings they give to them. From this perspective our culture may provide us with an identity and guidelines on how to live our lives, but we always have the choice of whether to accept this identity or to develop alternative values and beliefs. These arguments are examined further in Chapter 8.

Abercrombie et al.: a critique of the dominant ideology thesis

The first part of this chapter examined a number of attempts by Marxist and neo-Marxist writers to explain the relationship between the economic system of capitalism and its cultural institutions. In most cases Marxists have tended to see the culture of society as strongly influenced if not actually determined by its economic structure. In particular they see the culture of capitalist societies as representing a dominant ideology. However, the view that there is a single dominant ideology and that it has a powerful hold on the working class is rejected by the neo-Weberian writers Nicholas Abercrombie, Stephen Hill and Brian Turner (1980).

Abercrombie et al. criticize the view that the working class in capitalist societies can be characterized by any clear and coherent ideology. They refer to a range of ethnographic studies of working-class life (e.g. Beynon 1973; Willis 1977) which demonstrate that working-class people's attitudes are often based on a contradictory mixture of values; for example, support for the welfare state may coexist with a belief in economic freedom for the individual.

Abercrombie et al. argue that the working class is in many respects critical of the workings of capitalism yet reluctantly accepts it. This implies that Marxists have exaggerated the importance of ideology and cultural factors in explaining how the ruling class retains wealth and power in capitalist societies. Abercrombie et al. suggest it is the wealth and power itself that gives the ruling class its dominance. Workers accept their position because the alternatives are likely to be unemployment, poverty or even imprisonment, rather than because they necessarily subscribe to a dominant ideology.

Multiple ideologies

Abercrombie et al. reject the view that there is a single dominant ideology. Instead they suggest that different social groups advance their own ideologies in seeking to defend or advance their own position. For example, business people may support an individualist ideology favouring tax cuts and limited welfare spending because it assists them to make profits. This may be opposed by other middle-class interests, for example those who work in the health service or education, who may articulate a collectivist ideology in defence of the services in which they work and the clients they serve. Abercrombie et al. thus argue that modern capitalist societies are characterized by a number of competing ideologies rather than a single dominant ideology.

Savage et al.: middle-class lifestyles

The kind of perspective put forward by Abercrombie et al. has been elaborated by other neo-Weberian sociologists. Mike Savage, James Barlow, Peter Dickens and Tony Fielding (1992) point out the way in which social classes – in particular the middle class – have become socially and culturally fragmented. Savage et al. argue that it is now difficult to identify a single middle-class lifestyle. Using data from the British Market Research Bureau, they discovered three distinctive but overlapping middle-class lifestyles.

1   **Postmodern**. This is the section of the middle class who are most likely to experiment with new and innovative lifestyles, often described as 'yuppies' (young upwardly mobile professionals), for example advertising executives and stockbrokers. Some aspects of these lifestyles may be apparently contradictory, for example self-indulgence in the form of fast cars, exotic holidays and expensive wine and food may be combined with a degree of asceticism, for example a concern with fitness, exercise and healthier foods.

2   **Ascetic**. This is likely to be the lifestyle favoured by those who in Bourdieu's terms are high in cultural capital but low in economic capital, for example teachers, health workers and social workers. They are likely to pursue a more ascetic lifestyle, e.g. consuming less alcohol and having less expensive tastes but enjoying intellectual and individualistic activities such as the theatre, classical music hillwalking.

3   **Undistinctive**. Managers and administrators are probably closest to the conventional middle-class lifestyle. They tend to enjoy activities such as golf and visiting country houses and heritage sites.

Savage et al.'s study suggests that while there are economic divisions within the middle class, cultural divisions are also important. People with similar incomes may pursue different lifestyles and articulate quite different ideologies. Some sociologists have gone further and argued that class based on a person's job or relationship to the means of production has less significance as a source of identity. These authors claim that it is patterns of consumption that increasingly mark out social divisions and provide a source of class identity.

Consumption and identity

According to Peter Saunders (1990), the major division in the field of consumption is between those who mainly rely on the market and those who rely on the state to supply them with goods and services. For example, council tenants are supplied with housing by the state while home owners buy their houses in the market. Similar consumption divisions can be seen in education, healthcare, transport and welfare services (e.g. private and state pensions). According to Saunders, individuals are more likely to identify with others who share a similar consumption position than with those who share a similar class position based on occupation or income.

The death of class?

Jan Pakulski and Malcolm Waters (1996) take this type of argument even further and argue that class has ceased to be important either as a source of identity or as an influence on consumption patterns. They point to an Australian survey by Emmison and Western (1990), which found that out of fifteen possible sources of identity, class ranked only ninth. For respondents, occupation, family role, Australian citizenship, gender, ethnicity, age, region of residence and even being a supporter of a football team all beat class as important sources of identity.

Lifestyle and identity

They also argue that consumption is dictated by lifestyle rather than class. Thus how people dress, the clothes they wear, the music they listen to and the decor in their

homes are influenced by which lifestyle they aspire to rather than their social class. For Pakulski and Waters, class may have been significant in the past but it has ceased to have much relevance to culture and identity.

Pakulski and Waters' work, like that of many critics of class analysis, is influenced by postmodernism. Like other postmodern theorists they reject the view that culture and identity can be explained according to any single set of factors, for example the prominence accorded by Marxists to material factors such as class and ownership of wealth. Postmodernists see identity as shaped by a complex set of factors which vary from individual to individual. We return to these arguments in more detail in Chapter 9.

Application and evaluation activity
Using the pictures above and examples of your own, consider how far the concept of lifestyle is useful in understanding the cultural tastes of different social groups in British society.
In what ways might class still be important in influencing lifestyles?

The continuing relevance of class

Not all sociologists agree with the argument that class is declining in importance. Marxists in particular emphasize the potential for the working class to unite and take political action to change society given the right circumstances. They see the acceptance by workers of the capitalist system as simply evidence of the power of the dominant ideology or the hegemony of the ruling class.

Marshall et al.: class and identity

Non-Marxists, however, have also supported the view that class remains important as a source of identity. Gordon Marshall and his colleagues (1988), in a major study of class in modern Britain, found that the attitudes of working-class people were often ideologically inconsistent or even contradictory. For example, many respondents in Marshall's survey were critical of the idea of simply leaving the economy to market forces, but of these only 30 per cent said they supported state intervention to ensure an economic revival. This fits in with Abercrombie et al.'s view that the working class neither supports a dominant ideology nor exhibits a clear counter-ideology that opposes capitalism.

Nevertheless, Marshall et al. found that most people in all classes were prepared to identify themselves as members of a social class (see Table 3.1 below). Marshall et al. therefore question the view that British workers lack class consciousness or a critical stance towards social inequality. Instead they suggest that there is the potential for greater class consciousness and an awareness of social injustices. They argue that it was the Labour Party's failure to exploit the potential support for radical social change rather than the demise of class consciousness that was responsible for the Conservative Party's electoral success in the 1980s.

Table 3.1 Self-assigned class

Class	Number	Percentage	Cumulative adjusted percentage
Upper	4	0.2	
Upper middle	53	3.0	
Middle	419	23.7	
Lower middle	208	11.8	42 Middle
Upper working	197	11.1	
Working	665	37.6	
Lower working	74	4.2	58 Working
Refused	50	2.8	
Don't know	100	5.6	
Total	1,770	100.0	

Source: adapted from Marshall et al. (1988), p. 144

Interpretation and evaluation activity

1   *What conclusions would you draw from Table 3.1 about the extent to which British people identify themselves as members of social classes?*
2   *What other data might be useful in assessing the importance of class compared to other sources of identity?*

Michel Foucault: discourses and identity

For Marx, a person's class position is essential to understanding his or her identity – ultimately, our consciousness as human beings is determined by the production relations of our society. Theories influenced by Weber give class a lesser priority and point to a variety of social influences that can create a sense of personal and group identity. The work of the French philosopher Michel Foucault (1926–84) takes this a stage further. Foucault denies that there is any essential factor which determines our identity or sense of who we are. He sees our sense of self as determined neither by biological factors nor by any specific social factors such as class. Because of this, Foucault's work is often described as poststructuralist, since he denies any link between social structures (such as the class structure) and the way we see ourselves. Instead, Foucault sees the way we view ourselves and those around us as shaped by discourses or ways of seeing, describing and thinking about things.

Power and knowledge

Foucault's main interest is in the relationship between power and knowledge and how particular forms of knowledge come to count as truth at particular points in history. Like Marx, Foucault sees what counts as truth or as valid knowledge as reflecting power relations in society. However, he rejects Marx's view that power is linked to economic wealth. Foucault argues that power is seen not only in economic relationships but in all social relationships. He likens power to a net in that it does not have a centre but is more like a mesh enveloping all social relationships.

Foucault's work explores how knowledge has come to be constructed in particular ways at particular points in history through the development of discourses in the form of ideas and ways of interpreting the social world. He explores how discourses give rise to new forms of knowledge, which can be used to control groups such as those defined as sick, insane or criminal. A good example of this is medical discourse, which is the basis for how doctors interpret and treat symptoms of illness.

Medical knowledge and power

In *The Birth of the Clinic* (1973) Foucault traces how medical knowledge was transformed by the application of scientific approaches from the eighteenth century onwards. Doctors started to base their treatment more on observation of patients' bodily symptoms rather than textbook classifications of diseases. Medicine was also increasingly based on a distinction between healthy and diseased bodies. Foucault describes this as a process of **normalization**, whereby patients were compared with what doctors considered as a healthy norm to see how far they deviated from it. For example, from the eighteenth century onwards doctors developed a concept of normal sexuality based on heterosexual relations within marriage. Those who deviated from this norm, for example homosexuals, single mothers and young people who masturbated, were defined as sexually perverted and seen as in need of correction or treatment.

Foucault also develops the concept of **surveillance** to describe the way in which patients were subjected to regular examinations in order to ascertain whether they were healthy or diseased. Foucault's work points to the way in which new forms of knowledge in the form of medical discourses gave rise to new forms of power and control. For example, patients suffering from mental illnesses and even certain infectious illnesses such as tuberculosis could be forcibly isolated and treated in medical institutions.

 How might the picture above be used to illustrate Foucault's concepts of normalization and surveillance?

Disciplinary power

In a later study, *Discipline and Punish* (1977), Foucault extended these ideas to examining prisons and punishment. Here again, Foucault sees a change taking place in the early nineteenth century, when imprisonment replaced punishment of the body (for example, whipping, torture and public execution) as the main method of dealing with criminals. Again, Foucault sees this as a sign of the application of new forms of knowledge, in particular discourses based on criminology and other human sciences. Foucault suggests that new forms of punishment were seen as more efficient and effective by their advocates and involved the application of new technologies.

Bentham's panopticon was the basis for the design of many nineteenth-century prisons.

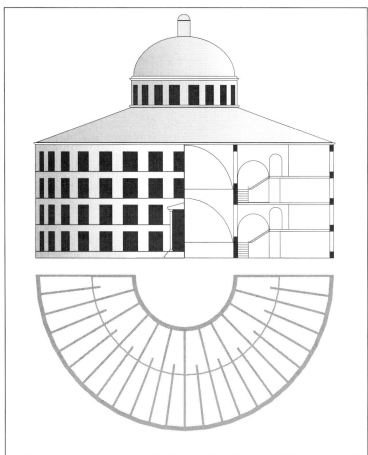

The most important of these were new techniques of surveillance. Foucault points to a design for a prison known as the panopticon by the philosopher Jeremy Bentham as an important influence. The panopticon had cells arranged in a circle around a central tower in which the guards were stationed. The guards in the tower could observe the prisoners in each cell at all times, but the prisoners could not see the guards or other prisoners. While Bentham's design was never fully put into practice, elements of his ideas can be seen in the layout of nineteenth-century prisons.

Prisons also came to be organized on the basis of strict rules and military-style discipline, which governed when prisoners could eat, sleep, exercise and so on. According to Foucault, power over convicted criminals ceased to be exercised through physical punishment of the body but came to involve moulding the prisoner to what was seen as normal behaviour through a disciplined regime and constant surveillance.

The disciplined society

Foucault's work implies that the kind of discipline and surveillance found in prisons and hospitals has now become part of social life in general. Foucault suggests that we live in a disciplined society in which all of us are subjected to surveillance and controls from above. For example, shoppers and football fans are monitored on closed-circuit television and the output of workers in offices and supermarkets can be monitored by computers connected to their work stations or tills. Even the success of teachers and pupils in schools is monitored in league tables of examination results.

 Application activity
Think of your own examples of ways in which people are subjected to surveillance and disciplinary power in contemporary society.

Foucault and Marxism

On the surface there appear to be some similarities between Foucault and Marx. However, Foucault rejects the Marxist view that this kind of discipline is simply a means of capitalist control. Foucault argues that disciplinary power is not exercised by one group or class over another but envelops all of us. He also suggests that this kind of power is only really visible when there is resistance to it, hence his interest in institutions such as prisons, where those subject to disciplinary power are most likely to fight back.

Also unlike Marx, Foucault rejects the idea that there is a form of knowledge that is ultimately true. For example, Marx believed that objectively capitalism was an exploitative and oppressive system and that workers only failed to realize this because they were led astray by false consciousness. Marxism is often portrayed by its advocates as an objective and scientific analysis of capitalism in opposition to bourgeois ideology, which is seen as based on a false or distorted view of things.

Foucault, however, rejects the idea that knowledge and discourses are true or false, and in this sense he presents a relativist view of truth. Thus he does not see modern medicine as necessarily better or truer than medieval medicine, nor does he see imprisonment as necessarily more humane than bodily punishments. For Foucault, the truth or falsity of how people see the world is irrelevant. What is interesting is how new forms of knowledge come to define the way we see things and how this results in shifts in the way knowledge is applied at particular points in history.

Evaluation of Foucault

In recent years Foucault's work has had enormous influence on sociology in a number of areas, notably the study of deviance, health and sexuality. Although Foucault was not a postmodernist, his work was important in paving the way for postmodernist theories in sociology. Like them he rejects the view that there is any essential source of identity for human beings. For Foucault, our sense of self is constructed through the discourses or ideas that are dominant in society at a particular time. Foucault's work has also encouraged sociologists to look at new areas, for example the importance of architecture and spatial arrangements in the exercise of power and control (as in the design of hospitals and prisons).

Genealogical method

Nevertheless, some sociologists find Foucault's approach difficult to accept. Foucault makes little use of conventional sociological methods but relies largely on examples drawn from historical sources to illustrate his ideas. Foucault developed an approach which he termed **genealogy**. This involved tracing the history of the emergence of new ideas and forms of knowledge in order and how they came to be applied through power relationships. However, it can be argued that Foucault's work is not systematic and relies on selective examples of evidence to support his arguments.

Ambiguity

Foucault's style of writing is also often ambiguous and elusive. This is perhaps deliberate, as Foucault wishes to show that the social world itself is indeed ambiguous and not reducible to any simple theory; however, it makes it difficult to pin down what he is really saying.

Theoretical explanation

Foucault offers little explanation for why things are as they are. He does not, for example, really explain why new forms of medical knowledge or punishment emerged at particular points in history. He would certainly reject the explanation of Marxists that these changes were in some way linked to the economic requirements of the emergent capitalist system. However, Foucault avoids providing any alternative theory. He in fact rejects any kind of grand theoretical explanation of how societies change.

Agency

Anthony Giddens (1982) points out that there is no theory of agency in Foucault's work. He tends to imply that those who built prisons or developed new forms of medical knowledge were unaware of what they were doing. Giddens asserts his support for Marx's famous statement that 'men make history, but not in conditions of their own choosing'. Giddens emphasizes that while new forms of knowledge may have produced consequences that were unintended by those who promoted them, we cannot deny that those who shaped historical events were knowledgeable agents who deliberately developed new forms of knowledge and systems of power because it in some way served their own interests.

Conclusion

This chapter has examined the way in which culture and identity are influenced by class and power relations. Marxist theories have made a major contribution to this field by developing concepts such as ideology and hegemony. These concepts point to the way in which those who exercise economic power in society play a decisive role in shaping cultural institutions. This can perhaps be seen most clearly in the mass media, where popular tastes are increasingly shaped (and possibly manipulated) by big business organizations engaged in producing cultural products such as television programmes, films, records and newspapers. However, the weakness of the Marxist approach would seem to be its tendency to economic determinism. Although writers such as Gramsci seek to avoid this, the logic of the Marxist argument tends to suggest that ideas and culture are ultimately shaped by the economic structure of society.

Theories based on a Weberian argument avoid this tendency. Weber's Protestant ethic thesis suggests that cultural influences (like Calvinism) can shape economic structures (like capitalism). Neo-Weberians also question the primacy of class as a source of identity and emphasize the way in which society is stratified in a variety of ways, creating a multiplicity of cultural divisions and a plurality of bases for conflict.

The risk of this type of analysis is that the significance of class in relation to other social divisions is lost. Class comes to be seen as simply another source of identity and cultural diversity. This ignores the significance of class and economic inequality in relation to culture. Not all groups in society have equal influence in defining cultural norms. Differences of power and wealth – in other words, class – remain significant, as in the example of control of the media mentioned above.

Finally, Foucault's work has little to say about class, but explores the relationship between knowledge and power. Foucault implies that forms of language, ways of looking at things and even the layout of buildings can embody power relations. This offers a radically different approach to the issues raised in the first part of this chapter. However, many sociologists would be unhappy about Foucault's refusal to link the power to define what counts as knowledge to other sources of power in society, such as economic wealth.

Class is not the only source of power in society. The next three chapters consider other important forms of social inequality – gender, race and age – and examine their significance in relation to culture and identity.

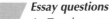

Essay questions

1 To what extent is social class significant as a source of identity in contemporary British society?

2 'The ideas of the ruling class are in every epoch the ruling ideas' (Marx and Engels). Explain and evaluate this statement.

Coursework suggestion

The importance of social class for identity offers many possibilities for coursework, particularly if you are studying social stratification elsewhere in your sociology course. One example would be to carry out a survey to investigate people's images of class and how far identification with a social class is important in relation to lifestyle, norms of behaviour (e.g. in family life), voting behaviour, attitudes to work and so on. Your study could draw on previously published research (e.g. Marshall et al. 1988; Goldthorpe et al. 1969). Your own primary research could use questionnaires or interviews to obtain data. You would need to operationalize concepts such as class for use in your study and you might also consider putting forward a hypothesis to be tested in the research.

References and further reading

Abercrombie, N., Hill, N. and Turner, B.S. (1980) *The Dominant Ideology Thesis*, London: Allen and Unwin.

Beynon, H. (1973) *Working for Ford*, Harmondsworth: Allen Lane.

Bourdieu, P. (1984) *Distinction: A Social Critique of the Judgement of Taste*, London: Routledge and Kegan Paul.

Bourdieu, P. and Passeron, J. (1977) *Reproduction in Education, Society and Culture*, London: Sage.

Bowles, S. and Gintis, H. (1976) *Schooling in Capitalist America*, London: Routledge and Kegan Paul.

Emmison, M. and Western, M. (1990) 'Social class and social identity: a comment on Marshall et al.', *Sociology* (24:2 pp. 241–53).

Foucault, M. (1973) *The Birth of the Clinic: An Archaeology of Medical Perception*, London: Tavistock.

Foucault, M. (1977) *Discipline and Punish: The Birth of the Prison*, London: Tavistock.

Garnham, N. and Williams, R. (1980) 'Pierre Bourdieu and the sociology of culture', *Media, Culture and Society*, vol. 2, no. 3, Academic Press.

Giddens, A. (1982) *Profiles and Critiques in Social Theory*, London: Macmillan.

Goldthorpe J., Lockwood D., Bechofer F. and Platt J. (1969) *The Affluent Worker in the Class Structure*, Cambridge: Cambridge University Press.

Gramsci, A. (1985) *Prison Notebooks: Selections*, New York: International.

Hall, S. and Jacques, M. (eds) (1983) *The Politics of Thatcherism*, London: Lawrence and Wishart.

Halsey, A.H., Heath, A.F. and Ridge, J.M. (1980) *Origins and Destinations: Family, Class and Education in Modern Britain*, Oxford: Clarendon Press.

Jones, M. (1996) 'The Protestant ethic revisited', *Sociology Review*, vol. 6, no. 1.

Kautsky, K. (1953) *Foundations of Christianity*, New York: Russell.

Marcuse, H. (1964) *One Dimensional Man*, London: Routledge and Kegan Paul.

Marshall, G., Newby, H., Rose, D. and Vogler, C. (1988) *Social Class in Modern Britain*, London: Hutchinson.

Marx, K. (1977) *Selected Writings*, ed. D. McLellan, Oxford: Oxford University Press.

Marx, K. (1982) 'Selections', in A. Giddens and D. Held (eds), *Classes, Power and Conflict*, Berkeley: University of California Press, pp. 12–49.

Marx, K. and Engels, F. (1970 [1846]) *The German Ideology*, London: Lawrence and Wishart.

Pahl, R. (1996) 'The future of success', *Sociology Review*, vol. 5, no. 4.

Pakulski, J. and Waters, M. (1996) *The Death of Class*, London: Sage.

Saunders, P. (1990) *A Nation of Home Owners*, London: Unwin Hyman.

Savage, M., Barlow, J., Dickens, P. and Fielding, T. (1992) *Property, Bureaucracy and Culture: Middle-class Formation in Contemporary Britain*, London: Routledge.

Waters, M. (1994) *Modern Sociological Theory*, London: Sage.

Weber, M. (1976) *The Protestant Ethic and the Spirit of Capitalism*, London: Allen and Unwin.

Willis, P. (1977) *Learning to Labour: How Working-class Kids Get Working-class Jobs*, Farnborough: Saxon House.

Wilson, B.R. (1966) *Religion in a Secular Society*, London: Watts.

4 Gender and sexuality

Key ideas	Key thinkers
Sexual development	E.O. Wilson
Instrumental and expressive roles	Sigmund Freud
Feminine mystique	Talcott Parsons
Patriarchy	Nancy Chodorow
Sex and gender	Betty Friedan
Gender socialization	Kate Millett
Social construction of sexuality	Margaret Mead
	Ann Oakley
	Jeffrey Weeks
	Michel Foucault

Introduction

The first question normally asked of a new parent is usually whether the baby is a boy or a girl. From the start of life a person's sex and the social role or gender associated with it is an important part of their identity.

This chapter examines the way in which gender identities not only reflect biological differences between the sexes but are also shaped by the culture of society. The first part of the chapter examines a number of theories of how gender identities develop. We then move to consider how feminism has highlighted the socially constructed nature of gender roles by examining the way in which gender is defined in different ways in different societies, and the process of gender socialization.

The next part of the chapter examines recent debates within feminism, including the influence of postmodern theory. Here we consider the way in which the categories of male and female are cut across by other divisions, such as those based on class, ethnicity, age and disability.

The final part of the chapter goes on to consider sexual identities and how human sexuality is not only the outcome of biological drives, but again is influenced by cultural norms and beliefs.

Theories of gender identity

Up until the 1960s most malestream sociology had little to say about issues of gender and sexuality. (Malestream sociology is the term used by feminists to describe traditional sociology dominated by men and masculine ways of looking at the world.)

Although sociology in general is concerned with examining how the social world is constructed through culture, differences of gender were often assumed to be simply natural or biological in origin.

Early feminism and gender roles

There were important exceptions to this view, often from outside sociology. Early feminists such as Mary Wollstonecraft challenged the then widely held view that women were naturally weaker, intellectually inferior and best suited to work within the domestic sphere.

In the nineteenth century Karl Marx's collaborator Frederick Engels argued that the subordination of women to men had only come about because men had invented monogamous marriage as a means of ensuring the inheritance of private property. Engels believed that in a socialist society women would be relieved of the role of producing heirs since private property would be abolished. Instead, male–female relations would be monogamous based on romantic love and women would be free to participate in paid work on an equal basis to men.

These writers recognized that gender differences were not necessarily natural and universal but were linked to the structures of particular societies at particular times; changing society might result in changes in the roles taken by men and women. Despite these arguments, most malestream social scientists continued to assume that gender was linked to biology rather than culture. In the first part of the chapter we examine three approaches to gender identity: sociobiology, psychoanalytic theory and functionalism, before moving to consider the impact of feminist ideas.

Interpretation and application activity

Give three examples of ways in which expectations about 'normal' behaviour for men or women have changed in British society in the last hundred years.

How are these changes related to wider changes in society?

What implications do these changes have for the view that men's and women's social roles are determined by biology?

Sociobiology and gender

The view that 'biology is destiny', in other words, that social behaviour is determined by biological drives and genetic programming, can be seen most clearly in sociobiology. Sociobiologists such as E.O. Wilson (1975) (see also pp. 4–6) argue that in the process of evolution each sex has developed different strategies for mating and reproduction and that these are reflected in a variety of aspects of social behaviour. Males, it is argued, are genetically programmed to be more promiscuous, while females are disposed to nurture their offspring and remain loyal to one partner.

Evolution and gender roles

Anthropologists influenced by sociobiology such as Robin Fox (1976) also reflect this view. Fox sees differences between men and women as a result of our evolutionary past. Throughout most of human history men were hunters, while women spent most of their adult lives burdened by pregnancy and nursing small children. In these circumstances, women developed skills of foraging and gathering wild foods and nurturing children rather than the strength and aggression required for hunting. Fox argues these differences in both physique and mental skills remain part of our genetic inheritance today.

The arguments of sociobiology remain controversial and criticisms of it are examined in Chapter 1 (see pp. 5–6). Most significantly, sociobiology ignores the ways in which culture shapes gender and sexuality; these are examined in more detail in this chapter.

 Interpretation and application activity

What are the implications of sociobiology for those who wish to remove barriers to women performing traditional male roles and men performing traditional female roles?

Does this help to explain why the claims of sociobiologists have been received more favourably by those on the political right and strongly opposed by most feminists?

Freud and psychoanalytic theory

Freud's model of personality has already been introduced in Chapter 1. One of Freud's major concerns was with understanding the psychosexual development of individuals. While children are often thought to have no sexuality until puberty, Freud argued that humans are sexual beings from the moment of birth, though sexuality manifests itself in different ways at different stages in development. Where this sexual development takes place in a normal way the child develops an adult sexual identity appropriate to his or her sex, in the case of a boy by identifying with his father and in the case of a girl by identifying with her mother. Freud sees this process as developing through five stages.

1 **Oral stage**. As a small baby the infant focuses on the pleasure derived from the lips and mouth, not only in feeding but in sucking a variety of objects.

2 **Anal stage**. Between the ages of one to three years the focus of pleasure shifts from the mouth to the anus and excretory functions. The child derives pleasure from being able to control its bowels and bladder by holding on to faeces and urine.

3 **Phallic stage**. In what Freud calls the **Oedipus complex**, boys develop a close relationship to their mother and come to see the father as a rival for the mother's love. Between three and six years old the boy realizes that his father is bigger and more powerful and develops a **castration anxiety** – a subconscious fear that his father will cut off his penis. The castration complex is resolved by the boy repressing his desire for his mother and identifying with his father. In this way boys cut their ties with their mother and take on a masculine identity.

   With girls this stage is quite different, as Freud argued that girls believe they have already been castrated since they observe they have no penis like boys. Girls develop **penis envy**, wishing for a penis like a boy, but in normal development this resolves itself into a wish for a baby instead. The father becomes the girl's love object as she hopes he will provide her with the baby. Freud was less clear over why girls eventually identify with their mothers, but he suggests this may be because of a wish to be loved by the mother and seek her approval.

4 **Latency stage**. From five or six years up to puberty the libido or sex drive is less obviously active.

5 **Genital stage**. From puberty onwards adult sexuality develops fully. By this time most individuals should have developed an identification with their own sex (via the father for boys and the mother for girls). During puberty the id in the form of the sexual drive becomes more demanding and individuals seek to satisfy their sexual desires through heterosexual relations.

For Freud, normal sexual development involves identification with a person's own biological sex. However, Freud was aware that human sexuality was not predetermined by biology and in many of his case studies showed how experiences in childhood could lead to individuals developing unusual sexual objects or fetishes. For example, some individuals may become sexually aroused by the sight of feet or the feel of silk or fur. Freud argued that babies are what he termed 'polymorphously perverse' when they are born – they are capable of finding sexual pleasure from all parts of their bodies. While for most people adult sexuality comes to centre on heterosexual genital sexuality, this is by no means predetermined or inevitable.

Evaluation of Freud

Freud's work has had enormous influence on both psychiatry and social sciences. Perhaps his major insight was in revealing the role of the unconscious in understanding identity. His work represents a move away from the Enlightenment conception of identity (see p. 21), which saw the subject as being fully in control of his or her self. Freud's work implies that there are forces at work in the unconscious of which we are not aware but which shape our behaviour and sense of self.

Nevertheless, Freud's work remains controversial. Many of his ideas are based on limited observations of patients showing symptoms of neurosis. It is difficult to prove or disprove concepts such as the unconscious or the castration complex since they are not things that can be directly observed; rather, they are inferred by Freud from his analysis of patients' behaviour, conversation and dreams.

Research and evaluation activity
The above is necessarily a brief summary of Freud's ideas. If possible, find out more information about his work: most psychology textbooks have a readable summary. Using your information answer the following questions:

Do you feel Freud's theory is effective in explaining any aspects of human sexual development? For example, can aspects of adult behaviour be related to childhood experiences?

What criticisms could be made of Freud's work? For example, does his work show an understanding of female sexual development?

Parsons and functionalism

The tendency of malestream sociology to view gender in biological terms can be clearly seen in the work of the famous functionalist sociologist Talcott Parsons. As noted in Chapter 2, Parsons made a distinction between **instrumental** forms of behaviour – involving concern with achieving a task or goal – and **expressive** forms of behaviour – concerned with affectivity or emotion. Parsons argued that in family life men tend to perform the instrumental tasks – for example, earning an income to support other family members – while women perform expressive tasks – for example, nurturing children and providing psychological support for the husband. Parsons's assumption that different roles for men and women were natural, inevitable and functional can be seen in the passage below.

The separation of the sex roles in our society is such as, for the most part, to remove women from the kinds of occupational status which is important for the determination of the status of the family. Where married women are employed outside the home, it is, for the great majority, in occupations which are not in direct competition for status with those of men of their own class.

Women's interests, and the standards of judgement applied to them, run, in our society, far more in the direction of personal adornment and the related qualities of personal charm than is the case with men.

(Parsons 1954, p. 80)

Evaluation question
Parsons was writing about American society in the 1950s. Do you think his ideas are still relevant to British society today?

Freud and Parsons

Although Parsons's explanation of gender differences is primarily in biological terms, he sees the socialization process as important here. In this respect, Parsons draws on Freud's work. Like Freud, Parsons suggests that the father necessarily has to prise the boy away from his mother's affections in the phallic or Oedipal stage. Because of this, boys are much more subjected to their fathers' discipline and are likely to react to deprivation of motherly love with aggression. Parsons suggests this is one reason why adolescence is often a difficult stage for boys. Girls remain closer to their mothers throughout, thus the experience of socialization is necessarily different for boys and girls.

Nancy Chodorow and feminist psychoanalytic theory

Nancy Chodorow's (1978) work is based on Freud's psychoanalytic approach, but she challenges the view developed by Parsons that sexual development for boys is necessarily a difficult process. Chodorow argues that this is only due to the way parenting is conventionally organized. Because mothers have the major responsibility for parenting and girls tend to maintain a more continuous relationship with their mothers, they can separate more gradually. Women grow up better able to sustain relationships and express their emotions. Men, by contrast, have to repress this feminine side to themselves as they separate from the mother. This makes men more independent and competitive, which may assist them in gaining better jobs than women. However, it means men are more likely to find it difficult to express their emotions and express intimacy.

Chodorow argues for a greater sharing of parental responsibilities between fathers and mothers. In her view this would mean that boys had fathers as role models who expressed tenderness and intimacy, and would help to resolve many of the emotional problems faced by men in their conventional masculine roles.

Evaluation activity
Do you agree with Chodorow's argument that men's upbringing makes it more difficult for them to express emotions and achieve intimacy? If so, is this inevitable or could it be changed by different styles of parenting?

Feminism

By the 1960s the women's movement in the United States and Britain was gathering strength. This movement is often referred to as the second wave of feminism, in contrast to the first wave of feminists in the nineteenth century, who campaigned on issues such as married women's property rights and women's suffrage. Many of the second wave feminists were concerned to challenge the view that women's destiny in life was governed by biology.

Betty Friedan: the feminine mystique

One of the leading feminists in the United States in the 1960s was Betty Friedan. She developed the argument that it was not women's biology that held them back from competing on equal terms with men but what she referred to as the **feminine mystique** (Friedan 1963). This was an ideology that defined what is was to be truly feminine. For example, the feminine mystique emphasizes that women are naturally intuitive, sensitive and close to nature. However, at the same time this implies that women are not naturally rational, logical and capable of independence and assertiveness.

Application activity
Give examples of beliefs or assumptions in our culture which reinforce the view that women naturally and inevitably have certain qualities.

For Friedan it was the feminine mystique that prevented women from realizing their full potential as human beings. Marx suggested that ruling-class ideology created a form of false consciousness in the working class which prevented it from realizing its potential for liberating itself from capitalist exploitation. In the same way, Friedan argued that the feminine mystique was an ideology that prevented women from seeing their potential and kept them locked into their traditional roles as wives, mothers and carers. Friedan highlighted the boredom and frustration many women experienced from being restricted to running a home and caring for children, and argued that problems such as marital dissatisfaction, depression and neurosis could be linked to the lack of rewards offered by married women's traditional role.

Kate Millett and patriarchy

Another leading American feminist, Kate Millett, developed many of these ideas. Millett is particularly famous for developing the concept of **patriarchy** or male domination (Millett 1970). Patriarchy had previously been used by anthropologists to describe family systems headed by the oldest male. Millett extended the meaning of the concept to describe the structures of male dominance which she saw as existing at every level of society.

Millett argued that ultimately male domination is underpinned by force and her ideas led to a range of feminist research on issues such as rape and domestic violence. However, like Friedan, Millett sees ideology and culture as playing an important role in persuading rather than coercing women to accept a subordinate role to men. Millet points to the way in which many religions have traditionally reinforced patriarchy. In the Christian book of Genesis, for example, Eve was seen as responsible for humanity's expulsion from the Garden of Eden and this was used to justify keeping women (who were particularly vulnerable to temptation) under the control and surveillance of their husbands or fathers.

Criticisms of the concept of patriarchy

The concept of patriarchy was useful according to feminists like Maria Mies (1986) because it was a 'struggle concept'. It provided something that would unite women in a common movement against male domination. However, in recent years the concept of patriarchy has been criticized by some sociologists for being too broad and vague. For example, the claim that patriarchy is a universal form of oppression ignores variations in the nature and degree to which women are oppressed and exploited in different societies. Emphasizing patriarchy also may mean that feminists overlook other forms of domination and oppression, for example those based on class, race and age.

Evaluation activity

Hold a class debate or discussion on the question: 'Does the concept of patriarchy have any relevance to understanding the role of women in contemporary society?'

Sex and gender

Many feminists emphasize the distinction between **sex** and **gender**, originally proposed by Robert Stoller in 1968. A person's sex is a biological status; they are male or female by virtue of certain reproductive organs and other biological characteristics. Gender refers to the person's social status and the cultural norms attached to their role, in other words, notions of masculinity and femininity. Women's ability to bear children is a biologically determined aspect of sex; however, many feminists believe that the idea that women should also be responsible for feeding, washing and socializing children is a culturally constructed gender role. A man's biological make-up does not prevent him from caring for a child any more than a woman's biological make-up prevents her from having a paid job. Women's and men's different social roles reflect cultural assumptions about gender rather than biological differences of sex.

Application activity

Take a sheet of paper and divide it into two columns headed 'sex' and 'gender'. In the first column list aspects of differences in male/female behaviour which you feel are natural or biological in origin. In the second column list those which you feel are social or cultural in origin. Compare your list with those of other students and discuss any areas of disagreement.

Anthropological studies of gender roles

In support of their view that gender is socially constructed rather than biologically determined, feminists have cited a range of cross-cultural evidence to prove that women (and men) are capable of a much more diverse range of roles than are traditionally found in a society like Britain.

Margaret Mead: cross-cultural evidence about gender

One of the earliest anthropologists to research the diversity of gender roles in other societies was Margaret Mead. In *Sex and Temperament in Three Primitive Societies* (1935) Mead described the gender roles in three New Guinea tribes. Among the Arapesh there was no sharp distinction between male and female roles; men were mostly gentle and placid and shared the responsibility with their wives for caring for children. The Mundugumor, by contrast, were a tribe of aggressive headhunters where men often obtained wives effectively by kidnapping them. Although men were extremely aggressive, even women in this tribe showed little maternal affection and were involved in the constant feuds and battles that were accepted as normal in their culture. Among the Tchambuli, women were the more assertive and businesslike sex. It was women who conducted most of the trade with other tribes and they normally made the first move in selecting a sexual partner. Men were more concerned with make-up and personal adornment and spent much of their time in special men's houses engaged in artistic activities, gossip and petty rivalry.

Mead argued that differences in temperament reflect differences in socialization. For example, the care and love lavished on Arapesh children produces gentle and loving adults. Mundugumor children, by contrast, are virtually neglected by their parents and thus grow into touchy and aggressive adults who take offence at the slightest provocation. Among the Tchambuli aggression in boys is frowned on while girls who are not assertive have a low status and find themselves dominated by the more typically bossy members of their peer group.

Criticisms of Mead

In recent years some of Mead's work has been called into question. A study of Samoa by Freeman (1983), which Mead had studied in the 1920s, produced very different results from her research. Mead found that sexual relationships were seen as a normal and acceptable part of life for adolescent Samoan girls. However, Freeman suggests that Mead was misled by her informants – virginity at marriage was highly valued in Samoa and adolescent girls were kept under close surveillance to ensure this. Although these criticisms were levelled at Mead's work in Samoa, rather than her New Guinea study, some social anthropologists have argued that it casts doubt on the reliability of all her research. Perhaps Mead was looking for evidence to fit her own hypotheses about the importance of culture in determining human temperaments.

Evaluation question

Do you agree that Freeman's criticisms of Mead's research in Samoa necessarily cast doubt on the validity of her research in New Guinea?

Further evidence from other cultures

Despite these criticisms, there exists a variety of other evidence to support the view that gender roles vary widely in human societies. Ann Oakley summarizes some of this evidence in her book *Housewife* (1974). While some anthropologists such as Murdock (1949) have argued that certain tasks are almost universally allocated to one sex – for example, hunting is done by men – Oakley disputes this. She points to the Mbuti Pygmies of the Congo, who have very little division of labour by sex; men and women hunt together and share responsibility for childcare. Similarly, among the

Australian aborigines of Tasmania it was women who were responsible for fishing and hunting seal and opossum. Oakley also notes that in many contemporary industrial societies heavy work is often done by women. Up until 1842 women in Britain were employed in mines pushing coal trucks and in many third world countries as much as a quarter of the labour force in mines is still female.

On the basis of this kind of evidence it is difficult to conclude that differences between women and men in social roles are purely the result of biology. Sociologists have therefore explored the role of culture in shaping male and female gender identities, in particular the part played by gender socialization.

Research and evaluation activity

Carry out research in your library on the roles played by men and women in other societies. If possible read the first chapter of Housewife *by Ann Oakley, together with any other sources you can find. Once you have completed your research, produce a summary of the evidence under the following headings:*

1 Evidence of universal male/female roles (examples of tasks or roles which are almost always the responsibility of one sex).
2 Evidence of cultural variations in gender roles (examples of differences between societies in assumptions about what are normal roles for males and females).
3 An evaluation of your evidence (this should conclude whether you think cultural or biological influences are more important in shaping gender roles and identities).

Gender socialization

Those writers who argue that gender is shaped by culture rather than biology have paid considerable attention to the process of socialization. We saw in Chapter 2 how human beings cannot function as members of society without socialization (see, for example, the case of Isabelle on p. 29). This suggests that much of our identity and behaviour is the result of experiences of interaction with other people, especially during childhood, and cannot be attributed solely to genes and biological drives.

Parents and children

As a result of the influence of feminism on sociology, a range of research has been carried out into the extent of differences in socialization between males and females. Some studies have suggested that parents begin to treat boys and girls differently from birth onwards. For example, Moss (1970) found that male babies were cuddled more than female babies and received more stimulation in general than girls. However, girls' noises and actions were repeated back to the baby by the mother more frequently than boys'.

In an experiment Will, Self and Datan (cited in Tavris and Wade 1984) gave six of a group of eleven mothers a six-month-old baby called Beth dressed in a frilly pink dress and observed their interaction. This was compared with the interaction of the other five of the group who were given six-month-old Adam in blue overalls. Beth received more smiles, was offered a doll to play with and was described by the mothers as 'sweet' and with a 'soft cry'. Adam was offered a train more often to play with. What the mothers in the experiment did not realize was that Beth and Adam were the same baby. The mothers all claimed that they treated their baby sons and daughters the same and ten of them said they encouraged their sons to play with dolls.

Ann Oakley: patterns of gender socialization

The feminist sociologist Ann Oakley (1981) argues that gender socialization takes place in four main ways.

1 **Manipulation**. Parents encourage behaviour seen as normal for the child's sex and discourage what is seen as deviant. For example, a mother may pay particular attention to girls' hair and clothes or scold her daughters more than her sons for getting dirty.

2 **Canalization**. This involves channelling the child's interests into toys and activities seen as normal for his or her sex. An obvious example is channelling girls into an interest in housework by giving them dolls, miniature kitchens and domestic appliances.

3 **Verbal appellations**. These are the names that children are called which teach them to identify with the appropriate gender, for example 'You're a naughty boy' or 'That's a good girl'.

4 **Different activities**. Children are encouraged to involve themselves in different activities. For example, girls are traditionally expected to take part in more indoor activities such as helping mothers with housework. Boys are given more freedom to roam around outdoors.

Development of gender identity

By the age of five most children have acquired a clear gender identity – in other words, they know which gender they belong to and are aware of gender-appropriate attitudes and behaviour. American psychologist William Damon (1977) asked children questions about a boy named George who liked to play with dolls. The youngest children felt George should go ahead and do what he wanted. However, five- and six-year-olds recognized that George's behaviour was likely to be viewed as deviant and attract punishment or ridicule. Older children of six to seven began to recognize that while George's behaviour might not be inherently wrong and deserving of punishment, he was perhaps unwise to play with dolls as it might cause him embarrassment.

Interpretation and evaluation activity
Examine the way you were treated by your parents compared to any siblings of the opposite sex. Compare your conclusions with those of other students. Do you feel any differences have affected your gender identity?

Education and gender socialization

In industrial societies educational institutions play an important role in socializing children and young people for adult roles. Since the 1970s there has been increasing interest in the significance of gender differences in education. Feminist sociologists in particular have pointed to evidence that girls' and boys' experience of education varies considerably, even when they sit in the same classroom.

Up until the 1980s it was common for girls and boys to study very different subjects, with science and technology taken predominantly by males. There was traditionally more emphasis on domestic subjects such as cookery and needlework for girls, together with arts and humanities in the academic subjects. The introduction of a National Curriculum up to the age of sixteen has helped to reduce differences in subject choice. Moreover, there is evidence that girls are beginning to achieve better than boys at A level and that the number of males and females entering higher education has almost equalized. Nevertheless, after the age of sixteen females are still less well represented in areas such as science, engineering and technical subjects and girls with higher-level qualifications often seem to have lower aspirations than boys with similar grades.

Research and interpretation activity

Try to obtain information about the subjects studied by males and females in your educational institution and compare these with national statistics (see for example Social Trends*). Are there any significant gender differences? Do these follow any patterns?*

Michelle Stanworth: gender in the classroom

Much of the research into gender and education in the 1970s and 1980s emphasized the importance of the **hidden curriculum**. This implies that pupils not only learn formal subjects such as English or physics but also receive hidden messages about their class, ethnicity or gender from their experience of schooling. Michelle Stanworth (1983) found in a study of a college of further education that staff had different attitudes towards and expectations of male and female students. One lecturer described one of the most academically successful female students as likely to become a 'personal assistant to someone rather important'. In class, male students appeared to get more attention from staff and even when girls were in the majority boys were allowed to dominate classroom discussion.

Dale Spender: invisible women

Dale Spender takes this type of argument further in her book *Invisible Women* (1983). Spender argues that women are made 'invisible' in our culture since their lives and achievements are not represented as being of any significance. Spender argues that this is reflected in the way knowledge in the school curriculum is from a male viewpoint. Economics, for example, studies paid employment but gives little consideration to the contribution of unpaid housework to the economy; in history the achievements of male kings, soldiers and politicians are highlighted, but the role of women in bringing up children and running homes is rarely considered; in science the achievements of male scientists receive more prominence than the role played by less well-known female researchers.

Application and evaluation activity

Are gender differences in classroom interaction apparent in your experience of education? To what extent do your experiences confirm or contradict Stanworth's arguments?

Examine the academic subjects you are studying. Do you agree with Spender that women are invisible in them?

Children's books

The invisibility of women highlighted by Spender is evidenced in a number of studies of books written for young children (Glynnis Lobban 1974; Grauerholz and Pescosolido 1989; Lesley Best 1993). Such studies show that male characters tend to outnumber female characters by up to three to one. Where females do appear they are more likely to be in subordinate or traditionally stereotyped female roles.

Research and evaluation activity
Examine a sample of children's books and consider the following questions:

1 *To what extent do male characters outnumber female characters?*
2 *To what extent does the way in which female characters are represented and the roles they play differ from male characters?*
3 *What significance would you attach to your findings?*

Changes in the 1990s?

Since the 1970s there have certainly been major changes in the education system as a result of the kind of criticisms levelled at schools by feminists. Some writers have argued that much of the research done over ten years ago is now dated. Certainly the improvements in girls' and women's educational achievement may reflect a greater commitment to equality of opportunity in the educational system. However, even recent studies suggest that differences remain.

Sue Sharpe: just like a girl

Sue Sharpe (1976) carried out a study of mainly working-class girls in schools in Ealing in 1972. She found that girls' priorities at school-leaving age were 'love, marriage, husbands, children, jobs and careers, more or less in that order'. Most girls' career aims were centred on traditionally female jobs such as office work, teaching, nursing and shop work. Sharpe's conclusion was that girls' education simply reinforced the messages they had received from primary socialization that their main roles in life were as wives and mothers.

Sharpe (1994) carried out a follow-up to this study in 1991 and acknowledged the significance of changes in the intervening years. She found that most girls in the 1990s were much more assertive about their rights and were more concerned about staying on at school or college after sixteen to acquire more qualifications. However, Sharpe also points to contradictions in the messages girls receive today. On the one hand there is greater emphasis on achieving qualifications, but on the other girls are still socialized to be future wives and mothers and are generally expected to help out far more with household chores than boys. This may help to explain why, even when girls achieve on equal terms with boys at school, they are less likely to progress to higher education and find it harder than males to translate academic success into success in careers.

Women and science

Another study by Kim Thomas (1990) points to the problems that women's gender identity poses for those who wish to compete on equal terms with men. Thomas is particularly concerned with why women are still under-represented on science courses in higher education. She argues that for many women the identity of scientist conflicts with their notions of female identity. She notes that 'women were only too aware of having to make a choice between following a career and raising a family: being a physicist or being a woman'.

Evaluation activity
How far have the models of gender identity offered to girls changed in the last twenty years?

Make a list of evidence which suggests things have changed and another list of evidence which suggests that girls are still encouraged into different roles. Use this to write a short evaluation on the question above.

Mass media and gender representations

One area which has attracted considerable analysis from feminist writers is the messages about gender carried in mass media. Feminists argue that, like education and other forms of socialization, the mass media carry ideological messages about relations between the sexes and the 'natural' roles of men and women. Much of the feminist research in the 1960s and 1970s explored the extent of gender stereotyping in mass media. Like the studies of children's books, they found that women tended to be portrayed in a limited range of traditional roles or were largely absent in certain forms of media, for example news and current affairs programmes.

Gay Tuchman and the annihilation of women

Gay Tuchman (1981) in a review of research argues that women are normally seen either in the confines of the home or in sexual or romantic situations. Those women who are seen in paid employment are often condemned or portrayed as incompetent or inferior to male colleagues. Tuchman describes this as the 'symbolic annihilation' of women, echoing Spender's argument about the 'invisibility' of women. She argues that this symbolic annihilation occurs through the absence, condemnation and trivialization of women. Women are rarely seen in positions of power or status, they are condemned for being interested in unimportant things and they are trivialized by being mainly presented in subordinate roles as either domestic workers or sex objects.

Pauline Clark, one of Britain's highest ranking operational policewomen (*left*).
Melinda Messenger modelling clothes by Tattoo at the Pure Womenswear Show in London (*right*).

Media images of women have arguably been transformed dramatically since the 1970s, with many more positive images of females now available in cinema, television and women's magazines. However, in 1993 the Broadcasting Standards Council monitored all evening television programmes for one week. It found that only 30 per cent of speaking roles were taken by women. In news programmes men appeared in the overwhelming majority, not just as reporters but also as interviewees, experts and studio guests.

Evaluation activity

Using the examples given and any other evidence, discuss how far the contemporary mass media simply reinforce traditional gender stereotypes.

Content analysis

Studies such as Tuchman's are based on **content analysis**. The studies of children's books mentioned earlier use a similar form of analysis. This method involves counting the number of occasions on which particular categories of representations appear in specified media, for example how often women appear in TV dramas as housewives, secretaries or nurses as compared to more traditionally male occupations. This method is useful for producing quantitative data; for example, it might show that women are consistently over-represented in some categories and under-represented in others. However, content analysis is poor at capturing the subtleties of media messages. For example, knowing that women appear as secretaries on *x* occasions out of a sample of *y* programmes tells us little about how they are presented or the context of the roles.

Research activity: content analysis

Carry out your own content analysis of how women are presented in mass media compared to men. Here are some suggestions:

- *Compare coverage of women's sport to men's on the sports pages of national newspapers.*
- *Analyse the roles played by men and women in a sample of popular soap operas.*
- *Analyse a sample of TV news broadcasts, looking at not only the proportion of male and female newscasters and reporters, but also the extent to which men and women are subjects of news stories/interviewed by reporters and so on.*

In each case you will need to devise categories to classify the media content you have analysed (for example, a classification of types of characters found in soap operas). You will also need to devise a way of quantifying your analysis (for example, measuring the column inches in newspapers, the number of occasions on which a particular feature appears or the amount of time devoted to categories by TV news programmes).

Women's magazines

While women are invisible or play a peripheral role in many branches of the mass media, some media are directed specifically at women, notably magazines for women and teenage girls. Angela McRobbie in her study of *Jackie* (1982) argued that magazines such as this provide a role model for teenage girls which reinforces conventional notions of femininity. She found that the theme of **romantic individualism** ran through many stories, with girls struggling single-handedly to win their man. Girls were portrayed as rivals and the notion of female solidarity was rarely explored. The main message for girls seemed to be that falling in love and getting married was the main aim in life for teenage girls.

Marjorie Ferguson's study (1983) focused on magazines for older women: *Woman, Woman's Own* and *Woman's Weekly* between 1949 and 1974. Like McRobbie, she suggests that women's magazines centre on certain themes and present role models of femininity for women to follow. Like *Jackie*, these magazines emphasized the theme of love and marriage and 'getting and keeping your man', albeit in a format aimed at older married women. A secondary theme was self-improvement, as seen in women's magazines' exhortations to 'lose a stone in two weeks on our new diet', 'brighten up your home with pastel colours' or 'cook our fabulous new pasta dish in twenty minutes'.

In a follow-up analysis of magazines in 1979–80, Ferguson found that self-improvement had taken over as the major theme, perhaps reflecting the increasing number of women in paid employment. Nevertheless, Ferguson argues that women's magazines provide what she calls a **cult of femininity**. They celebrate the ideal of what it means to be a woman in our culture. She suggests their message is that 'women are uniquely different' and 'require separate treatment and instruction in ways that men do not' (Ferguson 1983, p. 190).

> *Interpretation and evaluation activity*
> *Analyse a sample of magazines for either adult women or teenage girls. Have such magazines changed since the 1970s or are the same themes still dominant?*

Semiotics and gender

In recent years feminist analysis of the media has moved on from simply showing that women are presented in a limited range of stereotyped roles to analysing the symbolic messages carried by media products and the way in which these often reflect ideologies about gender. This type of approach is known as **semiotics** and is discussed further in Chapter 8. A good area to start analysing the media using semiotics is to study advertisements, whether on television, in magazines or on advertising hoardings. Advertisements aimed specifically at women often carry hidden assumptions about femininity, whether for household products (e.g. washing powder) or women's clothing (e.g. bras). Other advertisements are aimed more specifically at males (e.g. for cars or beer) and may carry hidden assumptions about masculinity.

> *Interpretation and application activity*
> *What messages about gender are contained in the advertisements above?*
>   *Give two other examples of advertisements which you feel carry hidden messages about gender and explain what they are.*

Interpreting images of women

The type of research into representations of women in education, literature and mass media discussed above has provided considerable evidence for feminist arguments about how gender identities are socially constructed. Feminists have argued that these representations offer traditional models of gender identity and reinforce the messages provided by other sources of gender socialization.

In recent years some feminists have criticized this kind of approach as too simplistic. Rosemary Betterton (1987) argues that the process whereby images of women are produced, circulated and interpreted is a complex one. Images of women do not always conform to crude traditional stereotypes but may still reflect traditional definitions of femininity. For example, fewer advertisers now rely on stereotypical images of women as housewives and sex objects. However, even when women are portrayed in more masculine roles they still have to be shown as attractive or desirable.

Betterton also argues that it cannot be assumed that all women will necessarily interpret images of femininity in the same way. She points to the example of popular press representations of women peace protesters at the Greenham Common missile base in the 1980s. These representations presented such women as not truly feminine, for example by highlighting the fact that some had left their families to join the protest. However, Betterton points out that for many feminists these images could be interpreted positively as offering 'new possibilities for women's lives and actions' (Betterton 1987, p. 10).

Romantic fiction and soap operas

Traditional feminists have tended to see women simply as victims of media representations of femininity. However, a growing body of research has explored how women use different types of media for their own pleasure. Romantic fiction and American soap operas such as *Dallas* and *Dynasty* can be seen as reinforcing conventional gender stereotypes but are also hugely popular with women themselves.

Ien Ang (1985) points out how many women are able to relate to the conflicts and dilemmas faced by women in soaps such as *Dallas*. In this sense *Dallas* highlights aspects of patriarchy which women are aware of in their own lives. Ang argues that we cannot assume that because women watch soaps like *Dallas* they will automatically be brainwashed into traditional roles. She insists that women's political allegiances cannot be read off from what they consume culturally. As a result of this kind of argument, recent feminist research into representations has shifted from content analysis to an examination of the different ways in which these representations are interpreted by female audiences. (These issues are explored further in Chapter 7, pp. 182–4.)

Gender research: new directions

Much of the research inspired by second wave feminism attempted to demonstrate how gender roles were socially constructed – culture was seen as the key determinant of gender identity. Women were seen as oppressed by the conventional roles ascribed to them in patriarchal culture. In recent years this sort of approach has been criticized for a number of reasons and this has led feminists to explore a variety of new directions in the study of gender and identity.

There has also emerged what has been variously described as **third wave feminism** and **postmodern feminism**. These new forms of feminism have been less concerned with emphasizing gender as the key source of oppression and identity for women, and have recognized the importance of differences between women based on class, ethnicity, nationality, age, sexual orientation, disability and so on.

An example of this approach is Elizabeth Spelman's (1988) book, *Inessential Woman*. In common with many postmodern thinkers, Spelman rejects the view that any single essence can explain personal identity. Just as class is the essential organizing concept for Marxists, for feminists it has been the category of gender. Spelman argues that feminists must 'deconstruct' the category of gender in order to expose the differences between women as well as their common identity.

An oversocialized concept of woman

In previous chapters we have encountered the criticism of a number of sociological perspectives for presenting an 'oversocialized concept of man' – human beings are seen as moulded by their socialization to fit an identity laid down by their culture. This ignores the degree to which individuals actively participate in their own socialization. This is a problem with certain feminist accounts of gender socialization, which tend to portray women as being passively moulded into traditional female roles by what they are taught by parents, schools and the media. This type of account ignores the degree to which women (and men) have some choice in developing their own identities and are able to resist aspects of socialization which they choose not to accept.

A sociological example here is Margaret Fuller's (1984) study of Black girls in a London comprehensive. She highlights the way in which the girls were able to resist negative stereotypes held by teachers about Black and female pupils. The girls adopted an indifferent attitude towards their teachers but worked hard to achieve success.

Sociologists have moved away from the idea that socialization is something which occurs in childhood and determines a person's identity for the rest of their lives. Instead it is recognized that socialization is a lifelong process in which an individual's identity can undergo sometimes radical changes. An American study by Kathleen Gerson (1985) revealed that the views women held in adolescence provided a poor guide to their later behaviour. For example, women who had started out planning to be wives and mothers often changed course as a result of events such as divorce and embarked on new careers and new identities.

 Application and evaluation activity
How far do you conform to traditional masculine or feminine roles?
You might start by considering examples of ways in which you do try to be masculine or feminine in traditional terms, and then go on to consider ways in which you reject traditional gender stereotypes in your appearance or behaviour.

Women as victims

A related problem is that orthodox feminist accounts frequently portray women as victims of patriarchy. Men are seen as the oppressors and women as the oppressed. This ignores the degree to which women may exert some degree of control, albeit in limited areas. For example, Julia O'Connell Davidson (O'Connell Davidson and Layder 1994) carried out research into prostitution, often regarded as the ultimate example of women as victims of patriarchy. However, O'Connell Davidson points out that prostitutes often relish the fact that no single man can claim ownership of their sexuality and are able to exploit and manipulate their clients as much as they are exploited and manipulated themselves.

Similarly, Emily Martin (1989) examines the way in which women deal with childbirth in a situation where the process is controlled by a mostly male-dominated medical profession. Martin shows how women employ a variety of strategies of resistance in order to gain some control for themselves. For example, some women delay going into hospital so that it is less likely doctors will order a caesarian section. In another case a woman described how she contaminated sterile scissors so they could not be used to give her an episiotomy (a surgical cut to widen the birth opening) just before delivery.

The significance of biology

Most feminist accounts have emphasized culture rather than biology as the source of gender differences. This can be seen in the concern to separate the concepts of sex and gender in order to show that social roles are not necessarily determined by biology. However, many feminists now recognize that it is important to acknowledge that women and men are biologically different. Linda Birke (1986) points out that biological experiences have an impact on the way in which gender is socially constructed. In recent years there has been a growth of interest among sociologists in the body and its importance in relation to personal identity.

Martin (1989) points to the fact that only women experience changes such as childbirth, menstruation and the menopause, which means that women's identity is influenced by biological as well as cultural factors. This is not to say that culture is unimportant – many feminists point out that it is patriarchal culture that defines women's biological role in reproduction as of relatively low status compared to men's roles in production, for example in paid employment.

Interpretation, application and evaluation activity
In a group discuss ways in which your body is important to your personal identity. For example, is it important that you are fat/thin, good looking/plain, tall/short, muscular/puny in how you see yourself and are seen by others? To what extent are the cultural meanings attached to these physical characteristics important?

Femininities

Traditionally feminism has emphasized the way in which women are channelled by their socialization into a limiting feminine role. In adolescence girls are expected to immerse themselves in a culture of romance in order to find a suitable marriage partner, while as mature married women they are expected to embrace the roles of wife and mother. In

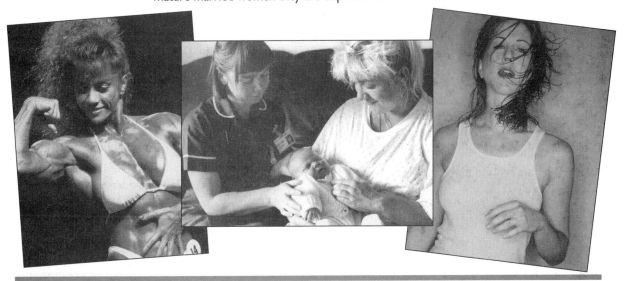

recent years feminists have begun to explore how women do not simply conform to a single stereotype of femininity. Instead there are a variety of femininities; for example, what is expected of women may vary between social classes, ethnic groups and generations. Women may also have opportunities to negotiate their own version of womanhood within the constraints offered by their culture.

> *Using the pictures on the previous page and any other evidence, evaluate the view that there is no longer a single stereotype of femininity.*

Black feminism

One sign of the diversity of femininities is the emergence of Black feminism as a distinctive voice within the feminist movement. Black feminists such as bell hooks (1982) have argued that the women's movement has traditionally been dominated by white middle-class women who have failed to address the concerns of their Black sisters. Thus for many Black women issues of race and ethnicity are as important as those of gender in their identity.

Asian women in Britain are often portrayed as victims of a patriarchal culture where women are largely confined to the home and are frequently expected to participate in arranged marriages. This kind of view is criticized by Helen Carby (1982), who argues that it fails to understand ethnic minority cultures from the perspective of insiders. Certainly sexism and patriarchy are a problem for Black women as they are for White women. However, the family and community in ethnic minorities often act as sources of defence and support for both women and men against racism and discrimination. Similarly, an institution such as arranged marriage is often viewed favourably by Asian women because it offers a high degree of security and support in a society where many marriages based on romance end in divorce and young parents are often expected to survive with little support from families and neighbours.

Feminism and disability

Another example of the emphasis on femininities is the emergence of a voice for disabled feminists. Writers such as Nasa Begum (1992) argue that disability is socially constructed in much the same way as gender. Like other women, disabled women are prevented from doing certain things more by the attitudes of society than by the fact that their bodies do not allow them. Begum argues that feminists can no longer ignore disabled women in their analysis of gender relations.

A different voice

Some feminists have argued that rather than seeing femininity as inferior and seeking to emulate men, women should celebrate their superior qualities. Carol Gilligan, in her book *In a Different Voice* (1982), argues that men approach moral problems in a rational way using 'reason' and are more concerned with personal achievement. Women are more concerned about relationships with others and place a higher emphasis on care and consideration to others.

Gilligan's argument at first seems to reflect popular stereotypes about natural differences between the sexes. However, Gilligan insists that these differences are not simply biological but are the result of socialization. Drawing on the work of Nancy Chodorow (see p. 86), Gilligan argues that girls learn feminine identity through intimacy with their mothers; they therefore come to value close and supportive relationships, especially with other women. Men by contrast must experience separation from their mothers in order to acquire masculine identity and thus learn to reject intimacy and emotion in favour of competitiveness and rationality.

Some feminists have been highly critical of Gilligan, arguing that women and men are more alike than she acknowledges and accusing her of perpetuating traditional stereotypes of gender. Nevertheless, there is some evidence that her ideas have had influence in the business community. Some management theorists now recognize that women may bring special qualities as managers, for example skills in building teams, empathy with subordinates and a greater awareness of people's emotional needs.

 Evaluation activity
Do you agree that men and women think in different ways? If so, what are the strengths and weaknesses of each sex's approach to problems?

Masculinities

One of the major feminist criticisms of malestream sociology is the invisibility of women. However, men are also arguably invisible in one sense in many sociological accounts, including those of feminists. Hearn and Morgan (1990) point out that while men are the subject of much research in sociology (for example, research into social mobility), much of this research has little to say about the experience of being a man or the concept of masculinity. Similarly, many feminist accounts emphasize the role of men as exploiters and oppressors of women and fail to look at the meanings that masculinity has for men themselves.

In recent years this issue has been addressed by a number of studies of masculinity. Many of them suggest that it is more useful to speak of masculinities rather than masculinity. While the traditional stereotype of masculinity is perhaps based on the kind of characters played in films by Clint Eastwood or Sylvester Stallone, there are a wider variety of models of masculinity than this stereotype would suggest.

Masculinism

Arthur Brittan (1989) argues that a distinction needs to be made between **masculinity** and **masculinism**. He suggests that masculinity is something that is always changing. For example, in the nineteenth century masculinity was associated with the notion of the male as provider and protector of his wife and family. By the 1970s the concept of the 'new man' who shared in housework and childcare was emerging. Similarly, there are differences in notions of masculinity between different classes, ethnic groups and localities. Brittan thus argues that masculinity is always constructed in particular social and historical circumstances. At the same time, Brittan argues that different masculinities can be seen as different expressions of masculinism, a form of dominant ideology. While men express their masculinity in a variety of ways, masculinism – in the form of male dominance – can be seen in all classes, ethnic groups and localities, although it expresses itself in different ways.

Changing men

Lynne Segal (1990) also shows how masculinity has been socially constructed in different ways in different historical periods. She suggests that the contemporary stereotype of the traditional 'macho' male emerged in the Victorian period. In the upper classes males were educated in public schools to cultivate a stiff upper lip, while the hard physical work of male manual workers encouraged a culture of masculinity based on the male peer group and activities such as drinking and sport.

Like Brittan, Segal notes that masculinity takes many forms. She also points out that some groups of men are denied full masculine status in our culture. Homosexuals, for example, are often portrayed as effeminate, as not real men. In recent years, however, some gay men have tried to assert homosexual identities as an alternative expression of masculinity. Similarly, a contradictory approach to the masculinity of Black men is apparent. Traditional myths in White culture represent Black men as enormously virile and as a threat to White women. However, the denial of status and power to Black men in White societies has meant that many feel emasculated and less than a man.

Segal also highlights the growth of a movement of men against sexism, with a minority of men becoming more willing to challenge conventional gender roles. Such men often see conventional male sexual identities as being as damaging to men as they are to women. Segal concludes that there is the potential to break down traditional structures of male power if groups such as feminists, anti-sexist men, gay men and lesbians continue to work for change. She concludes by pointing out that if they are successful it would 'spell the end of masculinity as we have known it' (1990, p. 319).

Evaluation activity

Using the pictures above and any other evidence discuss the extent to which men are moving away from traditional masculine identities.

The social construction of sexuality

Like gender differences, sexuality is often seen as something which is linked to nature and biology rather than part of culture. Freud saw the sex drive or libido as the most fundamental human drive. Sociobiologists argue that ultimately all species are programmed to try to ensure their own reproduction; in the case of humans this means finding a mate and having sex.

However, the way in which human sexuality is expressed and organized varies widely between human societies and even individuals. For example, heterosexuality is seen as being the norm in many cultures because it is linked to biological reproduction; however, homosexual behaviour is regarded as an acceptable alternative to heterosexuality in many others.

Among some native North American peoples such as the Cheyenne, a traditional practice known as the **berdache** allowed men to opt out of the traditional male gender role of hunting and fighting and instead to move in female circles, dress as women and even take husbands. Men who might be stigmatized as effeminate homosexuals in our culture were offered an institutionalized and socially accepted role in these societies.

Norms of sexual attractiveness also vary. In some cultures a plump body is seen as sexually attractive. In parts of West Africa, wealthy men frequently sent their daughters to fattening houses to be fed on fattening foods with minimal exercise in order to make them plump (Helman 1990). Western European paintings of female nudes from the seventeenth and eighteenth centuries by artists such as Rubens suggest an ideal of feminine beauty that would be judged as overweight by today's standards. This compares with the emphasis on slimness in contemporary western ideals of female beauty, seen in its most extreme form in waif-like supermodels who cultivate an almost emaciated figure.

Interpretation and application activity
Using the examples illustrated above and any other evidence, discuss the view that female beauty is constructed in different ways by different cultures and in different historical periods.

Kinsey and sex research

Research by sexologists has also revealed far more sexual diversity within contemporary western societies than was acknowledged in the past. Perhaps the most famous example of this is the research of Alfred Kinsey and his colleagues (Kinsey et al. 1948; 1953), who interviewed thousands of men and women about their sexual habits and experiences. Kinsey's research found that sexual activity before and outside marriage was far more prevalent than generally believed at that time, with 80 per cent of men and about 50 per cent of women having had sex before marriage. Similarly, Kinsey found that sexual practices such as masturbation, oral sex and homosexual relations were far from uncommon at a time when these were regarded by many people as in some way deviant. Kinsey also showed how even quite similar people might have completely different sex lives. He cited the example of two men who lived in the same town, met in the same place of business and had common social activities. One of these men had had one ejaculation in thirty years while another claimed to have thirty a week.

Kinsey's research has been criticized because of the unrepresentativeness of his samples and his interviewing techniques. However, subsequent studies suggest that the general picture of sexual diversity presented by his work is probably correct. A more recent study by Lillian Rubin (1990) in the United States found that in general sexual activity now begins at a younger age than in the recent past and women in particular have higher expectations of sexual pleasure in relationships. Significantly, Rubin found that many men found this threatening and felt a sense of inadequacy in sexual relationships.

Jeffrey Weeks: the regulation of sexuality

Jeffrey Weeks (1986) argues that because sexuality is expressed in so many different ways it must be seen as something which is socially constructed. He rejects the sociobiological view that sexuality can be reduced to the expression of a simple biological drive because this fails to account for the wide variety of ways in which human sexuality can be expressed. Weeks argues that sexuality needs to be studied from a sociological viewpoint because society organizes and regulates sexuality in a variety of ways.

1 **Kinship and family systems**. In all societies rules about marriage and incest define who we may mate with. While most societies have incest taboos, there is a wide variation in who this applies to. For example, in some societies marriage between cousins is the norm but in the Middle Ages this was forbidden in Europe. In the ancient Egyptian royal family marriage between brothers and sisters was permitted, though this is taboo in most cultures.

2 **Economic and social organization**. Wider changes in society are often reflected in changes in sexual behaviour and attitudes. For example, a rise in illegitimacy in the early nineteenth century was probably due to the disruption of traditional patterns of courtship and marriage caused by the industrial revolution.

3 **Social regulation**. In the last hundred years the regulation of sexual behaviour has shifted from the church via moral regulation to medicine, psychology, social work and welfare organizations. However, Weeks points out that attempts to regulate sexuality can have unforeseen consequences; for example, attempts to ban sexually explicit films have often given them additional publicity and led to more people going to see them!

4 **Political interventions**. The extent of regulation and intervention in sexual life often reflects the balance of social and political forces. In the 1960s a climate of political liberalism created an atmosphere of greater sexual permissiveness. However, in the 1980s the success of the New Right, especially in America, tipped the balance back towards sexual conservatism, with more condemnation of homosexuality, abortion and sexual permissiveness generally.

5 **Cultures of resistance**. Despite attempts to control and regulate sexual behaviour, there is a long history of opposition and resistance to prevailing moral codes. The best example of this is probably male homosexual subcultures, which have existed since the late Middle Ages. This has become more apparent in recent years with the development of a fully-fledged gay rights movement incorporating not only gay men but also groups representing lesbians.

Weeks thus argues that sexuality is the product of culture rather than biology. Sexuality is also an important component in many individuals' identities. As noted earlier, notions of normality in relation to masculine and feminine identities are bound up with notions of sexual normality, for example the notion that 'real men' are not homosexuals. Those whose sexuality does not fit into such norms may have a deviant identity imposed on them by others or may voluntarily embrace it as a rejection of the sexual norms of the wider society.

Homosexuality

Homosexuality provides perhaps the clearest example of the way in which 'normal' and 'abnormal' sexuality is defined by prevailing cultural norms. The term homosexuality itself was invented only in the nineteenth century. Before that a variety of other terms were used for homosexuals, such as 'sodomites'; however, this included men who engaged in sodomy with women and animals and did not recognize the idea of female homosexuality.

Michel Foucault and discourses about sexuality

The French philosopher Michel Foucault (1984) argues that new ways of classifying sexual behaviour first started to develop from the eighteenth century onwards as governments sought to regulate sexual behaviour and control population growth. Foucault describes ways of thinking, talking and writing about matters such as sexual behaviour as discourses. Discourses provide a framework for people to understand and make sense of the world.

The new discourses about sexuality were heavily influenced by scientific thinking and the wish to classify and label all matters of scientific study, including sexual behaviour. Thus not only was homosexuality invented as a deviant label in the 1860s, but thereafter researchers sought to distinguish a variety of different categories of homosexuals. One early sexologist, Clifford Allen, distinguished twelve types ranging from the compulsive and nervous to the psychopathic and alcoholic.

Homosexuality as abnormality

As homosexuality came to be defined as abnormal it became increasingly the topic of medical discourse, with researchers seeking to pinpoint the causes of homosexuality and other 'perversions' and to suggest cures for them. Theories about the causes of homosexuality ranged from those which stress some biological abnormality to those which have searched for some abnormality in social or psychological development.

For example, Freudian theories of homosexuality emphasize the lack of a strong father figure in male homosexuals' socialization, leading to a failure to develop a normal male sexual identity. In recent years, however, most experts have rejected the notion of homosexuality as a mental illness or abnormality. In 1972 the American Psychiatric Association removed it from its list of psychiatric disorders.

While there is more tolerance of homosexuality in Britain today than in the past (up until 1861 sodomy was theoretically punishable by death), homosexuality is still regarded as deviant by many. Clause 28 of the 1988 Local Government Act described homosexuality as a 'pretended family relationship' and forbade teachers or others employed in local government from portraying it as an equal alternative to heterosexuality in sex education.

Adrienne Rich (1984) uses the term **compulsory heterosexuality** to emphasize how in a variety of ways society makes it difficult for those who wish to develop a homosexual or bisexual identity. These range from legal sanctions such as Clause 28 to sexual harassment, gossip and jokes. Rich points out that just as women face discrimination because of sexism, lesbians and gay men face discrimination because of **heterosexism** (discrimination against homosexuals) and **homophobia** (fear of homosexuals).

Evidence from other cultures suggests that homosexuality is often regarded as normal. Among the people of East Bay in the Pacific Islands of Melanesia male homosexuality is common, especially among young men who live together in a men's house before marriage. However, older married men often continue to have sex with both younger men and boys and their wives. Men who are exclusively homosexual seem to be virtually unknown in this culture (Davenport 1965).

Interpretation activity
In cultures such as that of East Bay no distinction is made between homosexual and heterosexual men, while in our culture homosexuals are regarded as different and even deviant. What effect might regarding gay men as a distinct category have on their sexual identities?

Homosexual identities and gay subculture

Evidence from other societies suggests that the distinction made between homosexuals and heterosexuals in our culture is not a universal one but arises from the kind of discourses described by Foucault, which sought to identify homosexuality as a deviant category of behaviour in opposition to what was seen as the male norm of 'manliness' and exclusive heterosexuality.

The emergence of homosexuality as a deviant identity owes much to its emergence as a label used by doctors and psychologists to classify what was regarded as a deviant form of sexuality. However, to see homosexual identities as simply a label imposed by others ignores the extent to which homosexuals themselves have reacted to this kind of labelling by asserting their separate identity as a source of pride, accompanied by a claim to be treated as different but equal.

As mentioned above, there is a long tradition of male homosexuals organizing themselves in subcultures to resist attempts to suppress their sexual behaviour. Gay men have organized their own bars, clubs and meeting places and developed their own language, modes of dress and norms of behaviour. However, in recent times this resistance has taken a more open form with the development of the gay liberation movement in the 1970s and the emergence of organizations such as Stonewall, which campaigns for equal rights for homosexuals. This resulted in the lowering of the age of consent for homosexual relations from 21 to 18 in 1995, though not to 16 as called for by gay rights groups.

While many gay men have 'come out' and publicly embraced an alternative homosexual identity, it would be a mistake to see gay men as a single subculture. Research into gay men suggests a wide variety of sexual identities, ranging from 'camp' men who parody the traditional stereotype of the effeminate homosexual to 'super-macho' gays who present themselves as extremely masculine types with, for example, crew cuts, moustaches and leather trousers.

Research activity

If you have access to a CD-ROM, search back copies of a quality newspaper for articles about pressure groups or political movements representing gay men and lesbians. Write a short report summarizing the information you have found.

Lesbianism

Female homosexuals have always had a much lower profile than men and research by writers such as Kinsey suggests that lesbianism may be less common than male homosexuality. In recent years a more defined lesbian movement has emerged, but lesbians have been concerned to maintain a separate identity from gay men. Research suggests lesbians are more likely to stay in long-term relationships.

Many lesbian groups are also linked to sections of the women's movement, seeing both political and sexual separateness from men as necessary in resisting patriarchy. Nevertheless, some lesbian writers have criticized other feminists for failing to consider them as a distinct group of women. For example, Tamsin Wilton (1993) criticizes Christine Griffin (1981) for arguing that women are dependent on men for their leisure activities. Wilton points out that while heterosexual women's leisure may be organized around men, this is not true for lesbians.

Conclusion

This chapter has explored the related issues of gender and sexuality in relation to culture and identity. In both cases we have seen how people's gender identities and sexual orientations cannot simply be explained in biological terms. Both the roles we play as women and men and the way we express our sexuality are influenced by culture and are socially constructed. Nevertheless, it would be a mistake to ignore the influence of biology and see gender and sexuality as entirely cultural; there are real bodily differences between men and women. However, cultural norms have often used these as an excuse for limiting what women or men are able to do socially. Similarly, people's desires to express their sexuality can be seen as the expression of a fundamental biological drive. However, in order to understand why different people have different sexual preferences we must consider socialization and the influence of cultural norms.

These issues are part of the wider nature–nurture debate in the social sciences. Traditionally, sociologists have seen human identities as primarily a result of nurture or socialization and have rejected the view that who we are is determined by nature or biology. Biological reductionism – in other words, approaches which argue that human behaviour can be explained in terms of genetic tendencies or biological drives – clearly ignores the important role that culture plays in influencing who we are and how we think and behave.

To adopt a cultural reductionist approach would also be a mistake, for two reasons.

First, we should not ignore the importance of biology; for example, much of our sense of identity and self is linked to our bodies and how we feel about them. Second, neither biology nor culture completely determines who we are or how we think and behave. Many sociologists argue that within the constraints of our society and our biological capacities we have some freedom of choice to determine our own actions.

Coursework suggestion

Issues concerning gender socialization and gender identities offer numerous opportunities for coursework. For example, there is now a considerable body of research on images of women and men in the mass media using methods such as content analysis and semiotic analysis. This would provide useful background material and secondary data for your own research. This is a very broad area and you would be well advised to focus your research on a specific theme, for example one particular medium or genre, such as advertisements in women's magazines, gender roles in soap operas or images of masculinity in body-building magazines. Consult books on mass media, for example Paul Trowler's Investigating Mass Media *(1996), for examples of existing research. If you can look at examples of original studies, this will also give you background material and ideas for your own research.*

DATA RESPONSE QUESTION

Item A

The following quote comes from a speech made in 1852 by Sojourner Truth, a former Black slave and feminist activist.

> That man over there says women need to be helped into carriages, and lifted over ditches, and to have the best place everywhere. Nobody ever helps me into carriages, or over mud-puddles, or gives me any best place! And ain't I a woman? Look at me! Look at my arm! I have ploughed and I have planted and gathered into barns, and no man could head me! And ain't I a woman? I could work as much and eat as much as any man – when I could get it – and bear the lash as well! And ain't I a woman? I have borne thirteen children, and seen most of them sold off to slavery, and when I cried out with my mother's grief, none but Jesus heard me! And ain't I a woman?

(Quoted in bell hooks 1982, p.160)

Item B

> There is no one form of femininity but rather several, and the same applies to masculinities. They vary especially by age, marital status, class and ethnicity. For instance, the forms of masculinity among the working class lay more emphasis on physical prowess than those of the middle classes, where an appropriate career is more important because masculine status is defined in terms of success as husband–father breadwinner

(From Nicholas Abercrombie, Alan Warde et al. 1994, p. 227)

Item C

The following extract comes from Sara Delamont's field notes from her observation of a girl's PE lesson in a secondary school.

> [Teacher says] If you don't wear a leotard you must buy decent knickers for hockey because there are boys in the top field. Goes over the rules for taking showers and swimming. The teachers keep a record of who has a shower/goes swimming. If they are 'on period' they must tell her (about

showers and she'll put 'P' in book) and they are to tell swimming master – he won't be embarrassed as he is a married man. Just say 'I'm on period'. Discussing jewellery. Says it must come off for PE except sleepers. One girl says her ring won't come off. Told tight rings are dangerous … told that especially dangerous when you get swelling in pregnancy. If they have ring that is too tight they should get it cut off (try to get off with soap first). For PE must cover with plaster. (Later) Asks what can go into socks to protect legs in hockey. 'Shin pads.' 'Foam rubber.' 'Miss, newspaper.' 'Yes borrow your dad's page three from the *Mirror*.' Later, when inspecting kit the girls actually have, finds one girl with a home-made skirt. Says 'If your mum's quite handy at needlework there's no reason why you shouldn't make your own.' PE staff say they prefer a skirt to shorts because girls get 'fatter' as they get older and because a skirt will 'cover your Dr White's'. If they buy a skirt with an adjustable waist which wraps around it will last through their school life, and when they leave school, if they want to work in an office and want to play in the badminton team the skirt would do for that.

(Adapted from Delamont 1980, pp. 52–4)

1 In what ways does the extract from Item A suggest that the role of women is socially constructed rather than biologically determined? [5 marks]

2 Item B suggests that there is not just one form of masculinity but many. Identify and briefly explain two examples of variations in how masculinity is defined other than the example of class given in the extract. [4 marks]

3 Identify three examples of assumptions about gender in what teachers say to pupils in Item C and explain how these might influence the pupils. [6 marks]

4 Evaluate the view that girls and women are socialized into traditional gender roles by the process of socialization. [10 marks]

References and further reading

Abercrombie, N., Warde, A., Soothill, K., Urry, U. and Walby, S. (1994) *Contemporary British Society*, Cambridge: Polity Press.

Ang, I. (1985) *Watching Dallas*, London: Methuen.

Begum, N. (1992) 'Disabled women and the feminist agenda', in H. Hinds, A. Phoenix and J. Stacey (eds), *Working Out: New Directions for Women's Studies*, London: Verso.

Best, L. (1993) '"Dragons, dinner ladies and ferrets": sex roles in children's books', *Sociology Review*, vol. 2, no. 3.

Betterton, R. (1987) *Looking On*, London: Pandora.

Birke, L. (1986) *Women, Feminism and Biology*, Brighton: Wheatsheaf.

Brittan, A. (1989) *Masculinity and Power*, Oxford: Blackwell.

Carby, H. (1982) 'White woman listen! Black feminism and the boundaries of sisterhood', in Centre for Contemporary Cultural Studies, *The Empire Strikes Back*, London: Hutchinson.

Chodorow, N. (1978) *The Reproduction of Mothering*, London: University of California Press.

Damon, W. (1977) *The Social World of the Child*, San Francisco: Jossey Bass.

Davenport, W. (1965) 'Sexual patterns and their regulation in a society of the south west Pacific', in Beach, F. (ed.), *Sex and Behaviour*, New York: Wiley.

Delamont, S. (1980) *Sex Roles and the School*, London: Allen and Unwin.

Engels, F. (1972 [1884]) *The Origins of the Family, Private Property and the State*, London: Lawrence and Wishart.

Ferguson, M. (1983) *Forever Feminine: Women's Magazines and the Cult of Femininity*, London: Heinemann.

Foucault, M. (1984) *The History of Sexuality: An Introduction*, Harmondsworth: Penguin.

Fox, R. (1976) *Kinship and Marriage*, Harmondsworth: Penguin.

Freeman, D. (1983) *Margaret Mead and Samoa*, Harmondsworth: Penguin.

Freud, S. (1977 [1905]) *Three Essays on the Theory of Sexuality*, Pelican Freud Library (5), Harmondsworth: Penguin.

Friedan, B. (1963) *The Feminine Mystique*, London: Gollancz.

Fuller, M. (1984) 'Black girls in a London comprehensive school', in M. Hammersley and P. Woods (eds), *Life in School: The Sociology of School Culture*, Milton Keynes: Open University Press.

Gerson, K. (1985) *Hard Choices: How Women Decide about Work, Motherhood and Career*, Berkeley: University of California Press.

Gilligan, C. (1982) *In a Different Voice: Psychological Theory and Women's Development*, Cambridge, MA: Harvard University Press.

Grauerholz, E. and Pescosolido, B. (1989) 'Gender representation in children's literature', *Gender and Society*, March, pp. 113–25.

Griffin, C. (1981) 'Young women and leisure', in A. Tomlinson (ed.), *Leisure and Social Control*, Brighton: Brighton Polytechnic.

Hearn, J. and Morgan, D.H.J. (1990) 'Men, masculinities and social theory', in J. Hearn and D. Morgan (eds), *Men, Masculinities and Social Theory*, London: Unwin Hyman.

Helman, C.G. (1990) *Culture, Health and Illness*, London: Butterworth.

hooks, b. (1982) *Ain't I a Woman? Black Women and Feminism*, London: Pluto Press.

Kinsey, A., Pomeroy, W. and Martin, C. (1948) *Sexual Behaviour in the Human Male*, Philadelphia: W.B. Saunders.

Kinsey, A., Pomeroy, W., Martin, C. and Gebhard, P. (1953) *Sexual Behaviour in the Human Female*, Philadelphia: W.B. Saunders.

Lobban, G. (1974) 'Data report on British Reading Schemes', *Times Educational Supplement*, 1 March.

McRobbie, A. (1982) '*Jackie*, an ideology of adolescent femininity', in B. Waites et al., *Popular Culture Past and Present*, London: Croom Helm.

Martin, E. (1989) *The Women in the Body: A Cultural Analysis of Reproduction*, Milton Keynes: Open University Press.

Mead, M. (1935) *Sex and Temperament in Three Primitive Societies*, London: Routledge and Kegan Paul.

Mies, M. (1986) *Patriarchy and Accumulation on a World Scale: Women in the International Division of Labour*, London: Zed Books.

Millett K. (1970) *Sexual Politics*, New York: Doubleday.

Moss, H. (1970) 'Sex, age and state as determinants of mother–infant interaction', in K. Danziger (ed.), *Readings in Child Socialization*, Oxford: Pergamon Press.

Murdock G.P. (1949) *Social Structure*, New York: Macmillan.

Oakley, A. (1974) *Housewife*, London: Allen Lane.

Oakley A. (1981) *Subject Women* Oxford: Martin Robertson.

O'Connell Davidson, J. and Layder, D. (1994) *Methods, Sex and Madness*, London: Routledge.

Parsons, T. (1954) *Essays in Sociological Theory*, New York: The Free Press.

Rich, A. (1984) 'Compulsory heterosexuality and lesbian existence', in A. Snitow et al. (eds), *Desire: The Politics of Sexuality*, London: Virago.

Rubin, L. (1990) *Erotic Wars: What Happened to the Sexual Revolution?* New York: Farrar.

Segal, L. (1990) *Slow Motion: Changing Masculinities, Changing Men*, London: Virago.

Sharpe S. (1971, 1994) *Just Like a Girl: How Girls Learn to be Women*, Harmondsworth: Penguin.

Spelman, E. (1988) *Inessential Woman*, London: Women's Press.

Spender, D. (1983) *Invisible Women: Schooling Scandal*, London: Women's Press.

Stanworth, M. (1983) *Gender and Schooling*, London: Hutchinson.

Stoller, R. (1968) *Sex and Gender*, London: Hogarth Press.

Tavris, C. and Wade, C. (1984) *The Longest War: Sex Differences in Perspective*, London: Harcourt Brace Jovanovich.

Thomas K. (1991) *Gender and Subject Choice in Higher Education*, Milton Keynes: Open University Press/SRHE.

Trowler, P. (1996) *Investigating Mass Media*, London: Collins Educational.

Tuchman, G. (1981) 'The symbolic annihilation of women by mass media', in S. Cohen and J. Young (eds), *The Manufacture of News: Deviance, Social Problems and the Mass Media*, London: Constable.

Weeks, J. (1986) *Sexuality*, London: Routledge.

Wilson, E.O. (1975) *Sociobiology: The New Synthesis*, Cambridge, MA: Harvard University Press.

Wilton, T. (1993) 'Queer subjects: lesbians, heterosexual women and the academy', in M. Kennedy, C. Lubelska and V. Walsh (eds), *Making Connections*, London: Taylor and Francis.

Wollstonecraft, M. (1985 [1792]) *A Vindication of the Rights of Women*, Harmondsworth: Penguin.

5

Race, ethnicity and nationalism

Key ideas	Key thinkers
Self and Other	Robert Miles
Race	Edward Said
Racism	Paul Gilroy
Racialization	Martin Barker
Ethnicity	Phil Cohen
Hybrid cultures	Tariq Modood
Fragmented identities	Stuart Hall
Globalization	Benedict Anderson
Nationalism	Edward Shils
Imagined communities	Eric Hobsbawm
Difference	

Introduction

In this chapter we shall explore the significance of race, ethnicity and nationality as sources of identity and influences on culture. All three of these issues arouse strong feelings. Racial categories have long been used to identify distinct groups of human beings and in the past were used as a justification for slavery, colonial domination and even genocide. In the first part of the chapter we trace the history of ideas of race and how far they continue to shape identities in contemporary Britain.

The concept of ethnicity focuses more on groups who share a common culture. In the second part of the chapter we shall explore how Britain can be seen as a multicultural society and the significance of the coexistence of many ethnic groups providing a diverse range of cultural influences and sources of identity.

The last part of the chapter considers how belonging to a nation state has become important in creating identities in modern times. We also explore whether national identities are being undermined by the process of globalization or whether this is simply leading to the emergence of new forms of nationalism.

What's in a name?

Skin colour, language, religion and country of origin all play an important part in shaping people's identities. The terminology itself used to describe groups of people who have some of these factors in common is important in creating a sense of identity. Most people living in the United Kingdom might be described as British, but this excludes people from Northern Ireland, which is not part of Britain but is nevertheless part of the UK. Many Catholics in Northern Ireland see themselves as Irish anyway, while many Protestants wish to identify with the Union and refer to themselves as coming from Ulster. Even those who live in mainland Britain may see themselves as primarily Scots, Welsh, English or even Cornish.

Ethnic classifications

The problems are even greater when we try to consider racial or ethnic identities. For example, the British government has tried to obtain information on ethnic differences from surveys such as the Census. Your school, college or university may undertake ethnic monitoring of students and ask them to classify themselves as White, Black, Indian, Pakistani, Bangladeshi and so on. Although collecting such information is well intentioned – for example, it can be used to monitor whether equal opportunities policies are working – many people object to the classifications used.

Interpretation and evaluation activity

Why might it be useful to organizations such as employers' or educational institutions to collect information on the ethnic composition of their employees or students?

What criticisms could be made of the categories used to classify people in the question shown above?

Problems of terminology

Terminology in referring to people's racial, ethnic and national identities is a sensitive issue and sociologists working in this area need to be careful about the names they choose. For example, up until the 1950s it was regarded as perfectly acceptable to refer to Black Americans as negroes. However, later many Blacks objected to this term with its connotations of slavery and racial segregation.

In the 1960s the term 'Coloured' was used. For example, one of the main organizations involved in the American civil rights movement was known as the National Association for the Advancement of Colored People (NAACP). However, this too came under criticism as many Blacks felt that White people were as 'Coloured' as they were. In the 1960s the Black Power movement resurrected the term 'Black' but used it as a term of pride to emphasize that Black people should not try to emulate Whites but should be proud of their own blackness.

In recent years some groups have expressed dissatisfaction with the term Black. For example, Hispanic Americans and British Asians often feel unhappy at being included in the umbrella term 'Black' alongside those who have African ancestors. Some writers therefore prefer to use terms that indicate ethnic or cultural groups rather than groupings based on colour, for example Afro-Caribbeans, Pakistanis or East African Sikhs in Britain and African Americans, Native Americans and so on in the United States. Some writers now also refer to 'people of colour' as a generic term for people from racial or ethnic minority groups.

Such debates illustrate the importance of identities based on race, ethnicity and nationality to individuals. They also illustrate the way in which names carry meanings which change over time. Often the struggle for a new name symbolizes the struggle for a new identity for a social group.

Representations of the Other

Throughout history groups of humans have encountered other groups through trade, warfare and exploration. Robert Miles argues that as a result of such encounters groups develop a distinction between Self and Other, between their own group and the outsiders. He suggests:

> The consequence has been the production of 'representations' of the Other, images and beliefs which categorize people in terms of real or attributed differences when compared with self
>
> (Miles 1989, p. 11)

The Romans, for example, saw people who lived outside their empire as 'barbarians' – this term contrasted the outsiders with themselves, who they saw as being the peak of civilization. Similarly, in the Islamic world unbelievers were seen as 'infidels' – the Other were defined by their difference in religious belief from true Muslims.

Orientalism

In Edward Said's study, *Orientalism* (1985), he argues that similar conceptions of the Other can be seen in European encounters with the Orient, particularly the Middle East. Orientals were defined in terms of the way they were different from westerners. For example, they were seen as mysterious, exotic, unpredictable, cruel and lacking in sexual restraint. These were all characteristics of the Oriental Other which contrasted with the way Europeans liked to see themselves.

Images of the Other in pre-modern societies

Miles argues that there is little evidence that these images of the Other in the past corresponded to what sociologists today would describe as a concept of 'race'. Nowadays the idea of race is taken to imply the division of human beings into groups on the basis of innate biological differences, for example, skin colour, hair type and facial features. However, this idea of race only really emerged from about the seventeenth century onwards. Before this time physical differences, such as colour, do not seem to have assumed the significance that they achieved later in differentiating human beings.

The Romans, for example, recognized that Africans had dark skin but this was not a significant factor in differentiating them from Romans. Some Africans were admired by the Romans for their degree of civilization and social organization: the Carthaginian general Hannibal, for example, who crossed the Alps equipped with elephants and inflicted a crushing defeat on a much larger Roman army.

The concept of race

The concept of race in its modern form first emerged in the eighteenth century, when scientists began to try to produce racial classifications of humans just as biologists had produced classifications of plant and animal species. By the nineteenth

In the nineteenth century, and until quite recently, it was common to classify human beings into three main races: Caucasoid, Mongoloid and Negroid.

century writers were not simply classifying humans according to physical differences such as skin colour, hair type and facial characteristics, but were starting to suggest that some races might be superior to others.

One influential writer was Joseph Arthur, Comte de Gobineau (1816–82). Gobineau suggested there were three main racial groups – the white, yellow and black races – each with their own characteristics. Other writers used the terms Caucasoid, Mongoloid and Negroid to refer to these three main 'racial types'. Later writers developed these ideas; for example, Ernst Haeckel argued that some races had evolved further than others. He saw the Indogermanic race in particular as intellectually superior and the Negro race as closer to less highly evolved species. Haeckel's ideas were an important influence on the later development of the racial theories of Nazism.

Racism

The term **racism** is usually used by sociologists to refer to the belief that human beings can be categorized by innate biological characteristics such as skin colour. Racist beliefs often attribute certain social characteristics to different 'races'. For example, some nineteenth-century thinkers on race assumed that the 'Anglo-Saxon race' was naturally predisposed to democratic forms of government, tolerance and a belief in 'fair play'. Many sociologists see the origins of contemporary racist beliefs in the supposedly scientific theories of 'race' of the nineteenth century.

Slavery and racism

It was no coincidence that such ideas about race emerged at precisely the same period as European nations were developing colonial empires and the slave trade between Africa and America was flourishing. From the sixteenth century to the mid-nineteenth century slave traders pursued a triangular trade. Slave ships sailed from European ports such as Liverpool and Bristol with cargoes of European goods; these were traded for slaves in West Africa. The slaves were then transported, usually in very crowded and insanitary conditions, to North and South America and the Caribbean islands and sold in the slave markets of the new world. Slave ships then

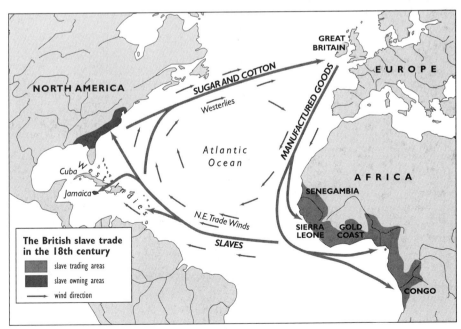

The British slave trade in the 18th century
slave trading areas
slave owning areas
wind direction

completed the third stage of the triangular route by returning to their home ports laden with goods from the new world such as sugar, tobacco and cotton, often produced by slave labour.

If Europeans had accepted that Africans were human beings just like themselves then it would have been difficult for them to justify slavery. People were forcibly transported thousands of miles in chains. Many died on the journey, while those who survived were forced to work on plantations in the new world for no more than basic food and clothing. Slaves were forced to adopt the language and religion of their masters and could be sold to another master at any time, even if this meant separation from their families. Racial theories suggested that Black people were less intellectually developed than Whites and particularly suited to manual labour. In these circumstances it was seen as natural that Whites should dominate and Blacks should act as servants. Theories of racial superiority helped to justify the institution of slavery.

Biology and race

In order to support this much scientific research in the nineteenth century and early part of the twentieth century attempted to prove that different races were endowed with different aptitudes and abilities. However, modern scientific research has largely disproved the supposedly scientific evidence for racial differences. Modern genetics shows that there is very little genetic difference between so-called 'racial groups' and genetic variations within 'racial groups' are far greater. Modern genetic fingerprinting techniques may enable us to classify human beings by genetic characteristics in the near future, but it seems likely that the genes for external features such as skin colour are only a tiny minority of the many pieces of genetic information that determine our physical make-up.

The social construction of race

On this basis contemporary sociologists and biologists argue that races do not exist in reality. While men and women exist as two sexes because of real biological differences, races exist only in the minds of those who perceive them. In this sense race is socially constructed. Some sociologists, such as Robert Miles (1989), therefore

While blackness has traditionally had negative associations in White culture, movements such as Black Power and Rastafarianism encourage Black people to take pride in their appearance and their culture.

reject the use of the term 'race'. Miles argues that by using the term sociologists give respectability to discredited racist ideas. Nevertheless, many sociologists argue that we cannot simply abandon the concept of race since race remains an important factor in defining many people's identities.

Paul Gilroy (1987) points out that White people continue to treat Black people as different and inferior on the basis of their skin colour. While this may have no basis in science it has real effects on the life chances of Black people. In Britain and other societies Black people are discriminated against or treated differently simply because of their colour. On the other hand, for some Black people blackness has become a source of pride as a means of resisting its traditional negative associations. Race thus has a reality in culture even if it does not exist as a biological fact.

Interpretation and application activity

Suggest other examples of ways in which members of ethnic minority groups may assert pride in their own identity.

Colonialism and racism

Slavery had died out in Europe and North America by 1865. However, by this time the major European powers were busy establishing colonial empires. Theories of race continued to provide a powerful ideological justification for the subordination of Black people by Whites. In Africa, for example, Europeans saw themselves as carrying out a civilizing mission. Africans were seen as a 'degraded race' and colonization was seen as bringing the benefits of European government, religion and technology.

Ellis Cashmore and Barry Troyna (1990) argue that ideas of race predate colonialism and slavery, but that colonialism and slavery obviously did much to encourage the idea that human beings could be divided into races ranked as superior and inferior to one another.

Racism under apartheid

Ideas of racial difference and superiority have not been confined to the colonial and slave-owning societies of the eighteenth and nineteenth centuries. In South Africa the idea of racial differences was developed into the doctrine of **apartheid** from 1910 onwards. Apartheid literally means 'separateness' in Afrikaans and was based on the belief that different races should develop separately. In practice this meant that every child in South Africa was classified at birth as a member of a racial group – White, Black, Indian or Coloured (those of mixed Black and White parentage). The arbitrariness of the system can be seen in the fact that while most Asian people were classified as Indian or Coloured, visiting Japanese business people were given 'honorary White' status.

In theory, each racial group was expected to develop separately. Indigenous African peoples were given their own 'homelands' and a measure of self-rule. In reality, the best schools, jobs, homes, land and even beaches were reserved for White people. Non-Whites could not become members of parliament or even vote in national elections and most of the wealth in South Africa was monopolized by a small White minority. While Blacks were supposedly confined to their own homelands White employers needed Black labour, so many Black workers settled in townships reserved for them on the outskirts of the large cities in White areas.

During the 1980s and early 1990s the worst extremes of apartheid were dismantled. In 1994 the first multiracial vote resulted in the election of Nelson Mandela as the first Black president of the country and the ending of apartheid. However, even today

South Africa suffers from political divisions within the Black population, notably the rivalry between the Zulu tribe's political party (Inkatha) and the African National Congress, the largest Black political party.

Apartheid illustrates how ideas about race have been important in different ways in different societies. While few would claim that Britain today in any way resembles South Africa under apartheid, ideas about race still persist and play an important role in understanding the treatment of ethnic minorities in the last forty years.

Migrant labour and racism in Britain

Britain – like many European countries – relied on workers recruited from other countries or **migrant labour** in the period after the Second World War. From the late 1940s onwards labour shortages encouraged employers to recruit migrant workers in industries such as hotels and catering, transport and the health service. The British Nationality Act of 1948 allowed citizens of the British Commonwealth (countries formerly in the British Empire) to come to Britain and work with few restrictions. Some sociologists such as Castles and Kosack (1973) argue that migrant workers helped to provide a **reserve army of labour**. Immigrants provide extra workers at times of labour shortage, helping to keep wages down to the benefit of employers.

The first wave of immigrants from the New Commonwealth came mainly from the Caribbean. They were joined later by those from the Indian subcontinent (India, Pakistan and Bangladesh). In the 1960s and 1970s many of the Asians entering Britain came from East African countries such as Kenya, Uganda and Tanzania. These were descendants of former immigrants from the Indian subcontinent. Many were forced out of positions in government, business and the professions as governments in those countries pursued policies of 'Africanization' in order to encourage Africans to take over positions of importance after independence.

Racial disadvantage in Britain

The new Commonwealth immigrants to Britain frequently met with hostility from white British people, despite the fact that many had been encouraged to come here to fill vacancies in low-paid jobs that White workers were reluctant to take. A study by Daniel (1968) between 1966 and 1967 revealed widespread discrimination against Black immigrants in employment, housing and commercial services (e.g. insurance and mortgages). Until it was outlawed by the 1965 Race Relations Act, Black people were often openly banned from using pubs, cinemas and theatres.

Since the 1960s there has been some progress in combatting racism in Britain. Two further Race Relations Acts were passed in 1968 and 1976 banning discrimination in areas such as housing and employment and setting up the Commission for Racial Equality to investigate cases of alleged discrimination. Many local authorities have developed equal opportunities policies in areas such as housing, education and social services. Black people have also become more involved in mainstream politics. In 1987 four Black MPs – the first since 1924 – were elected to Parliament.

Despite these developments there is still much evidence that Black people remain disadvantaged in a number of respects, though the picture is complicated by significant differences between and even within ethnic groups (see, for example, Brown 1992). In education, for example, Afro-Caribbean children, especially boys, continue to underachieve compared to Whites. Children from Indian backgrounds do relatively well in the education system, while some studies suggest those from Bangladeshi backgrounds fare even worse than Afro-Caribbeans.

In employment, too, the picture is not straightforward. The 1990–1 Labour Force Survey revealed that Indians are better represented proportionately than Whites in professional occupations, while Afro-Caribbeans, Pakistanis and Bangladeshis are over represented in semi-skilled and unskilled manual work. Many commentators attribute at least part of the disadvantage of ethnic minorities in areas such as employment, housing and education to racism leading to racial discrimination (treating people defined as racially different in an unfavourable way).

Research and interpretation activity

Using information from your sociology books or sources of statistics such as Social Trends, *collect evidence about the extent to which ethnic minorities are socially disadvantaged in Britain in areas such as housing, education, employment and law enforcement. Compare your findings with other students and consider the following questions:*

> *Are all ethnic minorities equally disadvantaged compared to Whites? If not, how can differences between minority groups as well as between minorities and Whites be explained?*

Cultural racism

Paul Gilroy (1987) suggests that in recent years cultural characteristics have become as important as physical features in identifying racial groups. For example, it has been argued that cultural differences between white British people and groups such as South Asian Muslims have been a source of racial tensions as much as differences of colour.

Martin Barker (1981) describes this as the **new racism**. Barker argues that biological racism based on physical differences has been largely replaced by cultural racism. Barker suggests that racism is increasingly expressed in terms of support for a traditional British way of life based on freedom of speech, tolerance and fair play. Ethnic groups are portrayed as threatening this culture with their demands to preserve their own cultural identity. Barker argues that the new racism avoids explicitly racist language and does not claim that Whites are physically or mentally superior to Black people. However, ethnic minorities are portrayed as aliens who perversely fail to integrate into British culture.

Barker argues that new racism has become part of the discourse of the New Right, an important influence on the Conservative Party since 1979. Norman Tebbitt MP illustrates this approach with his famous observation that many ethnic minorities would fail the 'cricket test' – true Britons would support England at cricket rather than India, Pakistan or the West Indies. Margaret Thatcher, the former Conservative Party leader, expressed similar views when she said:

> Some people have felt swamped by immigrants. They've seen the whole character of their neighbourhood change … Of course people can feel they are being swamped. Small minorities can be absorbed – they can be assets to the majority community – but once a minority in a neighbourhood gets very large, people do feel swamped. They feel their whole way of life has been changed.
>
> (*Observer*, 25 February 1979)

Evaluation question

Is there any justification for Mrs Thatcher's statement about swamping by immigrants? Bear in mind that ethnic minorities make up about 5 per cent of the United Kingdom population and about 40 per cent of them have been born and brought up in Britain.

Mass media and racism

A number of studies have argued that cultural racism is reinforced by the mass media. Van Dijk's (1991) analysis of reporting of ethnic issues in British newspapers revealed a tendency for the press to portray ethnic minorities as a problem. Minorities were often seen as abusing British tolerance and reporting of events such as muggings and riots disproportionately emphasized the involvement of young Black people. The following quote from a *Daily Mail* editorial is used by Van Dijk to illustrate this type of media style:

> We have to be more brisk in saying no, and showing the door to those who are not British citizens and would abuse our hospitality and tolerance. To do this is not to give way to prejudice, but to lessen the provocation on which it feeds.
>
> (*Daily Mail*, 28 November 1985)

Feminists have used content analysis to demonstrate media bias and stereotyping in relation to representations of women (see pp. 95–6). Van Dijk used a similar technique to analyse media coverage of ethnic minorities. He found that negative representations of ethnic minorities considerably outnumbered positive ones and that coverage of ethnic minorities in the context of crime and violence was one of the most frequent categories in his analysis.

Research activity

Collect cuttings of newspaper stories on issues of race and ethnicity over a period of time, perhaps a month. Carry out a content analysis of these stories. You could categorize the articles by subject: for example, immigration, crime, racial attacks, racial discrimination. You could then compare the frequency with which people from minorities are represented in different contexts.

Criticisms of the concept of new racism

The concept of new racism has been useful in drawing attention to the way in which ideas about race and ethnicity have been modified and expressed in new ways. However, some critics such as David Mason (1992) suggest that notions of cultural incompatibility have always been present, even in traditional discourses about race. Similarly, some versions of new racism contain ideas about biological racial differences, for example Herrnstein and Murray's (1994) claim that African Americans are innately less intelligent than Whites.

Institutional racism

Some writers have used the term **institutional racism** to describe the way in which racism is built into institutional practices and ways of thinking. For example, anti-racist critics of the British education system have argued that schools often consistently fail to provide an education which is appropriate to the needs of ethnic minority children and have low expectations of their abilities. The concept of institutional racism implies that racism is not simply a matter of individual prejudice but can be seen in procedures, practices and assumptions built into the working of institutions which result in disadvantages for ethnic minorities.

However, critics of this approach argue that the term racism has now been extended too widely. Jeffcoate (1984) argues that the tendency of subjects such as literature, geography and history to emphasize British and European culture at the expense of minorities' cultures is more likely to be due to ignorance or inertia amongst teachers in introducing new curricula than deliberate racism. Jeffcoate argues that the concept of institutional racism is more appropriately applied to situations such as apartheid in South Africa, where racism was deliberately institutionalized in the operation of the state.

Nevertheless, the concept of institutional racism can be useful in highlighting the operation of racist practices which are not necessarily the result of individual prejudice. For example, critics have argued that Britain's immigration rules are racist because they make it much more difficult for Black immigrants to enter Britain than Whites. Immigration officers operating such rules may not be personally prejudiced but nevertheless enforce laws which can be seen to have a discriminatory effect.

Debates over the concepts of race and racism

The terms race and racism have been used in a number of different ways to describe different ways of classifying and thinking about human beings. Because of this some sociologists argue that we should abandon the term race altogether. Robert Miles (1989) argues that the term has been used so widely that it has become meaningless. Moreover, he suggests that race is a purely ideological construct and its use only serves to give respectability to discredited racist ideas.

Miles is similarly critical of the concept of racism. He argues it is now no longer clear whether racism applies only to beliefs based on biological classifications or also those relating to cultural differences. Similarly, it is not clear whether racism has to be intentional or whether it can be unintentional, whether racism is always something White people are guilty of or whether Black people can be racist too.

Racialization

Miles suggests we should instead use the concept of **racialization**. He defines this as 'a representational process whereby social significance is attached to certain biological (usually phenotypical) human features, on the basis of which those people possessing those characteristics are designated as a distinct collectivity' (1989, p. 74). Miles thus suggests that attention should shift from the issue of whether races actually exist or not to the social processes whereby people come to see certain groups in racial terms. He points out that in the process of racialization there is not always explicit reference to the term race. This would certainly be true of the new racism, where distinctions between the Self and Other are largely in cultural terms and only coded references are made to race.

Miles's argument does, however, present some difficulties. For example, it is difficult to see how it is possible to talk about racialization without talking about race, though we may wish to put the term in quotation marks to indicate that we see it as a socially constructed category. Moreover, it is not clear whether we could legitimately refer to the way in which Catholics are treated in Northern Ireland as a process of racialization, since they are not identified as a group on the basis of physical features. Nevertheless, there are strong parallels between the discrimination that has been practised against Catholics in Northern Ireland and the treatment of Black people on the UK mainland.

Multiracist Britain

Other writers have rejected Miles's view, arguing that since race and racism have a reality in many people's minds, sociologists cannot afford to ignore their existence. Many sociologists have recognized that racism manifests itself in different ways in different social groups and situations. Phil Cohen (Cohen and Bains 1988) argues that it is more useful to talk about **racisms** than racism. Cohen suggests that different social groups in Britain use different 'codes' embodying different strands of racist thinking. The upper class are more likely to emphasize their own breeding and purity and the threat posed by the 'animal-like' qualities of Black people. Working-class people, by contrast, are more likely to become racist when they feel their territory is threatened, for example when ethnic minorities are seen as competing for jobs and housing in what they perceive as 'their area'.

A similar approach is apparent in Ellis Cashmore's study, *The Logic of Racism* (1987). Cashmore studied four housing areas in and around Birmingham and found different forms of racism reflecting differences of class, housing tenure and degree of contact with ethnic minorities. For example, young Whites in inner-city Newtown were more likely to recognize that they had common problems with young Blacks while also resenting the fact that they were in competition for jobs. In Chelmsley Wood on the edge of the city Whites had less contact with Blacks and were more influenced by crude racist stereotypes. Middle-class respondents, by contrast, were more likely to stress ideas such as the need for ethnic minorities to assimilate into British society and achieve success by personal effort. Cashmore's work reflects a growth in interest among researchers in understanding White racism rather than simply dismissing it as irrational and bigoted.

Ethnicity

Because of the association of the term race with discredited biological theories, some sociologists prefer to use the term ethnicity. Ethnic groups normally share a common language, religion or nationality and may have distinctive customs in terms of food, dress, music and traditions. Thus ethnicity is based on shared culture rather than physical characteristics. Thus Protestants and Catholics in Northern Ireland or Muslims, Serbs and Croats in Bosnia may be seen as ethnic groups, although indistinguishable in terms of physical appearance. Many ethnic groups also claim a common origin, for example all Jews see themselves as originating from Israel. Ethnicity is often a much more powerful basis for identity than race. Members of supposed racial groups often share little apart from a common skin colour. Members of an ethnic group are bound together by a shared culture and sense of belonging.

 Interpretation and application exercise
Ethnic groups are usually seen as having the following characteristics: (a) a common culture; (b) belief in a common origin; (c) a sense of group identity; (d) social ties and interaction within the group. Select any ethnic minority group in contemporary Britain and show how far it exhibits each of these characteristics.

Criticisms of 'ethnicity' research

Some anti-racist writers have been suspicious of the concept of ethnicity because it has been used as a basis for 'victim blaming' theories. For example, in the 1960s and 1970s underachievement amongst ethnic minority children was often blamed on the culture of their home background, for example the high proportion of lone parents among Afro-Caribbeans and the tendency of Asian families to speak minority languages at home. Critics argued that, by focusing on ethnic minority culture, such theories absolved schools from blame and ignored the institutional racism in the education system.

The new sociology of ethnicity

In recent years, however, there has been renewed interest in the concept of ethnicity and many sociologists have acknowledged that it is simplistic to see all ethnic minorities as part of a homogeneous Black population who are all equally victims of racism. Seeing minorities as members of ethnic groups offers certain advantages in understanding their identity and position in British society. For example, if we view Asians in Britain as a single category, this ignores the ethnic diversity among British Asians. Asians can be distinguished by language (Bengali, Gujarati, Punjabi, Urdu and Hindi speakers), religion (Hindus, Muslims and Sikhs) and national origin (Bengali, Indian and Pakistani). Moreover, these categories do not coincide; thus Punjabi speakers may be Sikhs or Muslims and may originate from India or Pakistan.

Tariq Modood (1992a) argues that many writers are guilty of **racial dualism** – simply dividing the population into Black and White. Modood points to important variations in the economic position of British Asians. He contrasts the relative success of many Indians – mainly Hindus and Sikhs – in achieving educational success, entering professions and building businesses, with the more disadvantaged position of Muslims from Pakistan and Bangladesh. Modood does not deny that all Black people are to some extent disadvantaged because of racism. However, he suggests that we should pay more attention to the significance of cultural differences within the ethnic minority population and how these might be factors in understanding their social situations.

Table 5.1 Religion and language in the City of Leicester	
English-speaking Christians	183,000
Gujarati-speaking Hindus	36,000
English-speaking – no religion	29,000
Punjabi-speaking Sikhs	9,600
Gujarati-speaking Muslims	5,200
Kutchi-speaking Muslims	2,900
Urdu-speaking Muslims	1,200

Source: Survey of Leicester 1983, adapted from Hides (1995)

Interpretation and application exercise

1 *How can the statistics in Table 5.1 be used to illustrate the problems of referring to Asians as a single ethnic group?*

2 *If you were carrying out a sociological study of ethnic groups in Leicester, what other kinds of data would be useful to you in classifying people into ethnic groups?*

Case Study the Rushdie affair

The significance of ethnic and cultural differences in British society was brought into sharp focus in 1988 with the publication of Salman Rushdie's book, *The Satanic Verses*. The book caused grave offence in many sections of Britain's one-million-strong Muslim community.

Muslims argued that, although the book was a work of fiction, it represented their prophet Muhammad in an offensive and blasphemous manner. Protests against the book were initially peaceful but escalated into firebomb attacks against bookshops. Subsequently the Iranian reli-

The Rushdie Affair – a trauma of identity for British Muslims?

gious leader Ayatollah Khomeini published a *fatwah* or religious death sentence on Rushdie and the author has had to live in hiding ever since.

Mike O'Donnell (1990) argues that the Rushdie affair 'raised the issue of ethnic cultural *incompatibility* in a way that cannot be avoided'. Two contradictory principles asserted themselves; the right of religious groups to punish blasphemers versus the right of artists and other citizens to freedom of speech.

The issue also polarized opinion in unexpected ways. While most Muslims were critical of Rushdie and called for his book to be withdrawn, many were unhappy with the *fatwah* and the more violent protests. Some Muslims even showed support for Rushdie, notably a Muslim women's group, Women Against Fundamentalism, who staged a demonstration supporting Rushdie and opposing sexism and fundamentalism in their own communities.

The opinion of white British people was also divided. Some Christian religious leaders felt the protection afforded by Britain's blasphemy laws to Christian beliefs should be extended to other faiths. On the other hand, many white liberals who were opposed to racism strongly criticized Muslim fundamentalists for attempting to suppress freedom of speech. For example, Michael Ignatieff compared the totalitarianism of Khomeini to that of Hitler.

However, on visiting Bradford, Britain's largest Muslim community, Ignatieff expressed himself as follows:

> I expected a community in a bell jar, sealed off from the rest of British society … and instead I found a community that is deeply, militantly British, down even to the Yorkshire accent. But I'm also finding the Rushdie affair has been a trauma for them, leading them to draw back from us, to defend a heritage they feel we don't understand.
>
> (*Guardian*, 9 May 1989)

While the attitudes of British Muslims over the Rushdie affair were heavily criticized by many whites, some writers have suggested that their feelings were misunderstood. Tariq Modood (1992b) argues that it is mistaken to identify British Muslims as fanatical fundamentalists. He points out that most British Muslims belong to the Deobandi and Barelevi sects of Islam, which have little sympathy for the Shiite fundamentalism represented by the Iranian Ayatollah Khomeini. These communities were deeply hurt when the prophet they revered was, in their view, slandered and misrepresented in Rushdie's book.

The Rushdie affair does bring into question the assumptions of **multiculturalism** – the belief that ethnic conflicts can be reduced by greater tolerance and understanding of cultural differences. It may be that some cultural beliefs are simply directly opposed; for example, Muslims' belief in the absolute truth of the Koran and western liberals' belief in the right to question all established ideas. The Rushdie affair also illustrates the importance of ethnicity. The attitudes and behaviour of British Muslims cannot be understood solely in terms of race but require consideration of their culture, in particular their religious identity.

Interpretation and evaluation questions

1 *Why does the Rushdie affair suggest that sociologists should consider issues of culture and ethnicity as well as those of racism and colour in examining relations between ethnic minorities and the white majority in British society?*

2 *What suggestions can you make for dealing with conflicts such as this in the future?*

The social construction of ethnicity

At the beginning of this chapter it was argued that races are socially constructed – people are grouped together as races in people's minds, not because there is any real biological basis for these groupings. Ethnic groups, too, can be seen as socially constructed. Ethnic groups exist because people identify themselves or others as members of such groups and reinforce the boundaries between such groups in a variety of ways in their social lives.

Paul Gilroy is one writer who has emphasized this view. In his work he argues that ethnic groups are not fixed entities but are constantly changing, with no fixed boundaries. Like Modood, he challenges the idea of a single Black culture; however, he emphasizes the fluid and kaleidoscopic nature of ethnic cultures. Gilroy's work challenges the assumptions of new racism, which assumes that there is such as thing as a pure and uncontaminated 'British culture' that is threatened by multiculturalism. However, he also challenges the approach of some multiculturalists who have presented ethnic minority cultures as somehow pure and separate and in need of preservation from being assimilated into the dominant culture.

Diaspora and hybrid identities

In *The Black Atlantic* (1993) Gilroy particularly focuses on the culture of what he calls the **African diaspora** – the descendants of African slaves in North America, the Caribbean and Britain. Gilroy argues that elements of these cultures have constantly influenced each other as well as influencing and drawing on White cultures. For example, Jamaican reggae music had its origins in ska and bluebeat, which drew on North American blues as well as African musical styles. Reggae in turn has influenced Black music styles in Britain and even Africa, as well as White artists such as UB40 and the Specials. As a result, Gilroy argues that we are seeing the emergence of **hybrid cultures**. Thus many young Blacks have incorporated elements of both Black and White cultures into their own youth culture. Young Whites, too, have borrowed elements of Black culture in their own dress, music, language and so on.

Evaluation exercise

The following is an extract from a lyric by British Afro-Caribbean band Earthling.

London's my city, Jamaica's my country, Africa's my history ... I know who I am, I'm not who you think I am ... I'm Marcus Garvey, I'm Harvey Keitel ...

(Quoted in Bradley 1996)

Using the quote and cartoon above, and any examples of your own, assess the usefulness of Gilroy's concept of hybrid cultures.

Black culture as resistance

The last two chapters considered ways in which subordinate groups in society may use an alternative culture to resist a dominant culture. For example, Gramsci emphasized the need for the working class to develop its own radical culture in order to counter ruling-class hegemony. Feminists argue that the women's movement plays an important role in raising women's consciousness of their subordination in order to resist patriarchy. In the same way, Paul Gilroy focuses on the significance of Black cultures as a form of resistance to racism and capitalism.

Gilroy argues that both traditional working-class political organizations, such as trade unions, and official anti-racism policies have achieved little for Black people. Gilroy points to the success of Black culture in subverting capitalism – for example in the lyrics of Black music – and of the emergence of new political movements often using unconventional tactics, for example the 'uprisings' of both Black and White youth in British cities in the 1980s.

Evaluation activity
Find examples of lyrics by Black musicians which might illustrate Gilroy's argument
that Black culture can play a subversive role.
What criticisms can you think of for this argument? For instance, can you find
examples of Black popular music which simply reinforce the existing social order?

Ethnic identities in contemporary Britain and the United States

Gilroy's work exemplifies an increasing interest among sociologists in ethnicity as a source of identity and an influence on culture rather than as simply a source of social disadvantage. Another example is Shaun Hides's (1995) research into the Asian communities in Leicester.

Material culture and ethnicity

Hides focuses on how ethnic minorities use material culture (for example, clothing, jewellery, home decor and other artefacts) to create a sense of ethnic identity. Hides emphasizes that ethnic groups entail an 'ongoing process of construction of collective identities'. Thus the wearing of traditional dress by members of ethnic minorities is a symbolic affirmation of group membership and of links with tradition and country of origin. Hides also notes variations in the importance of such cultural symbols. For example, Asian women are much more likely to wear traditional dress than men, symbolizing the traditional association of women with the home and the private domain in both Hindu and Muslim culture.

Hides argues that aspects of material culture such as dress are part of a symbolic order. The artefacts possessed or worn by certain individuals in traditional cultures often symbolize their role or social status, for example, distinctions between men or women or different castes in Hinduism. He points out how this increasingly conflicts with the individualistic values of modern western societies, where material commodities are more likely to symbolize a chosen lifestyle or identity rather than an ascribed social position in a fixed social order.

Postmodernity and identities

Recent thinking about ethnicity reflects the influence of postmodernism in sociology (see also Chapter 9). Postmodern theorists see identities in contemporary societies as increasingly 'decentred' or 'fragmented'. It is argued that in traditional societies identities were rooted in stability and certainty, for example, in class, nationality and religion. The rapid pace of change in postmodern societies has undermined certainty about identities. Mass migration and the creation of multicultural societies have called into question the notion of a unitary society with shared core values. However, postmodernists argue that contemporary societies are not simply fragmented along ethnic lines but that many other sources of identity – including class, gender, age, sexual orientation, disability, locality, religion, nationality and even musical styles and dress codes – compete for our allegiance. Different sources of identity will come to the fore in different circumstances.

Case Study — fragmented identities

Stuart Hall uses the following example to illustrate this fragmentation of identities and its political consequences.

In 1991, President Bush, anxious to restore a conservative majority to the US Supreme Court, nominated Clarence Thomas, a Black judge of conservative political views. In Bush's judgement, White voters (who may have been prejudiced about a Black judge) were likely to support Thomas because he was conservative on equal-rights legislation, and Black voters (who supported liberal policies on race) would support Thomas because he was Black. In short, the President was 'playing the identities game'.

During the Senate 'hearings' on the appointment, Judge Thomas was accused of sexual harassment by a Black woman, Anita Hill, a former junior colleague of Thomas's. The hearings caused a public scandal and polarized American society.

Some Blacks supported Thomas on racial grounds; others opposed him on sexual grounds. Black women were divided, depending on whether their identities as Blacks or as women prevailed. Black men were also divided, depending on whether their sexism overrode their liberalism. White men were divided, depending not only on their politics, but on how they identified themselves with respect to racism and sexism. White conservative women supported Thomas, not only on political grounds, but because of their opposition to feminism. White feminists, often liberal on race, opposed Thomas on sexual grounds, and because Judge Thomas is a member of the judicial elite and Anita Hill, at the time of the alleged incident, a junior employee, there were issues of social class position at work in these arguments too.

(Hall 1992, pp. 279–80)

Interpretation and application activity

1 Take a sheet of paper and divide it into two columns. In the first column list those groups who supported Thomas and in the second those who supported Hill (some groups may appear on both lists).

2 Discuss the following questions:
(a) Why might the way these groups were aligned be quite different on another political issue? Give examples of possible issues to illustrate this point.
(b) Stuart Hall states 'No single identity – e.g. that of social class – could align different identities into one overarching "master identity", on which a politics could be securely grounded'. What does he mean by this and how does the case study illustrate this argument?

Identities of young Muslim women

The case study of the Thomas–Hill affair illustrates how contemporary societies can be seen to be fragmented into a variety of groups with contradictory identities. We will now examine the conflicting identities of one group in British society. Charlotte Butler

(1995) notes how a variety of identities are important to young Muslim women in Britain. For most of the young women she studied adherence to Islam was a central part of their lives; however, many felt a broader identification with British Asians generally. Age was also important, as most young Muslims were aware of the conflicts between their parents' expectations and the wider culture of British society, for example over issues such as clothing and arranged marriages. Most young women were also acutely aware of gender issues, notably the traditional role ascribed to women in Pakistani and Bangladeshi culture. However, many felt this had more to do with traditions brought from their parents' countries of origin than the true teachings of Islam on women's roles. Butler concludes that for most young Muslim women Islam remains a major guide to life. However, she describes them as sorting and choosing the elements of both British and Asian culture which they feel are compatible with Islam in order to construct roles that give them more freedom and choice.

Globalization and nationalism

One reason offered by many sociologists for the fragmentation of identities in contemporary societies is the acceleration in the process of **globalization**. Globalization implies that the boundaries between nation states become less significant in social life. One example of this can be seen in economic life, where world trade is increasingly dominated by transnational corporations and capital can be moved rapidly by investors from one country to another as the international financial markets are connected by computerized technology. Globalization can also be seen in culture, where television programmes, films and books are made for an international market. This cultural globalization can also be seen in the worldwide spread of tastes in food; for example, hamburgers, pizzas and curries, while identified as American, Italian or Indian, can be found in restaurants all over the world.

Evaluation activity
Think of examples of evidence for the globalization of culture. You could start by using the following as headings, but try to think of some others of your own: (a) television and films; (b) music; (c) fashion/clothing; (d) sport; (e) food.
Once you have completed the above activity consider examples of evidence which might suggest that national and regional cultures remain important despite globalization.

Modernity and nationalism

It might be expected that the advance of globalization would herald the end of the nation state and our sense of national identity. Ironically, many sociologists argue that the opposite is true. Nationality has a central place in many people's identities in the late twentieth century and some of the most significant social movements of recent years have been those based on nationalism. For example, nationalism could be seen as a factor in the outbreak of both world wars, in anti-colonial struggles, in the downfall of communism in Eastern Europe in 1989 and in contemporary debates over the role of the European Union.

The division of the world into nation states is a relatively modern phenomenon. During the Middle Ages most kingdoms had very fluid boundaries. Medieval France, for example, was made up of many feudal territories ruled over by great nobles. The King of France exercised only nominal control over much of this area. It was only from around the sixteenth century onwards that European monarchs started to exercise centralized control over a territory with definite territorial boundaries – what we think of today as a nation state.

While nation states are a comparatively recent phenomenon in Europe, some sociologists argue that nations existed in the past. Certainly, civilizations such as the ancient Egyptians, the Chinese Empire, the Aztecs and the Inca had highly developed systems of government and administration. Edward Shils (1957) argues that human beings have always formed bonds based on a sense of common identity. On this basis, he argues that modern nations are simply the development of a natural tendency of human beings to group themselves together.

While some kind of nation state may have existed in ancient societies, many sociologists see nation states as characteristic of the modern world. Moreover, many would reject Shils's view that the grouping of human beings into nations is a natural phenomenon. Ernest Gellner reflects this view when he writes:

> Nationalism is not the awakening of nations to self-consciousness; it invents nations where they did not exist.

(Gellner 1964, p. 169)

Gellner argues that nations and nationalism are essentially a modern invention. In traditional societies rulers and ruled had little in common and thus could not be united in a common national identity. For Gellner, nationalism developed as a result of the development of a common culture in modern society and provides a means of uniting the diverse populations of the nation states that emerged with industrialization.

Germany did not emerge as a nation state until the end of the nineteenth century. Before that it was composed of a loose association of principalities and city states.

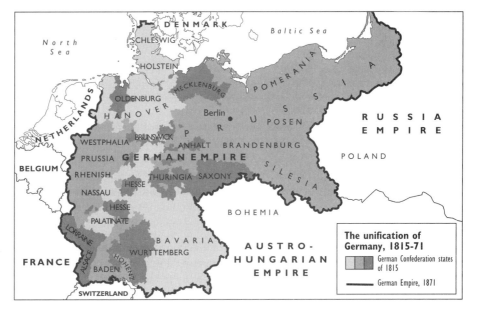

The unification of Germany, 1815-71

German Confederation states of 1815

German Empire, 1871

Nations as imagined communities

Other writers, like Benedict Anderson (1983), have developed the view that nations and nationalism are socially constructed. Anderson describes nations as **imagined communities**, since unlike real communities their members do not know one another or interact regularly. Anderson argues that modern nations emerged in Europe after the Protestant Reformation with the invention of printing. In pre-print Europe people spoke thousands of different dialects; printed books required that a single standardized language be adopted in each country. Anderson argues that a common language was a powerful force in creating a sense of common identity or imagined community in each nation state. According to Anderson, a sense of national identity is a social construction in much the same way as identities of gender or ethnicity.

Anderson argues that nationalism has become increasingly important in modern times as a source of identity and group formation. He links this to the decline of religious certainties, which in the past helped to explain the meaning of birth, suffering and death. Anderson suggests that feeling part of a larger community in the form of a nation gives people's lives meaning and coherence and a sense of belonging, in the same way as religion did in the past.

Research activity

Investigate the emergence of any modern nation state. Consider the following questions:

- *When did the nation come to have its present form?*
- *How have the boundaries and identity of the nation state changed historically?*
- *What brought into being the present nation state (e.g. nationalist movement, colonialism and decolonization, creation of a national empire, etc.)?*
- *To what extent do citizens of the nation identify with it, or are there nationalist divisions within the nation state?*

If possible, report your findings back to your group and compare similarities and differences between the nation states you have chosen to investigate.

Common culture and national identity

Michael Schudson (1994) analyses how the promotion of a common culture has been important in many nation states in creating a sense of national identity. Schudson identifies a number of mechanisms by which a national culture can be disseminated.

1 **Language, print and schooling**. Like Anderson, Schudson argues that the creation of a common language spread through the printed word helped to create an 'assemblage of readers connected with one another through their common texts' (1994, p. 28). The spread of formal state education in most industrial societies from the late nineteenth century also encouraged this. Children were educated in the standard version of the national language and were often socialized into respect for their nation's history and culture. Hobsbawm (1990) notes how in 1789 over half the population of France spoke no French at all, while in 1863 at least a fifth of the population did not speak what officials recognized as French. As state schooling spread, standard French replaced local dialects and other languages such as Breton and Basque.

2 **Consumer culture and national markets**. Schudson also points to the development of national markets for consumer goods such as clothes and food. By the end of the nineteenth century, people were buying food, clothing and other goods which had been mass produced rather than produced at home or in the immediate locality. Fashions, tastes in food and even leisure activities such as sport became organized on national rather than local lines.

3 **National rituals**. The significance of civic religious rituals in promoting social solidarity has already been discussed in Chapter 2. However, more secular rituals may also be important in promoting national identity. Both the communists and the Nazis were skilled in stage managing impressive rallies and parades, such as the May Day parades in Moscow or the Nuremberg rallies. Schudson suggests that in democratic societies elections may have a similar ritual significance, acting as a reaffirmation of the legitimacy of the democratic state.

4 **Broadcasting and mass media**. Schudson argues that mass media, especially broadcast media (radio and television), have the capacity to both reinforce and

undermine a sense of national identity. Television in particular has contributed to the process of globalization, as it gives individuals access to programmes from all over the world and allows them to experience and interact with the lives of many other people, even when they are physically isolated. However, many national television networks see part of their mission as the promotion of national identity. Television also allows many more people to partake in the kind of national rituals discussed above, for example President Kennedy's funeral or Prince Charles and Lady Diana's wedding. Daniel Dayan and Elihu Katz (1992) describe how an Indian family washed themselves and dressed in long clothes with their heads covered to watch Prime Minister Indira Ghandi's funeral on television, as this is what they would have done if they had been physically present at the event. People often view such events in groups with family and friends, reinforcing the sense of seriousness and communion characteristic of such occasions.

Interpretation and application exercise
Take the four aspects of national culture identified by Schudson and give examples of how the cultural institutions in Britain or any other nation might help to promote a sense of national identity.

Theories of nationalism

Functionalism

Functionalist sociologists such as Emile Durkheim and Edward Shils see nationalism as the means by which large-scale and heterogeneous industrial societies are integrated or bound together. Durkheim saw collective beliefs and rituals such as national ceremonies as helping to unify citizens in a sense of loyalty to their society, as represented by the nation state. Shils (1975) makes a distinction between the cultural **centre** of society and the **periphery**. Individuals may feel that they are at the periphery or margins of society. However, if the state can make them feel part of a wider society, for example through nationalist symbols, values and beliefs, individuals will be better integrated and feel closer to the 'centre'. The work of Durkheim and Shils on civil religion (see pp. 40–2) illustrates one way in which national rituals can help to create a sense of national unity.

Marxism

Marxists, like Gramsci (see pp. 61–4), however, reject the view that shared values and beliefs are for the benefit of society as a whole. For Gramsci, nationalism was simply another aspect of the hegemony of the ruling class, a means of winning the consent of the working class to its rule.

Invented traditions

The Marxist approach is reflected in the work of Eric Hobsbawm and Terence Ranger (1983). They argue that in the nineteenth century newly emerging nation states sought ways of binding together their citizens in allegiance to their governments and motivating people to fight wars. Hobsbawm and Ranger argue that flags, national anthems and national rituals were important in this process. However, they show that much of what appears to be traditional in national rituals and emblems are what they call **invented traditions**. For example, many of the rituals surrounding the British monarchy appear to be ancient because old-fashioned clothes and language are used to create this impression. However, ceremonies such as the Coronation and the Investiture of the Prince of Wales are largely modern creations, although traditional elements have been incorporated to give them authenticity. For Hobsbawm and Ranger, nationalist traditions have been invented by the dominant groups in most nation states in order to legitimate the existing political system by making it appear natural and based on long-established traditions.

Traditional rituals such as the State Opening of Parliament may be modern inventions, but they provide a sense of national tradition.

Evaluation exercise
Discuss the following question: 'Is nationalism a beneficial or a destructive force in contemporary societies?'

Giddens's typology of nationalism

While nation states are socially constructed, different nations have emerged in very different circumstances. Anthony Giddens (1993) argues that they can be classed into three types.

1 **Classical nationalism**. This is the type of nationalism associated with the emergence of the modern nation state in Europe from the eighteenth century onwards. In some cases this nationalism was an ideology imposed from above supporting the position of an existing ruling class. However, in some cases, as in Italy, nationalism was a popular movement that overthrew existing ruling elites.

2 **Post-colonial nationalism**. Many nation states outside Europe only came into being because of colonialism. For example, most of Africa was 'carved up' by the European great powers at the end of the nineteenth century with little consideration for existing ethnic and tribal divisions. As former colonial states have achieved independence they have often sought to use nationalism as a means of binding together disparate communities and cultures.

3 **Subcultural nationalism**. This refers to nationalist movements that emerge within nation states. These nationalist movements often seek to break away from the established nation state, for example Quebec nationalists in Canada, Basque nationalists in Spain and Chechen nationalists in Russia.

The future of nationalism

Eric Hobsbawm (1990) argues that classical nationalism was most influential in the nineteenth and early twentieth centuries. As nation states became more democratic and the vote was extended to the working class they needed to legitimate themselves. Nationalism provided an ideology which presented ruling-class interests as being in the national interest. For example, in the First World War thousands of young men on both sides were persuaded to fight and in many cases die for their country motivated by nationalist sentiments.

Hobsbawm, however, argues that this type of nationalism now has no future. The heterogeneous or diverse nature of most modern nation states makes it difficult to appeal to a national identity, which may have little meaning to many of a nation's population. The former Soviet Union, for example, was held together by the force of communist rule, but once communism collapsed the Soviet Union disintegrated into a number of smaller states. Interestingly, many of these have used the invented traditions referred to by Hobsbawm and Ranger to make connections between the contemporary state and kingdoms and peoples of the past. For example, in 1996 the passports of Russian citizens ceased to carry the hammer and sickle emblem of communism, which was replaced by the double-headed eagle, formerly the emblem of the tsars of Russia.

Nationalism in contemporary societies

While Hobsbawm is sceptical about the future of nationalism, there has been a resurgence of subcultural nationalism at the end of the twentieth century. Mark Kirby (1995) cites an article in the *Guardian* in 1993 giving fourteen examples of nationalist movements seeking their own breakaway nation states.

Nationalist conflict in Bosnia

One example of this can be seen in the former Yugoslavia. After the collapse of communism the constituent states from which Yugoslavia had been formed after the Second World War separated and became independent states. However, in Bosnia-Herzegovina a civil war between ethnic groups in the country resulted in the further fragmentation of even this new nation. Serbian nationalist forces have captured about 70 per cent of the country and driven out members of the other main ethnic groups – Croats and Muslims – in a process of so-called 'ethnic cleansing'. In UN-sponsored elections in 1996, the leading political parties were extreme Serb and Croat nationalist parties committed to partitioning the country into ethnically pure Serb and Croat mini-states.

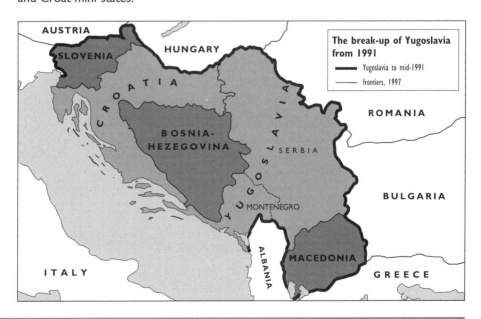

Nationalism in the UK

It is not only in other countries that nationalism is significant. In the United Kingdom, English nationalism has always tended to be identified with British nationalism. However, in other parts of the United Kingdom subcultural nationalist movements have been significant.

The Scottish National Party (SNP) has held seats in Parliament since 1970. While a referendum failed to achieve an assembly for Scotland, there is now considerable support for one, not only in the SNP but also in the Labour and Liberal Democrat parties. In Wales nationalism has focused more on cultural issues, notably the preservation of the Welsh language. Like the SNP, Plaid Cymru (the Welsh nationalist party) has achieved some political success since the 1970s. Welsh nationalists also secured their own Welsh-language TV channel – S4C – which was established as a Welsh alternative to Channel 4.

Both Scottish and Welsh nationalism provide examples of what Hobsbawm and Ranger call 'invented traditions'. According to Hugh Trevor-Roper (1983), the kilt was invented in the eighteenth century by an Englishman. Similarly, the Eisteddfod was a medieval Welsh festival revived in 1780 by the Welsh Society based in London.

Irish nationalism

Northern Ireland provides perhaps the clearest example of the significance of nationalism for identities in the contemporary United Kingdom. Since the settlement of Ireland by English and Scottish Protestants in the seventeenth century, the population of Ireland has always divided between the Catholic community – who mainly identified with Irish nationalism – and the Protestant community – who favoured union with the United Kingdom. Agitation by Irish nationalists and an uprising in 1916 eventually resulted in the partition of Ireland into the independent republic in the south and Northern Ireland, which remained part of the United Kingdom. As a result, Protestants became a majority in the province.

In the late 1960s conflict between the two communities erupted when Catholics demanded equal civil rights with Protestants, for example an end to religious discrimination in employment. In 1969 the Provisional Irish Republican Army (IRA) was formed, the main paramilitary organization pursuing the political aim of a united Ireland. In response a number of Protestant loyalist paramilitary organizations have been established, such as the Ulster Volunteer Force (UVF). Both sides have been responsible for bombings, shootings and other acts of violence in 'the Troubles', which have continued to the present apart from a ceasefire in 1994–5.

Research activity

Using a CD-ROM or back copies of newspapers, investigate the background to recent events in Northern Ireland. Consider the following questions:

- *What is the background to the sectarian conflict in Northern Ireland?*
- *Which political groups are involved in the conflict and negotiations to achieve a peaceful settlement?*
- *What are their aims and how much support do they have?*
- *What role has the British government played both in creating the conflict and in attempting to resolve it?*

British nationalism

While Scottish, Welsh and Irish subcultural nationalism are associated with clearly identified political movements, English or British nationalism is less clearly linked with a particular political ideology or movement. Some parties of the far right have been associated with nationalist sentiments, notably the neo-fascist British National Party (BNP). The BNP has campaigned on overtly racist policies, blaming ethnic minorities for problems such as unemployment and crime and calling for the repatriation of Black immigrants.

Far right parties such as the BNP have usually only attracted a tiny minority of votes in general elections. However, in a council by-election in Tower Hamlets, London in 1993, a BNP candidate, Derek Beackon, was elected for the Isle of Dogs ward. Some observers suggest that this reflected a long tradition of racism in the East End of London. However, the result may simply have been a protest vote against the failure of the mainstream parties to combat problems such as unemployment and housing shortages in the area.

While British nationalism has been associated with neo-fascist political parties, nationalist sentiment is not exclusively associated with the far right. In Britain the monarchy has always played an important role as a focus for nationalist feeling. International sporting events also provide occasions on which nationalist feelings come to the fore. Interestingly, in some sports there are teams representing the United Kingdom, for example the Olympics. In other sports England, Scotland, Wales and Northern Ireland compete separately, for example in World Cup football, often provoking nationalist rivalries between the United Kingdom's constituent nations.

England v. Scotland, Wembley 1996

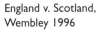 **Interpretation and evaluation activity**
Using the picture above and any other examples, discuss why sport often arouses strong nationalist feelings.

Britain in Europe

Britain's entry into the European Union (EU), and with it the closer economic and political integration of European states, has also provoked a nationalist reaction, most notably in sections of the Conservative Party. Many so-called 'Euro-sceptics' fear that the monetary union of EU states may lead in the long run to a political union – a United States of Europe. Those opposed to European integration fear that it will undermine the sovereignty of the British Parliament in Westminster and destroy the United Kingdom's national identity. Ironically, many of those who support British withdrawal from the European Union on the grounds of lack of sovereignty are also most fiercely opposed to independence or devolution (self-government) for Scotland and Wales.

Evaluation activity

Does closer integration of Britain into the European Union mean a loss of Britain's national identity? If so, is this a bad thing?

Race, ethnicity and nationality

While this section of the chapter has focused on nationality and nationalism as sources of identity, these concepts are closely intertwined with the concepts of race and ethnicity discussed earlier. Technically, a person's nationality can be defined in terms of his or her citizenship of a nation state – in theory a person with a British passport is British. However, a number of sociologists have pointed to the difficulties which members of ethnic minorities in Britain face in asserting their Britishness. As the title of Paul Gilroy's book, *There Ain't No Black in the Union Jack*, implies, one of the characteristics of the new racism is its tendency to portray blackness and Britishness as mutually exclusive. Black people have been portrayed in the press and in statements by leading politicians as alien and a 'threat to our way of life' (see the quote from Margaret Thatcher on p. 119).

Interpretation and evaluation exercise

The following quote from a speech by a British MP made in 1989 illustrates the tendency to see ethnic minority cultures as incompatible with Britishness.

> The fact that the Hong Kong Chinese are very hard-working and hold British passports does not make them British. If millions of Chinese come to the UK, they would not integrate and become yellow Englishmen. They would create another China, another Hong Kong in England, just as former immigrants have created another Pakistan in Bradford.
>
> This possibility should make us consider what has already happened in this green and pleasant land – first as a result of waves of coloured immigrants and then by the pernicious doctrine of multi-culturalism … Every year that goes by the English are battered into submission in their own country and more strident are the demands of ethnic nationalism. The British people were never consulted as to whether they would change from being a homogeneous society to a multi-cultural society. If they had, I am sure that a resounding majority would have voted to keep Britain an English-speaking white country.

(Townsend, quoted in Pilkington 1993)

1 Why does Townsend question the view that British nationality automatically makes a person British?

2 What does Townsend mean when he refers to the change 'from being a homogeneous society to a multi-cultural society'? How could the view that Britain was ever a homogeneous society in the past be questioned?

Postmodernity and nationalism

Nationalism in the world today appears as a paradox. On the one hand, nation states appear to be undermined by the process of globalization. Writers such as Lash and Urry (1987) argue that while early capitalism was organized around competition between nation states, we are now entering a period of **disorganized capitalism**. A key feature of this is that transnational companies have become more significant in influencing the world economy than individual nation states.

On the other hand, nationalist movements have become more politically significant in many parts of the world. In many states nations within nations have become crucial sources of political identity. Examples of this include Palestinians in Israel, Tamils in Sri Lanka and Quebecois in Canada.

For many commentators the two trends are not as contradictory as they appear. As discussed earlier in this chapter, the erosion of traditional certainties and sources of identity is seen by some sociologists as characteristic of postmodern societies. While nation states were an important part of modernity, they have become less politically and economically significant as societies move towards postmodernity. However, the undermining of traditional sources of identity has led individuals to seek new sources of stability and certainty in a rapidly changing world. Nationalist movements, the reassertion of traditional ethnic identities and religious fundamentalism are all examples of this process.

Conclusion

Many of the issues involved in debates about postmodernity and fragmented identities are considered in more detail in the final chapter of this book. However, this chapter has attempted to illustrate not only how race, ethnicity and nationality can be important in the construction of identities, but also the broader issue of how identity is based on what sociologists refer to as **difference**. People are categorized as belonging to a particular group because they have characteristics that differentiate them from another group. We define people as Other because they are seen as in some way different from ourselves. Thus difference can be seen not only in terms of skin colour or cultural beliefs but also in terms of economic position, gender or sexual orientation, as we have seen in previous chapters. The next chapter considers one more important aspect of difference: age.

Coursework suggestion

Like gender, the topic of race and ethnicity offers numerous opportunities for research. You could of course research media images of race and ethnicity in a similar way to the suggestions about gender in the previous chapter.

The concept of 'hybrid identities' put forward by Gilroy also offers interesting research possibilities, particularly if you live in an area where there is a mixture of young people from different ethnic backgrounds. You could, for example, interview a sample of young people from different ethnic backgrounds or from one specific ethnic group in order to find out how far they are influenced by the culture of their parents and their religious beliefs as well as by the dominant culture of the wider society.

You would need to focus your research on clearly formulated questions, perhaps centring on one or more hypotheses. You would also need to think about how you could operationalize sociological concepts. For example, if you were interested in the degree of hybridization of cultures, you would need to think about how you would measure this in practice.

Essay questions

1 How would you explain sociologically the apparent growth in the significance of nationalism and national identity?

2 Evaluate the claim that racism is an inevitable feature of a multicultural society.

(Both questions from Interboard Syllabus Specimen Paper)

References and further reading

Anderson, B. (1983) *Imagined Communities: The Origin and Spread of Nationalism*, London: Verso.

Barker, M. (1981) *The New Racism*, London: Junction Books.

Bradley, H. (1996) *Fractured Identities: Changing Patterns of Inequality*, Cambridge: Polity Press.

Brown, C. (1992) '"Same difference": the persistence of racial disadvantage in the British employment market', in P. Braham, A. Rattansi and R. Skellington, *Racism and Anti-racism: Inequalities, Opportunities and Policies*, London: Sage.

Butler, C. (1995) 'Religion and gender: young Muslim women in Britain', *Sociology Review*, February.

Cashmore, E. (1987) *The Logic of Racism*, London: Allen and Unwin.

Cashmore, E. and Troyna, B. (1990) *Introduction to Race Relations*, Basingstoke: Falmer Press.

Castles, S. and Kosack, G. (1973) *Immigrant Workers and Class Structure in Western Europe*, Oxford: Oxford University Press.

Cohen, P. and Bains, H. (eds) (1988) *Multi-Racist Britain*, Basingstoke: Macmillan.

Daniel W. (1968) *Racial Discrimination in England*, Harmondsworth: Penguin.

Dayan, D. and Katz, E. (1992) *Media Events and the Live Broadcasting of History*, Cambridge, MA: Harvard University Press.

Gellner, E. (1964) *Thought and Change*, London: Weidenfeld and Nicolson.

Giddens, A. (1993) *Sociology*, Cambridge: Polity Press.

Gilroy, P. (1987) *There Ain't No Black in the Union Jack: The Cultural Politics of Race and Nation*, London: Hutchinson.

Gilroy, P. (1993) *The Black Atlantic: Modernity and Double Consciousness*, London: Verso.

Hall, S. (1992) 'The question of identity', in S. Hall, D. Held and T. McGrew (eds), *Modernity and Its Futures*, Cambridge: Polity Press.

Herrnstein, R. and Murray, C. (1994) *The Bell Curve: Intelligence and Class Structure in American Life*, New York: Free Press.

Hides, S. (1995) 'Consuming identities: ethnicity and material culture', *Sociology Review*, November.

Hobsbawm, E. (1990) *Nations and Nationalism since 1780*, Cambridge: Cambridge University Press.

Hobsbawm, E. and Ranger, T. (eds) (1983) *The Invention of Tradition*, Cambridge: Cambridge University Press.

Jeffcoate, R. (1984) *Ethnic Minorities and Education*, London: Harper and Row.

Kirby, M. (1995) *Investigating Political Sociology*, London: Collins Educational.

Lash, S. and Urry, J. (1987) *The End of Organised Capitalism*, Cambridge: Polity Press.

Mason, D. (1992) 'Some problems with the concept of racism', Discussion Papers in Sociology, S92/5, University of Leicester.

Miles, R. (1989) *Racism*, Milton Keynes: Open University Press.

Modood, T. (1992a) *Not Easy Being British: Colour, Culture and Citizenship*, Stoke-on-Trent: Trentham.

Modood, T. (1992b) 'British Muslims and the Rushdie affair', in J. Donald and A. Rattansi, *'Race', Culture and Difference*, London: Sage.

O'Donnell, M. (1990) 'Culture and identity in multi-ethnic Britain', *Social Studies Review*, January.

Pilkington, A. (1993) '"Race" and Ethnicity', in M. Haralambos (ed.), *Developments In Sociology*, vol. 9, Ormskirk: Causeway Press.

Said, E. (1985) *Orientalism*, Harmondsworth: Penguin.

Schudson, M. (1994) 'Culture and integration of national societies', in D. Crane (ed.), *The Sociology of Culture*, Oxford: Blackwell.

Shils, E. (1957) 'Primordial, personal, sacred and civil ties', *British Journal of Sociology*, vol. 8, pp. 130–45.

Shils, E. (1975) *Centre and Periphery: Essays in Macrosociology*, Chicago: University of Chicago Press.

Solomos, J. (1993) *Race and Racism in Contemporary Britain*, Basingstoke: Macmillan.

Trevor-Roper, H. (1983) 'The invention of tradition: the Highland tradition of Scotland', in E. Hobsbawm and T. Ranger (eds), *The Invention of Tradition*, Cambridge: Cambridge University Press.

Van Dijk, T. (1991) *Racism and the Press*, London: Routledge.

6

Age, generation and subculture

Key ideas	Key thinkers
Social construction of age	Philippe Ariès
Generation	Margaret Mead
Life cycle	S.N. Eisenstadt
Adolescence	Albert Cohen
Youth culture and youth subcultures	The Centre for Contemporary
Status frustration	Cultural Studies
Resistance	Stuart Hall
Magic	Stan Cohen
Incorporation	Angela McRobbie and Jenny Garber
Moral panic	
Subcultural capital	

Introduction

The last three chapters have focused on class, gender and ethnicity as important sources of identity and cultural differentiation. This chapter considers a fourth aspect of identity: age, with particular reference to the culture and identity of young people.

We start this chapter by looking at the idea that age is socially constructed. Different cultures have different assumptions about the significance of age and differentiate individuals by age in different ways. We then examine the transition from childhood to adulthood in industrial societies and consider why some sociologists have seen adolescence as a particularly problematic period as far as identity is concerned. From this we move on to review some of the research into youth subcultures, which represent some of the responses by young people to their social situation. We also consider how young people are differentiated not only by age but also by class, gender and ethnicity, linking in with some of the issues explored in previous chapters.

The social construction of age

Every society divides its members according to age. In many cases these age divisions have a biological basis. Young children may be too small to undertake adult tasks, while elderly people may be too infirm to perform some kinds of work. However, sociologists argue that age, like gender and 'race', is socially constructed. Different societies divide their members into age groups in different ways and the roles assigned to them vary widely and cannot always be attributed to biological abilities. In western industrial societies children and young people spend a relatively long period undergoing socialization into adult roles before entering the adult world. Elderly people enter a phase of retirement at a legally specified age and are again excluded or excused from the world of work. In other societies children start working alongside adults much earlier and there may be no formal retirement age – elderly people simply continue working for as long as they are physically able.

Age divisions in traditional societies

In most traditional societies there are no formal records of births or ages, thus while age may be very important to social status it has little to do with chronological age. In many such societies people only have a very rough idea of how old they are. In some societies males and in some cases females are divided into age grades. Children born around the same time are grouped together into an **age set**. This age set will then pass through important stages in life – for example, initiation into adulthood – at the same time, even though its members may be spread over several years in chronological age.

In many traditional African societies there are three main stages in men's lives – as children, warriors and elders – though there may be subdivisions within each of these. Boys of roughly the same age are normally initiated into adulthood around puberty and then become warriors. In many African societies initiation is preceded by instruction by older men on tribal lore and in the responsibilities of an adult. This is followed by a

Skin decoration is one of the rites of passage into adulthood in some African tribes.

ceremony in which the young men are admitted to adult status. In such societies initiation often requires a test of a man's physical strength or ability to resist pain. In some tribes boys are circumcised at initiation; amongst the Nuer of the southern Sudan, boys must submit without flinching to having six cuts made in their temples. Many societies have an initiation ceremony for girls too. Like boys, girls are usually instructed in adult roles with emphasis on sexual matters and their duties as wives. For girls, initiation allows them to marry and take on the role of an adult woman.

Interpretation activity

In what ways might an initiation ceremony such as the one illustrated above assist young people in the transition from childhood to adult status?

In contemporary British society there is no real equivalent of this type of ceremony. Discuss how young people in Britain today acquire adult status and what problems they might face in this process.

Age grades among the Arusha

In some societies age divisions are quite complex. Among the Arusha of Tanzania each of the main age groups – warriors and elders – is further divided into a junior and senior division. There is friendly competition between the junior and senior divisions of each age grade. Age grades are also linked; the junior elders act as patrons for the junior warriors and the senior elders for the senior warriors. Where a dispute arises a man expects members of his age grade to support him and may appeal to elders of the allied age grade to adjudicate in his favour. In a society where there are no courts or police, age grades act as a form of social control and a means of resolving disputes.

In societies such as the Arusha age is obviously a major source of identity for individuals. What is expected of an individual will depend to a large degree on his or her age and sex. For example, young men in many traditional African societies are responsible for fighting and herding cattle. Young women look after children and perform agricultural work; older men are responsible for making important decisions and adjudicating over disputes; older women have authority over younger women and direct the affairs of their households.

Age divisions in industrial society

In western industrial societies age is important in different ways. In tribal societies status usually increases with age and young people are expected to defer to their elders. While elderly people may be physically infirm they are often regarded as the source of knowledge and experience and take responsibility for directing the affairs of their tribe or village. In western societies the pace of change is much more rapid and traditional forms of knowledge handed down by word of mouth from the old to the young are seen as outdated and irrelevant. Consequently, elderly people do not seem to be accorded the same respect as in traditional societies. Status in industrial societies tends to be closely related to occupation and income and, as most elderly people are retired from work and may be on a reduced income as a result, old age is often a period in which people experience a decline in status compared to their working lives.

Most western societies legally regulate what a person is allowed to do at a particular age. For example, most industrial societies insist on a compulsory period of schooling during childhood. Legal rights such as the right to marry, vote or drive a car are usually restricted to those over a certain age. In Britain as in many other countries there is no single age at which a person achieves these adult rights. Instead there is a long period of growing up in which children gradually acquire the rights and freedoms associated with adulthood.

Legal age limits in England and Wales

Age	Permitted behaviour	Age	Permitted behaviour
5	Go to school	14	Pawn something
7	Withdraw money from a post office account		Be held fully responsible for a crime
10	Be convicted of a criminal offence (but not fined)		Own an air rifle
13	Buy a pet		Perform in public without a licence
	Buy fireworks	15	Possess a shotgun if supervised by someone over 21
	Be employed for certain hours of the week		Enter a knackers yard
	Be fingerprinted if in custody charged with an offence		Open a National Giro account
			Enter into some contracts (e.g. apprenticeships)

Age	Permitted behaviour	Age	Permitted behaviour
16	Buy premium bonds	18	Age of majority
	Join a trade union		Marry without parents' consent
	Leave school		Leave home without parents' consent
	Consent to sexual intercourse (girls)		Get a mortgage
	Leave home with parents' consent		Be tattooed
	Marry with parents' consent		Vote
	Enter or live in a brothel		Bring and defend accusations in court
	Sell scrap metal		Sue and be sued in the courts
	Choose your own doctor		Make a will
	Work full-time		Act as executor of a deceased person's estate
	Hold a licence to drive certain tractors, ride a		Change your name
	motorcycle or invalid carriage		Be a full legal owner of house and land
	Enter a bar of a pub (can only buy beer or wine if		Go abroad for the purpose of singing, playing,
	you are also ordering a meal)		performing or being part of an exhibition without a
17	Drive a car		licence
	Have a firearms licence		Buy alcoholic drinks
	Enter a betting shop		Pay adult contributions to National Insurance
	Fly a private aircraft		schemes
	Engage in street trading		Sit on a jury
			Consent to homosexual relations
		19	Join the police
		21	Be a local councillor or Member of Parliament
			Sell alcohol with a licence
			Hold a licence to drive any mechanically propelled
			vehicle

Interpretation and evaluation activity

In a group study the table above.

    Do you agree with the legal age limits in force at present or should any of them be changed? Justify your proposals.

    Discuss in your group at which age you think a person becomes an adult in Britain today. Give reasons for the age you have chosen.

It should be clear from the activity above that in Britain today the age at which a young person becomes an adult is by no means clear cut. This contrasts with many of the tribal societies discussed earlier, where a young person's initiation ceremony marks a sharp break with childhood and full entry into adult status with all its associated duties and privileges.

Age groups and generations

Although formal age grades do not exist in industrial societies, many sociologists recognize the importance of belonging to an age group in a person's identity. Most industrial societies are characterized by economic systems where the young and the elderly are economically dependent on those in the intermediate group of working age. Thus a person's status and economic position are heavily influenced by age. Harriet Bradley (1996) suggests that most sociologists distinguish five main age groupings: childhood; youth (or adolescence); young adulthood; mid-life; and old age. Some writers further subdivide the last category between the 'young old' (60 or 65 to 74) and the 'old old' (those aged 75 and over).

Individuals may identify with a particular age group because they share a common status and lifestyle. However, some sociologists suggest that members of an age group share a common experience of growing up at the same point in history – they are members of the same **generation**. Thus the generation who fought in the Second World War had a very different experience from those who enjoyed the affluence and full employment of the postwar period. They in turn differ from the young of the 1980s and 1990s, who have entered a labour market with much higher levels of unemployment.

The concept of generation highlights the fact that the experience of being a member of a particular age group changes from generation to generation. Adolescents in the 1990s share many of the same problems and pleasures of growing up experienced by their parents and grandparents. However, they also have experiences which are quite different from those of previous generations. The German sociologist Karl Mannheim (1952) argued that in some circumstances a generation may act as a unified social collectivity to change society in the same way as a social class. For example, the student radicals of the 1960s may have helped to end the Vietnam war and introduced a variety of new and radical ideas that helped to change society.

There are also problems in using the concept of generation. For example, where does one generation end and the next one begin? Also, emphasizing that members of a generation share a common experience of growing up or ageing may obscure important differences within a generation, particularly those of class, gender and ethnicity. For example, most of the student radicals of the 1960s were middle class, male and white.

Case Study four generations

Albert is 74. He is now retired but worked as a farm labourer in Suffolk from the age of fourteen. He was educated at the village elementary school and served in the army in North Africa during the Second World War. After the war he married his childhood sweetheart Amy and they had four children. He now lives with his wife in a council flat in Ipswich. Their only source of income is their state old age pension. Albert still cultivates his own allotment, though he finds the digging more difficult now. He occasionally meets up with old friends for a drink in the ex-servicemen's club.

Jenny is 45. She was born in Sussex and passed the 11+ exam in order to obtain a place at the local grammar school. She did well at school and went on to train as a teacher. At college she met her ex-husband and after graduating they travelled overland to India together. On their return they found teaching jobs in London and got married. Jenny has a teenage girl and boy but is now divorced from her husband. Although she gave up work for six years when the children were born, she is now back in full-time teaching. She also receives monthly maintenance payments from her ex-husband. Jenny is taking evening classes in watercolour painting and enjoys visiting the theatre with friends.

Linton is 22. He was born in Birmingham but his parents came to Britain from Jamaica as children in the 1950s. Linton never really liked school and left at sixteen with only a few qualifications. He found it hard to get a job and tried a Youth Training course to train as a car mechanic. However, at the end of the scheme he could not find an employer who would help him complete his training. After being unemployed and doing odd jobs for two years, Linton got a job working in a local filling station. He now lives with his girlfriend Chantelle, who recently found out she was pregnant. Until now Linton and Chantelle have enjoyed going drinking and clubbing with friends at weekends, but they don't know how they are going to manage financially when she gives up her job in a supermarket.

Harriet is eight. Her father is a commodity broker in London and her mother runs her own catering firm from home in Surrey. Until she started school Harriet was looked after by a nanny. Now she attends Cuthbert House, a private preparatory school. At weekends Harriet has ballet and riding lessons. Her parents have put her name down for Millfield, a public school with an excellent reputation for its sports facilities. Apart from riding and ballet, Harriet enjoys playing computer games and watching *Home and Away*. She also looks forward to the family's annual skiing holiday in Switzerland.

Interpretation and evaluation activity

1 What is the significance of age and generation in the social position, lifestyle and experience of each of the four people described above?

2 To what extent are class, gender and ethnicity also important in understanding these people's lives?

Age and life cycle

The importance of age is recognized by sociologists in the concept of **life cycle**. In most societies individuals undertake different roles at different times in their lives. For example, sociologists studying family life acknowledge that the family changes in importance as individuals move through the life cycle. The nuclear family of parents and children is most important to young children who are dependent on their parents, and the parents who are raising the children and who depend on each other for emotional support. As children grow they are likely to become less dependent on their parents and eventually leave the family home.

Robert Chester (1985) points out that as people live longer, being a child and raising children takes up a smaller proportion of people's lives and thus people spend less of their lives in nuclear families. This does not necessarily mean that the nuclear family is less important in people's lives, simply that at any one time a significant proportion of the population will be young single adults, lone parents, divorcees and elderly people. Family life thus provides a good example of how an individual's identity will vary depending on their age and the stage they have reached in the life cycle.

Briefly compare your identity and relationships to other people today (e.g. your family) with ten years ago. Where do you see yourself in another ten years' time? If possible, compare your answers with other students' and consider reasons for any similarities and differences.

Historical changes in childhood

Historical research suggests that the way age is socially constructed in Western Europe has changed considerably in the last 500 years. The French historian Philippe

Breughel's 'The struggle between Carnival and Lent' (1559).

Children as mini adults?

Ariès (1973) argues that in the Middle Ages the conception of childhood that we have today did not exist. Children were not seen as very different from adults or as needing special treatment. Children were portrayed by artists as wearing the same clothes as adults and with similar facial features. Once a child was old enough to enter the adult world – usually by the age of seven – he or she would start to work and play alongside adults. Ariès points out that most adults had no formal education and were illiterate, thus the entertainments and amusements of adults were very similar to those of children.

 Interpretation and application activity
Ariès uses paintings such as this one by Breughel to illustrate his arguments about how children were viewed in the Middle Ages. Why is it significant that the children wear the same clothes and are portrayed with similar features to adults?

Formal education and childhood

Ariès argues that it was the spread of formal education that separated children from the adult world. The invention of printing meant that to become an adult in the higher social classes (and eventually in all classes), a person had to be able to read and write. From the sixteenth century onwards wealthy families began to have their children educated by tutors or at schools. By the nineteenth century education was coming to be seen as important for all children. In 1870 the first state schools were established in England and Wales and in 1880 education was made compulsory for children up to the age of ten. Children could no longer learn about the adult world by being part of it; instead they were socialized for later life in schools separated from the adult world.

Ariès argues that the idea of children as separate and different from adults has been reinforced by the emergence of a variety of professions specializing in children's needs, for example teachers, paediatricians, child psychiatrists, child social workers, educational psychologists and so on. These experts base their work on the assumption that children are not yet fully developed people, and that they are vulnerable and in need of protection and guidance. For Ariès, this view of children as different from adults never existed in the Middle Ages and is a modern invention.

Criticisms of Ariès

Critics of Ariès argue that he has overstated his case. They point out that even in medieval times children were seen as vulnerable and innocent. There is also evidence that parents often had close and affectionate relationships with their children and this is not simply a modern invention as Ariès suggests. Nevertheless, Ariès points to important changes in the role and status of children in society in modern times.

The end of childhood?

Some writers have developed Ariès's argument by suggesting that the division between the worlds of children and adults is once again being eroded in the modern world, this time by the mass media. Neil Postman (1985) agrees with Ariès that the invention of the printed word meant that children needed to read before they entered the adult world. However, modern electronic media such as television, video and computers have brought the adult world into children's lives and meant that children can no longer be kept isolated from and innocent of the adult world. As evidence to support his argument Postman cites recent increases in child crime, together with the tendency for children to dress and behave sexually more like adults. In his view, all this indicates that children are once again joining the adult world and losing their innocence.

Evaluation question
Do you agree that modern mass media have destroyed children's innocence? If so, is this a bad thing?

Adolescence

Some sociologists have suggested that not only is childhood a product of modern societies, but so is **adolescence**. Adolescence can be defined as the period between physical maturity or puberty and the attainment of full adult status. In many traditional societies initiation into the status of a young adult comes soon after puberty. Girls may get married and take on domestic responsibilities, boys may become young warriors. In industrial societies young people may have to wait a long time between reaching physical maturity and achieving full adult status, often only attained when a young person gets their own home, a job and financial independence.

Biological theories of adolescence

It is often thought that adolescence is inevitably a difficult period of transition for young people because of the biological changes associated with puberty. This view was popularized at the turn of the twentieth century by G. Stanley Hall (1904). He suggested that puberty led to greater aggression and an awareness of sexuality, which meant that adolescence was inevitably a period of 'storm and stress'. Hall suggested that the lack of physical outlets for these feelings and the more sedentary life of industrial societies intensified these problems. His ideas influenced the development of youth movements, such as the Scouts, which aimed to channel young people's energy into constructive pursuits. However, Hall's emphasis on the biological basis of adolescent problems ignored the importance of social factors.

Margaret Mead: growing up in Samoa

For the anthropologist Margaret Mead the difficulties associated with adolescence in western societies have more to do with the role assigned to young people by western culture than with the biological changes involved in puberty. Traditional cultures usually assign young people a much more clear-cut role than western societies and adult status comes at a defined point often marked by an initiation ceremony. Western teenagers have to endure a long period in which they are neither children nor adults. They are not required to take on the responsibilities of adulthood but are also excluded from many of its privileges. Mead suggests that it is no wonder that in this situation adolescence is viewed as a period of 'storm and stress'.

Mead (1943) described how in Samoa teenage girls were expected to take on responsibility for many activities associated with adult women in our society, for example washing, cooking and looking after younger children. Mead argues that girls of this age entered into sexual relationships much earlier than was common in the west at the time she was writing in the 1920s. On this point, Mead's work has come in for some criticism in recent years (see p. 89), but she points out that Samoan girls seem to have far fewer problems in moving through adolescence into adulthood.

Evaluation activity
Compare your own experience of being a teenager with other students. Do you agree that adolescence is a problematic stage in life? If so, is this due to the social role assigned to teenagers by our culture?

The transition from childhood to adulthood in industrial society

In the 1950s functionalist sociologists such as S.N. Eisenstadt developed Mead's argument. Eisenstadt argued that industrialization had altered the way in which young people underwent the transition from childhood to adulthood. In pre-industrial societies most people's status was **ascribed** or determined by birth. Children followed in their parents' footsteps, whether as peasants or as nobles. In industrial societies status is more likely to be **achieved**. Schools and other educational institutions become more important as a means of sorting and grading students for future occupational positions. In these circumstances, Eisenstadt argues, young people become less certain about their status.

Adolescence is a period of limbo between the ascribed status provided by the child's parents and the achieved status he or she attains in adult life. As a result, young people turn to their peers – young people of their own age who are experiencing the same problems and anxieties. In this way, Eisenstadt argues that peer groups fulfil an important function in providing support for young people in making the difficult transition from childhood to adulthood in industrial society.

The emergence of 'youth culture'

Eisenstadt saw young people as developing their own **youth culture** with its own styles of dress, music, speech and behaviour. The postwar period witnessed for the first time the emergence of styles specific to teenagers. Before the Second World War young people mostly listened to the same popular music as their parents and wore similar clothes and hairstyles. The 1950s saw the development of distinctive teenage fashions and styles of music such as rock and roll, which were shocking to many of the older generation.

At this time the British sociologist Mark Abrams (1959) carried out a survey of young people's spending and estimated that by the late 1950s, young people had a spending power of about £850 million per year, 5 per cent of national consumer spending. With little unemployment, teenagers and young adults could earn high wages on leaving school and did not have the responsibilities of adults. Big business realized the opportunity to market new products specifically aimed at young people, such as records, clothes, cosmetics, magazines and entertainment.

A generation gap?

The sociological view that young people were acquiring a separate identity from both children and adults with their own distinctive 'youth culture' echoed the widely expressed sentiment that a 'generation gap' was emerging, in other words, that the norms and attitudes of the young were diverging from those of their parents' generation. This view is often reflected in media representations of young people which tend to focus on examples of youthful rebellion and delinquency. Nevertheless, most attitude surveys of young people suggest that the majority are remarkably conformist. A study by Thelma Veness (1962) in 1956 revealed that most school leavers believed that hard work was the key to getting on in life. They placed a high value on property and material possessions and hoped to settle down, get married and have children. More recent surveys (Coffield et al. 1986; Davis 1990) present a remarkably similar picture, suggesting most young people are conformist, conservative, share their parents' values and generally get on well with them.

▍ *Evaluation activity*

In a group discuss arguments for and against the view that the emergence of a distinctive teenage identity has created a 'generation gap'.

On a sheet of paper, summarize the points you have considered and decide in conclusion whether you agree or disagree with this view.

Youth culture or youth subcultures?

Writers such as Eisentadt emphasized the extent to which age and generation were important in the culture and identity of young people in industrial societies. Young people were seen as more likely to identify with other young people and share common norms and attitudes with them than with older people, even those from a similar social background. This view, however, ignores the extent to which young people are separated by other social divisions. By the 1970s much of the research on young people was beginning to explore the importance of social class in their experience of moving from childhood into adulthood. Later writers also emphasized the significance of gender and ethnicity.

As a result many researchers began to speak of **youth subcultures** rather than a youth culture. The concept of a youth culture implies a set of norms, values and attitudes shared by most young people which contrasts with or is even in opposition to the wider adult culture of society. The concept of subculture implies a culture within a culture – in other words, a group of people who share some of the norms and values of the wider culture but who are in some way culturally distinctive. By referring to youth subcultures, these writers wished to emphasize the way in which young people were influenced by the culture of the wider society and their own position in it, while in some respects rejecting or rebelling against some of the norms and values of the dominant culture.

It was also becoming increasingly difficult by the 1970s to talk of a single youth culture. Since the 1950s a succession of youth styles had rapidly succeeded one another. For example, in the 1950s there were teddy boys and beatniks, in the 1960s mods, rockers and hippies, and in the 1970s glam rockers, skinheads, rastas and punks. Each style had its own dress codes, hairstyle, favoured type of music and recreational activities.

Subcultural theory and youth

The concept of subculture has been used extensively in sociology as a means of understanding the behaviour of groups who in some way deviate from the norms and values of the dominant or mainstream culture of society. Individuals who may appear as deviants in the eyes of the wider society may in fact be conforming to the alternative norms and values of a subculture. Subcultural theory has been used in a variety of forms to explain the distinctive styles, attitudes and behaviour of groups of young people.

Albert Cohen: delinquent subcultures

The American sociologist Albert Cohen (1955) used the concept of subculture to explain the delinquent or law-breaking behaviour of certain sections of working-class youth. Cohen argues that many lower-working-class males see little to be gained from educational qualifications and achieve little at school. Schools in turn offer little status to such pupils. These boys come to suffer from what Cohen calls **status frustration**. They are unable to achieve status or recognition in terms of the values of the wider society, where success is equated with educational qualifications, a good job and material success.

Cohen suggests that such boys turn to a **delinquent subculture**, hanging out with other boys in a gang on street corners. While the 'college boys' who remain in the education system can achieve status according to the values of the wider society, the 'corner boys' create their own subculture in which many of the norms of the wider society are reversed. Stealing, fighting, vandalism and rowdiness, which are condemned by society at large, become a way of earning status as a young gang member proves his toughness or daring to his peers. In this way the delinquent subculture solves the problem of status frustration since its members are able to gain status, albeit by methods condemned as delinquent by the wider society.

Evaluation of Cohen

Cohen's theory was subsequently criticized by other writers for overestimating the degree to which the values of delinquents represent a rejection of society's values. Matza and Sykes (1961), for example, point out that many delinquents show genuine remorse and may attempt to use what they call **techniques of neutralization** to excuse what they have done. These involve justifications of delinquent behaviour in terms of wider cultural values. For example, a shoplifter may claim that he only steals from big shops that make excessive profits, not from small corner shops. Matza and Sykes argue that if delinquents really subscribed to different norms from everyone else they would feel no need to justify their actions in this way.

Nevertheless, Cohen's version of subcultural theory was important in establishing a link between social class and delinquent subcultures. Most middle-class and more respectable working-class boys have no need to turn to delinquency; they achieve success through the system. It is mainly the lower-working-class boys who are educational failures and who feel the need to prove themselves by turning to delinquency. Unfortunately, Cohen – in common with most writers of the period – has little to say about girls. It is not clear why girls who fail to achieve status in the education system far more rarely turn to law-breaking behaviour.

While Cohen's work explored the links between class and delinquent subcultures, it had little to say about the behaviour of young people who appeared to be rebelling against wider social norms without being specifically criminal. Many youthful styles such as the mods and the punks have been seen as a rebellion against adult society but were not specifically focused on delinquent behaviour, although activities such as consumption of illegal drugs could bring members of such subcultures into conflict with the law.

Application and evaluation exercise
Assess the usefulness of Cohen's theory of status frustration in explaining the attitudes and behaviour of the two groups of young people illustrated above.

The CCCS: working-class youth subcultures

The links between class and youth subcultures were explored more fully by the Centre for Contemporary Cultural Studies (CCCS) in the 1970s. CCCS scholars were strongly influenced by Marxism. They argued that cultural features such as youth styles are ultimately manifestations of structural features of a society, notably the economic system and its associated class relations. They claimed that it was no coincidence that most post-war youth subcultures attracted predominantly working-class young people because it was working-class youth who experienced most acutely the problems and contradictions of growing up in a capitalist society.

Phil Cohen: the semiotics of youth subcultures

The CCCS also made use of **semiotics** or the science of signs (see also pp. 00–0). This involves reading (interpreting) subcultural elements, for example dress or hairstyle, in order to understand their underlying meaning. For example, Phil Cohen's (1972) study of the traditional working-class community in the East End of London attempted to decode the mod and skinhead youth subcultures. Cohen argues that the traditional working-class community of the East End was in decline by the 1960s, as traditional industries and small businesses were destroyed by economic change. Rehousing, redevelopment and the influx of immigrants meant that traditional communities were broken up. In these circumstances young East Enders sought to establish new identities for themselves. The skinheads and the mods represent alternative routes.

According to Cohen, the skinhead subculture symbolizes an attempt to recover the working-class community which was passing away. Skinheads' dress, with shaved heads, heavy boots, baggy trousers and braces, represents an exaggerated version of traditional working-men's clothes. Similarly, their attitudes and behaviour, typified by use of aggression and violence to defend their territory, combined with dislike of Black people and middle-class youths such as hippies, could be seen as an exaggerated version of traditional working-class male values.

Figure 6.1 Semiological interpretation of skinheads

Class: clothes are just like dad's but dramatized – style 'on the cheap'.

Attitudes: defensive of their 'own' territory, macho, often anti-immigrant, anti-authority.

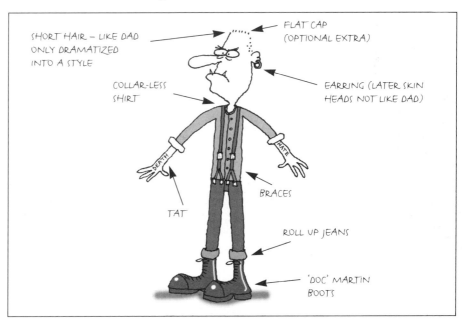

The mods, by contrast, reflected the upward aspirations of a more affluent section of the working class, who sought to copy the middle class. Mods wore flashy Italian suits and drove scooters if they could afford them. They aspired to a glamorous lifestyle centred on nightclubs and dance music, using drugs such as 'uppers' and 'downers' to keep them going. In reality, few working-class mods could afford to indulge fully in this lifestyle. However, Cohen suggests that the style reflects a rejection of traditional working-class culture and an attempt to embrace a more glamorous and cosmopolitan style.

Resistance through rituals

Later work by the CCCS made use of Gramsci's concept of **hegemony**, the way in which the ruling class secures the consent of the working class to its rule by ideological means (see also pp. 61–3). Like Gramsci, the CCCS argued that the majority of society accepts the hegemony of the ruling class. While members of the working class may be critical of the existing social system in some respects, they mostly accept it as fair, just and legitimate. For example, most people accept inequalities between rich and poor as inevitable, they see the political system as democratic and assume the educational system provides equal opportunities for all. Gramsci, however, argued that ruling-class hegemony is never complete, that there are always groups who reject ruling-class ideology and resist this hegemony.

For Stuart Hall and Tony Jefferson (1976) of the CCCS, working-class youth subcultures represent one source of such **resistance**. Working-class youth experience the contradictions of capitalism more acutely than middle-class youth, since they are far more likely to experience schooling as a waste of time ending in failure. Many of them will end up in dead-end, low-paid jobs that offer little satisfaction. It is precisely at the point of transition from school to work, from childhood to adulthood, that working-class youths experience most acutely their structural position at the bottom of the pile in the capitalist system. Unlike older workers, they are not yet tied down by the responsibilities of jobs, mortgages and families. In these circumstances rebellion and resistance are still a real possibility.

While Hall and Jefferson suggest that working-class youth subcultures represent a form of class resistance, they also acknowledge that this resistance is purely symbolic. It does little to change the structural position of the young people involved and represents little more than a symbolic V-sign to the wider society. It is for this reason that Hall and Jefferson describe youth subcultures as 'resistance through rituals'. However, Hall and Jefferson argue that working-class youth subcultures are not simply an unconscious reflection of existing working-class norms, but rather each youth subculture actively creates its own style and attitudes based on a reworking of existing elements.

Youth subcultures as magic

In Cohen's study the East End mods and skinheads were faced with a situation where traditional working-class values were being eroded along with the communities on which they were based. Alongside this there existed a middle-class culture of affluence based on educational opportunity and individual ambition and a media culture emphasizing fun and consumption. None of these cultures were immediately relevant to working-class youths in the 1960s, so their solution was to create their own subculture which 'magically' resolved the contradictions.

The CCCS uses the term **magic** to suggest that youth subcultures do not in reality solve the contradictions of young people's situation; however, they provide the appearance of a solution. The solidarity provided by being a member of a subculture may offset the sense of alienation felt by many young people, while rebellion in the form of appearance or behaviour may provide a chance to kick back at society without actually changing anything.

Dick Hebdidge: the incorporation of youth subcultures

One of the problems associated with the CCCS approach is that many youth styles appear to be no more than fashions created by the mass media and commercial interests. Dick Hebdidge (1979) explains this by arguing that there is a tendency for authentic youth subcultures to become **incorporated**. For example, the punk subculture of the later 1970s represented a conscious rejection of high street fashion. Clothing and jewellery were do-it-yourself, made out of ripped old clothes, safety pins and even bin liners. Punk bands took pride in the fact that they rehearsed in garages and could hardly play their instruments. Yet, within months of the emergence of punk, high street stores were selling mass-produced fashions based on punk styles and big record labels were queuing up to sign their own punk bands to counter the threat of small independent labels. Hebdidge quotes a *Cosmopolitan* headline of 1977 – 'To Shock is Chic' – to illustrate this process. Punk was transformed and tamed from a form of rebellion to simply another fashion and another music style. Hebdidge argues that this process of incorporation represents the way in which capitalism neutralizes or makes safe youth subcultures.

Application and evaluation activity
To what extent are youth styles created by young people themselves and to what extent are they creations of big business interests such as the fashion and music industries?

Try to give examples of youth subcultural styles which you think are 'authentic' styles developed on the street rather than created by big business. To what extent have these authentic styles subsequently been 'incorporated', as described by Hebdidge?

Evaluation of the CCCS

The work of the CCCS is generally regarded as a major contribution to theorizing about youth subcultures. It represented a number of major innovations. First, the CCCS went beyond the functionalist accounts of writers such as Eisenstadt to point out how youth subcultures represented a response not only to the transition from childhood to adulthood, but also to other structural features of young people's position, notably their class position.

Second, the CCCS attempted to make use of the methodology of semiotics to suggest that youth styles were not simply random and meaningless fashions but could be seen as constructed from symbolic elements whose meaning could be read by the skilled observer.

Third, the CCCS drew on interpretive sociology (see Chapter 8) in arguing that youth subcultures needed to be understood from the position of young people themselves. Young people were not seen as passive fashion victims but as actively constructing their own identities and creating their own culture in an attempt to make sense of the often contradictory messages coming from the society around them.

The CCCS's arguments have also provoked a range of criticisms.

The problem of meaning

One of the major criticisms of the CCCS is that it reads meanings into the behaviour and appearance of young people which the young themselves would not recognize.

Stan Cohen (1980), for example, suggests that there is a tendency among such theorists to interpret the behaviour of young people as a form of class resistance, even when such behaviour is either conservative (for example skinheads attacking Asian immigrants) or simply an expression of a dominant commercialized culture (young people buying punk gear from high street boutiques). In using methods such as semiotics there is a risk that researchers impose their own meanings on the subcultural elements in an interpretation that would make little sense to the young people themselves.

> *Take any youth subcultural style since 1945 and attempt to decode its meaning using a semiotic approach. What problems are there in using such an approach? You may find it useful to consult pp. 167–70, which provide a brief summary of the approach of semiotics.*

Middle-class youth

Mike Brake (1980) argues that youth subcultures can be classified into three types:

1 Delinquent youth.

2 Cultural rebels.

3 Politically militant youth.

He suggests that working-class young people have generally formed delinquent youth subcultures, while cultural rebellion and political militancy are more typical of middle-class youth.

Most of the CCCS research focused on working-class youth subcultures. These were explained as a form of resistance to young people's subordinate class position. This theory, however, provides little explanation of middle-class youth subcultures such as the beatniks or the hippies (cultural rebels) and the student movement of the 1960s or anti-road protesters in the 1990s (political militants). These subcultures arguably offered a much more coherent alternative set of values to the dominant culture than working-class youth subcultures such as the mods or the skinheads. Hippies, for example, rejected the work ethic and materialism, while radical students were in the forefront of protests against the Vietnam war. Yet most students and hippies were from middle-class backgrounds and their transition from school to work was eased by the relatively privileged world of higher education. Why such young people should reject the dominant culture is not clear from the CCCS approach.

Ordinary youth

The other major problem with the work of the CCCS, as with much of subcultural theory, is its concern with exotic and rebellious youth and its lack of consideration of 'ordinary youth'. The vast majority of young people are never members of youth subcultures or simply adopt subcultural styles because they are the fashion rather than as an expression of real rebellion. As pointed out above, most young people appear to be remarkably conformist and the majority of youth styles are creations of the mass media and marketing by big business rather than authentic creations of young people.

Since the 1980s there has been more research into the everyday problems of young people. For example, Tom Kitwood (1980) examines the way in which different groups of young people dealt with parents' attempts to restrict their freedom to go out on their own. Christine Griffin (1985) studied the aspirations of teenage girls and how they coped with the transition from school to work. Paul Willis (1984) carried out a survey of unemployed young people in Wolverhampton which describes the problems of coping with the postponement of adult status because of joblessness. While the CCCS's work provides some fascinating research into more exotic youth subcultures, these subsequent studies are perhaps more representative of the experience of the majority of young people.

Subcultures as moral panics

For the CCCS, youth subcultures represent an authentic form of resistance to the dominant culture of capitalist society. However, Stan Cohen (1980) sees youth subcultures as more often a creation of the mass media. His study of the mods and rockers in the 1960s illustrates this.

Stan Cohen: folk devils and moral panics

Before 1964 few people in Britain had heard of mods and rockers, but press reports of a clash between rival groups of youths in Clacton that Easter first brought the groups to public attention. Cohen suggests that because there was little news that weekend, the events of Clacton were given heavy coverage and exaggerated to create interest – a minor scuffle became a 'riot'. Newspapers predicted similar events on future bank holidays and sent reporters to seaside resorts to ensure they collected evidence to fulfil these predictions. Young people attracted by the media publicity flocked to towns such as Brighton, Margate and Hastings to join in the fun.

The media publicity also provoked what Cohen calls a **moral panic**. Local councillors demanded heavier policing and stricter action against youthful misbehaviour. Newspaper editors preached against the moral decline of the younger generation. There was a wave of concern amongst their readers about the irresponsible behaviour of young people. As a result, young people were often arrested for very minor offences and given heavy sentences by magistrates as an example to others.

In Cohen's terms mods and rockers came to be seen as **folk devils**. He suggests they were used as scapegoats who could be blamed for other problems in society. Mods and rockers had never really been enemies until the media created an imaginary rivalry which became a reality in the minds of many young people. This created a **self-fulfilling prophecy**. Rival subcultures emerged in reality and young people who saw themselves as mods or rockers felt obliged to live up to the fearsome reputation created for them by the media.

Rave subculture and moral panic

Cohen's concept of moral panics has been very influential and other writers have identified a variety of subsequent moral panics (see, for example, discussion of Hall et al.'s work on mugging in the 1970s, below). A more recent example is a series of studies by Redhead et al. (1993) of the rave subculture of the late 1980s. The mass media dubbed rave subculture 'acid house' and particularly focused on the use of illegal drugs such as Ecstasy, amphetamines and LSD. As with the mods and rockers, media attention provoked a moral panic and a punitive reaction. From 1988 onwards raves often suffered from police harassment. In 1990 a backbench MP's bill resulted in stiffer penalties for organizers of illegal raves. Redhead et al. suggest that, ironically, as with many other moral panics, the reaction had the effect of amplifying the deviance. Publicity for raves increased their popularity and criminals, alerted to the profits to be made, moved in to organize raves and sell illegal drugs to those attending them.

Interestingly, Sarah Thornton (1995), in another study of the rave/club subculture, describes how the alternative music media ridiculed the moral panic in the tabloid press over raves. While papers such as the *Sun* reported on the dangers of young people taking Ecstasy or 'E', music magazines ran spoof scandals about millions of kids 'hooked on a mind-bending drug called "A"' (for alcohol) or stories about the new designer drug 'T' on sale in supermarkets in small perforated bags. By contrast, the *Sun* briefly celebrated acid house, advising readers to wear smiley face T-shirts and day-glo colours like ravers. Thornton suggests that if this had really caught on most ravers would have abandoned the style immediately as being 'uncool'. It would seem that it is often the condemnation of subcultures by the popular media that makes them so attractive to young people.

Criticisms of moral panic

The concept of moral panic has been criticized by some writers. For example, it is not entirely clear why certain groups or events are selected for media attention. Moreover, the theory implies that the young people who are the subjects of moral panics are relatively harmless and that the threat they pose is exaggerated by the media. In some cases deviants are a genuine problem. For example, the 'joy riding' craze which received extensive media coverage in the late 1980s and early 1990s resulted not only in destruction of property for those whose cars were stolen but also the deaths of innocent people. Finally, moral panics are alleged to lead to deviance amplification. However, in some instances a punitive reaction by social control agencies may actually prevent a minor problem from being amplified. It is also not clear why moral panics come to an end – presumably the media and society at large lose interest and move on to other concerns.

Figure 6.2 The development of a moral panic

Original deviant act.
↓
Media pick up story and identify a 'problem' group.
↓
Story is exaggerated and sensationalized to create interest. Viewers and readers become interested in story, encouraging media to cover further stories.
↓
Deviants come to be seen as folk devils and stereotyped as having certain undesirable characteristics.
↓
Public and police are sensitized. Hostility towards deviants spreads and there is preparation for trouble.
↓
Deviants start to live up to their reputation. May react with further deviance because they feel 'picked on'.
↓
Further interest, increased fear and calls for stronger measures against the deviants.

Interpretation and application activity
Figure 6.2 illustrates the stages in the development of a typical moral panic. Take any example of a moral panic in recent years and show how it might fit into this sequence of events.

Gender and youth subcultures

While the CCCS addressed the issue of class in relation to youth subcultures, its work had little to say about gender. Feminist writers such as Christine Griffin (1985) argue that much of the sociology of youth subcultures has been almost exclusively concerned with males: women and girls – as in much traditional sociology – are invisible. Griffin argues that it cannot be assumed that the transition from childhood through adolescence to adulthood is experienced in the same way by girls as by boys.

McRobbie and Garber: girls and the bedroom subculture

One of the few exceptions to this was a study by Angela McRobbie and Jenny Garber (1976). This highlights how most research into youth subcultures ignores girls and, indeed, boys' relationships to girls. The question of why most of those who become teddy boys, mods, skinheads and so on are not only young and working class but also overwhelmingly male is never really addressed.

McRobbie and Garber argue that girls do have a female subculture of their own, but it is less obviously rebellious than that of males. They describe this as a **bedroom subculture**, since it typically involves girls spending time in their bedrooms, often in pairs, rather than in gangs on the street. Girls listen to music, experiment with make-up and discuss sex, pop idols and the latest gossip. McRobbie and Garber were describing the teenybopper subculture of the 1970s, centring on idols such as Donny Osmond and David Cassidy. However, there are perhaps contemporary equivalents, for example the teenage following of boy bands such as Take That and Boyzone in the 1990s.

To many observers this type of teenybopper culture would appear to be simply a form of manipulation of impressionable teenage girls by commercial interests. However, McRobbie and Garber argue that they offer teenage girls a chance to create a space which they control themselves. The bedroom is a private place where girls are not harassed by either boys or adults and this is symbolized by the decor, which includes posters of teenage idols. The teenybopper subculture is also accessible and safe for young girls; there are no entry qualifications and compared to going out with boys, the risks of personal humiliation involved are minimal. For McRobbie and Garber the teenybopper subculture represents a form of resistance to sexual subordination rather than class subordination.

Commercial manipulation or an accessible and safe subculture?

Interpretation activity

Suggest reasons why the subcultures of teenage girls differ from those of boys. You may find it helpful to refer back to Chapter 4 in answering this question.

Black youth

Not only have mainstream subcultural theories focused mainly on males, they have also concentrated on White youth subcultures. However, since the 1970s there have been a number of studies of young people from ethnic minorities. Afro-Caribbean youth have probably attracted most attention, perhaps because of the negative images of them presented by the mass media.

Policing the Crisis

One study illustrating this was Hall et al.'s *Policing the Crisis* (1978), which focused on a wave of media reports about the crime of mugging in the early 1970s. Hall et al. argue that street robbery had been in existence for centuries, but appeared as a new crime when the term 'mugging' was imported from America by the media. Reports on mugging reached a peak in 1972 after the conviction of three youths of mixed ethnic origin from Handsworth in Birmingham. Many of the reports emphasized that the muggers were Black and their victims White. Black youth came to be seen as a threat to law and order in British society.

Moral panic and the crisis of hegemony

Hall et al. argue that Black youth provided a convenient scapegoat. They use Cohen's concept of moral panic to describe the way in which public concern about mugging was whipped up by sensational media reports. However, unlike Cohen, Hall et al. develop a Marxist explanation of the emergence of the moral panic over mugging. They use Gramsci's work to suggest that the British state in the 1970s faced a **crisis of hegemony**. Britain was facing economic decline and growing class conflict in the form of industrial unrest. In these circumstances the state, supported by the mass media, sought to shift the blame for Britain's problems from the economic crisis of capitalism onto a crisis of law and order. Black youth, portrayed in the media as a threat to law and order, were used as scapegoats for the problems of society. In this way White working-class people were encouraged to support the state in its call for tough law and order policies. This resulted in heavy sentences for muggers and harsher policing of the inner-city communities where most Black people lived.

Hall et al. acknowledge that the media's portrayal of Black youths as muggers may have contained a grain of truth. Many young Blacks were disillusioned with the discrimination and unemployment they faced in Britain and turned to crime as a survival strategy. However, the reality of mugging was much exaggerated by the media. The reaction of the police may also have amplified the problem, since a special British Transport Police Squad was set up to deal with mugging and may have justified its existence by making large numbers of arrests.

While Hall et al. use Cohen's concept of moral panic, they go beyond his explanation of moral panics as simply a means of creating news when journalists cannot find a good story. Their work follows in the tradition of the CCCS in arguing that capitalist society depends on hegemony to maintain an apparent consensus. They suggest that the 1970s were a period of escalating concern about industrial unrest and class conflict: in this situation ruling-class hegemony was threatened as working-class people began to question the fairness of the existing distribution of wealth and income. The moral panic about mugging provided a means of reasserting ruling-class hegemony by mobilizing public support for the state's tough law and order policies.

Criticisms of Hall et al.

Critics such as Downes and Rock (1988) have suggested that there are weaknesses in Hall et al.'s argument. First, Hall et al. argue that Black crime was only rising because it was amplified by the police and media. However, they also suggest that unemployment and racial discrimination may have encouraged Black youths to turn to crime, implying a real increase. This appears contradictory. Second, Hall et al. explain the moral panic over mugging in terms of the crisis of capitalist hegemony in Britain. It is not clear that this provides an adequate explanation and it seems unlikely that it would also explain other moral panics, for example those over the mods and rockers or raves.

Afro-Caribbean youth

Subsequent studies (Pryce 1979; Gilroy 1983) of Afro-Caribbean youth have, like Hall et al., emphasized the way in which Black youth subcultures need to be seen as a form of resistance, not only to young Blacks' class position but also to racism and the structural disadvantages of being members of a subordinate ethnic minority.

A number of studies have focused on the Rastafarian subculture inspired by the Black leader Marcus Garvey. Rastafarians are notable for their long dreadlocks and woolly hats in Ethiopian colours (red, green and gold). Rastafarianism combines religious beliefs (God is called Jah) with a political rejection of White society (described as Babylon). Rastafarianism has also become associated with the musical style of reggae and encourages pride in being Black and a rejection of White culture. While only a minority of Afro-Caribbean youth were or are Rastafarians, the movement has encouraged a sense of pride in being Black in many young Black people.

In recent years a variety of other Black youth subcultures have emerged, for example rude boys and hip-hoppers, which suggest that for many young Black people ethnicity as well as age is important in developing a cultural identity. Black youth subcultures have also been an important influence on White young people, with many young Whites adopting Black styles of dress, speech and music.

Application and interpretation activity

Black youth subcultures have been an important influence on youth styles generally in British and American society in recent years. For example, rap music, wearing branded trainers and using terms like 'wicked' all have their origins in Black youth styles.

Think of as many examples as possible of ways in which Black youth culture has influenced the mainstream culture of British society.

Asian youth

There have been fewer studies of Asian youth in Britain and until recently the popular stereotype was that Asian youths were more conformist than Afro-Caribbeans. Asian young people have traditionally been part of close-knit extended families and religious communities which have tended to integrate them into the culture of their ethnic communities. However, there is evidence that in recent years young Asians are developing their own identities. While many young Asians feel a sense of loyalty to their parents' culture, many are also influenced by western youth culture and combine elements of both in creating their own subcultures. (See, for example, discussion of Charlotte Butler's study of young Muslim women in Chapter 5, pp. 127–8.)

Anti-school subcultures are traditionally seen as characteristic of white working-class and Afro-Caribbean youth. However, Martin Mac an Ghaill's study, *Young, Gifted and Black* (1988), describes how an Asian anti-school subculture called the Warriors existed alongside an Afro-Caribbean group, the Rasta-Heads. Because of the conformist reputation of the Asians, the Warriors got into trouble with the teachers far less than their Afro-Caribbean rivals.

The emergence of new youth subcultures amongst British Asians can also be seen in the emergence of new music styles such as bhangra, a cross-over between traditional Asian music and western pop. Asian young people have also been active in campaigns against racism, for example the Anti-Nazi league. In the late 1980s young Bangladeshis in the East End of London formed vigilante groups to defend members of their community against racial attacks.

Subcultures in the 1980s and 1990s

Many of the classic studies of British youth subcultures were written in the 1960s and 1970s and in some ways have become dated. Young people in the 1980s and 1990s have grown up in a very different set of circumstances from their parents. The transition from school to work is even more problematic for young people today than in the past. Unemployment has increased since the end of the 1970s and young people's entitlement to many social security benefits has been withdrawn.

Much of the research into young people in recent years has therefore switched from concern with youth subcultures to a focus on how young people cope with unemployment, juggling part-time work with further education, or their experience of government training schemes that offer little in the way of worthwhile qualifications.

Nevertheless, the concept of youth subcultures may still have some relevance. Arguably, since the 1980s there has been a proliferation of subcultures. In the mid-1960s the mods and rockers were perceived as the two main rival working-class subcultures, while the beatniks or early hippies attracted rebellious middle-class youth. In the 1990s there are scores of subcultural styles, often difficult to distinguish from one another. This explosion of styles is apparent not only in the dress and appearance of young people but also in styles of music. Mainstream chart pop music has now become confined largely to children up to the age of thirteen. Most teenagers and young people now graduate to a diverse range of musical tastes from indie, through hip-hop and techno to heavy metal.

Application and evaluation activity
Identify some contemporary youth subcultures or youth styles.
    To what extent does membership of these groupings reflect factors such as class, gender, ethnicity and locality?
    Do you think that sociological theories developed about youth cultures in the 1960s and 1970s have any relevance to the youth cultures of today?

Clubbers, ravers and subcultural capital

A recent study that illustrates how subcultural theory has been applied in a novel way to contemporary youth is Sarah Thornton's *Club Cultures* (1995), a study of the club and rave scene. Thornton draws not only on subcultural theory but also on Bourdieu's concept of cultural capital (see pp. 67–70). Bourdieu sees cultural capital as something that is an asset of the dominant social class. Those with cultural capital are those with the cultural knowledge of what constitutes good and bad taste according to the standards of the elite. Using the example of the club/rave subculture,

Thornton points out that youth subcultures also make distinctions between good and bad taste and that those who are 'in the know' have what she describes as subcultural capital: they acquire status and admiration from other members of the subculture for their 'cool' attitude or inside knowledge. Thornton explores three forms of cultural distinction that are apparent in the club subculture.

1 **Authenticity versus inauthenticity**. Up to the 1970s authenticity in music tended to be equated with live music – recorded music was seen as inferior or inauthentic. Club cultures, however, celebrate the new technologies of advanced recording techniques, synthesized sound, sampling and mixing. Thus what was previously seen as artificial music has come to be defined as the authentic article; sound engineers, remixers and DJs are admired as much as lead vocalists or virtuoso guitarists.

2 **Hip versus mainstream**. Many youth subcultures have maintained a distinction between their own sometimes obscure brands of music and mainstream pop music. This is apparent in the club subculture, where knowledge of often obscure dance records is a sign of status, as is being able to dress in the appropriate style, for example T-shirt, baggy jeans and kicker boots. Followers of mainstream fashion and pop music are described as Sharons and Tracys and seen as lacking subcultural capital.

3 **The underground and the media**. Much of the information about club culture and forthcoming raves is disseminated by word of mouth, flyers, fanzines and other more-or-less informal media. Members of the club subculture disparage the mass media as failing to understand their culture, and as often giving distorted or sensationalized accounts focusing on issues such as drugs rather than what clubbers define as important, i.e. the music and dancing. This again preserves the insider status of clubbers, since they feel that only they understand the club culture so misrepresented by the mass media. However, clubbers also resent it when the media release authentic information about the club scene, as this makes available exclusive knowledge – a source of subcultural capital – to outsiders (see also p. 156).

Saturdays at The Pod, Dublin. June 1997

classic clubs: old and new

Thornton argues that the existence of subcultural capital creates hierarchies within youth subcultures. Those who possess most subcultural capital or understanding and knowledge of these kinds of distinctions gain status and rise in the subcultural hierarchy. Those with less subcultural capital are given a lower status or even treated as outsiders. For example, many clubs will not admit those who are not dressed appropriately and only insiders will have access about information on how to get to raves.

Application activity

Can Thornton's concept of subcultural capital be applied to any other subcultures? Think of other subcultural groups who might make similar distinctions to those Thornton outlines.

Conclusion: youth subcultures and postmodernity

For many sociologists the diversity of contemporary youth subcultures is evidence of the influence of postmodernity on youth. It is argued that the modern society that emerged with industrialization was based on standardized mass-produced cultural products, for example Hollywood films and early pop music. Thus youth culture itself was relatively homogeneous and mass produced. In postmodern societies, by contrast, there is greater cultural choice and diversity. Individuals can freely select their own identity and have an increasingly diverse range of lifestyles and consumer products to choose from. In these circumstances the proliferation of youth styles is no surprise. The young are in the forefront of experimenting with new forms of consumption and inventing new lifestyles and identities for themselves.

Postmodern theories also reject the search for meaning characteristic of earlier subcultural research, for example the CCCS's claim that youth styles symbolize a form of class resistance. Instead they see youth styles as having multiple meanings which cannot be reduced to a single essential. For example, in his research on rave subculture Steve Redhead (1993) emphasizes that rave is more about pleasure and fun than rebellion against the adult world. Arguably, that has always been an important element in youth subcultures.

Debates about postmodernity are discussed in more detail in the final chapter of this book. However, many sociologists argue that postmodernity theories have exaggerated the degree to which social change has broken down traditional sources of identity. For example, much recent research suggests that factors such as youth unemployment and restrictions on student grants and social security for young people have widened class inequalities among the young and made the transition to adult status more difficult. Although new opportunities for young women and Black people have been opened up in recent years, there is evidence that they remain disadvantaged. For most young people class, gender and ethnicity, as well as age, remain important as cultural influences and sources of identity.

Coursework suggestion

The study of young people and youth subcultures has immediate relevance for many sociology students. You may have an interest in investigating a newly emergent youth subculture. This offers numerous possibilities for research, including participant observation (if you are part of a subculture yourself), interviews with young people and semiotic analysis of youth styles. It is a good idea to start out with clear aims or questions that you intend to investigate in order to give your research a focus. For example, you might investigate the hypothesis that contemporary youth subcultures are more concerned with hedonism and pleasure than with resistance to a dominant culture. You also need to be aware of your own values: if you identify with a particular youth style or subculture this may affect your analysis of it, though it may also give you insights which are not available to outsiders!

DATA RESPONSE QUESTION
Item A

In contemporary British society, older people are encouraged to conceal grey hair, wrinkles and other signs of ageing. In other cultural traditions, however, less negative interpretations are placed upon physiological aspects of old age. For the Sherbo people of Sierra Leone, incoherent or incomprehensible speech is perceived as a positive sign. Their incoherence indicates their close communication with ancestors who are regarded as important arbiters of destiny.

(Pilcher 1995, p. 13)

Item B

We can summarise the sub-cultural argument like this, then. Youth groups use their own area of power – their 'free time' – to make a gesture against their lot. Their material situation (school failure, unemployment, no future), is at one level accepted – there is nothing they can do about it – but, at another level, rejected – deviant styles symbolise a refusal to accept dominant accounts of their position. Youth sub-cultures can only cast spells against the boring powerlessness of the daily routine, but such magic does have cultural consequences. It challenges the ideology that normally keeps the social machinery working.

(Frith 1985, p. 349)

Item C

Going out dancing crosses boundaries of class, race, ethnicity, gender and sexuality, but not differences of age. The most avid clubbers and ravers are between fifteen and nineteen, followed by those aged between twenty and twenty-four. The age boundaries of clubbing are tight, framed at the younger end of the scale by practical factors such as being allowed out of the house after eleven, having enough money to pay the substantial entrance fees, and successfully negotiating a loosely enforced drinking age of eighteen. A loss of interest in clubbing coincides with moving out of the parental home, which has repercussions for young people's desire to get out of the house and escape the family. Most importantly, however, clubbing declines when people form partnerships by either living together or marrying. Market research repeatedly finds that single people are ten times more likely to be frequent clubbers than married people.

(Thornton 1995, pp. 15–16)

1 *With reference to Item A and any other evidence, explain what sociologists mean when they claim that age is socially constructed.* [5 marks]
2 *Item B states that: 'Youth sub-cultures can only cast spells against the boring powerlessness of the daily routine'. In what ways can youth subcultures be seen as a 'magical' solution to young people's problems?* [4 marks]
3 *Using evidence from Item C and elsewhere, explain how the concept of life cycle might help to explain age differences in consumption and leisure activities.* [4 marks]
4 *Item C suggests that going out dancing is more closely associated with age than with class, gender, ethnicity, race or sexuality. Critically evaluate the argument that age, rather than any other social division, is most significant in shaping young people's identities.* [12 marks]

References and further reading

Abrams, M. (1959) *The Teenage Consumer*, London Press Exchange Papers, 5.

Ariès, P. (1973) *Centuries of Childhood*, Harmondsworth: Penguin.

Bradley, H. (1996) *Fractured Identities: Changing Patterns of Inequality*, Cambridge: Polity Press.

Brake M. (1980) The *Sociology of Youth Culture and Youth Subcultures,* London: Routledge and Kegan Paul.

Chester R. (1985) 'The Rise of the Neo-Conventional Family' *New Society, 9* May.

Coffield, F., Borrill, C. and Marshall, S. (1986) *Growing up at the Margins*, Milton Keynes: Open University Press.

Cohen, A. (1955) *Delinquent Boys*, New York: The Free Press.

Cohen, P. (1972) *Subcultural Conflict and Working Class Community*, Working Papers in Cultural Studies no. 2, Centre for Contemporary Cultural Studies, University of Birmingham.

Cohen, S. (1980 [1971]) *Folk Devils and Moral Panics*, Oxford: Martin Robertson.

Davis, M. (1990) *City of Quartz*, London: Vintage Books.

Downes D. and Rock P. (1988) *Understanding Deviance,* Oxford: Clarendon Press.

Eisenstadt, S.N. (1956) *From Generation to Generation*, New York: The Free Press.

Frith, S. (1985) 'The sociology of youth', in M. Haralambos (ed.), *Sociology: New Directions*, Ormskirk: Causeway.

Gilroy, P. (1983) 'Police and thieves', in Centre for Contemporary Cultural Studies, *The Empire Strikes Back*, London: Hutchinson.

Griffin, C. (1985) *Typical Girls*, London: Routledge.

Hall, G.S. (1904) *Adolescence: Its Psychology and Its Relation to Physiology, Anthropology, Sociology, Sex, Crime, Religion and Education*, New York: D. Appleton & Co.

Hall, S. and Jefferson, T. (eds) (1976) *Resistance Through Rituals*, London: Hutchinson.

Hall, S., Critcher, C., Jefferson, T., Clarke, J. and Roberts, B. (1978) *Policing the Crisis: Mugging, the State and Law and Order*, London: Macmillan.

Hebdidge, D. (1979) *Subculture: The Meaning of Style*, London: Methuen.

Kitwood, T. (1980) *Disclosures to a Stranger*, London: Routledge and Kegan Paul.

Mac an Ghaill, M. (1988) *Young, Gifted and Black*, Milton Keynes: Open University Press.

McRobbie, A. and Garber, J. (1976) 'Girls and subcultures', in S. Hall and T. Jefferson (eds), *Resistance Through Rituals*, London: Hutchinson.

Mannheim, K. (1952) *Essays in the Sociology of Knowledge*, London: Routledge.

Matza, D. and Sykes, G. (1961) 'Juvenile delinquency and subterranean values', *American Sociological Review*, October.

Mead, M. (1943 [1928]) *Coming of Age in Samoa*, Harmondsworth: Penguin.

Pilcher, J. (1995) 'Growing up and growing older: the sociology of age', *Sociology Review*, September.

Postman, N. (1985) *The Disappearance of Childhood: How TV is Changing Children's Lives*, London: W.H. Allen.

Pryce, K. (1979) *Endless Pressure*, Harmondsworth: Penguin.

Redhead, S. (1993) *Rave Off: Politics and Deviance in Contemporary Youth Culture*, London: Avebury.

Thornton, S. (1995) *Club Cultures: Music Media and Subcultural Capital*, Cambridge: Polity Press.

Veness, T. (1962) *School Leavers*, London: Methuen.

Willis, P. (1984) 'Youth unemployment, a new social state', *New Society*, 29 March.

7

Signs, symbols and structures

<table>
<tr><td>

Key ideas

Semiotics

Signifier and signified

Structuralism

Polysemy

Deconstruction

Mass society theory

Encoding and decoding

Preferred, negotiated and oppositional
  readings

</td><td>

Key thinkers

Ferdinand de Saussure

Claude Lévi-Strauss

Roland Barthes

Jacques Derrida

Stuart Hall

David Morley

</td></tr>
</table>

Introduction

This chapter explores the way in which aspects of culture carry signification or meaning for members of societies. The chapter starts by considering the approach of semiotics, which examines the social meaning attached to signs. Words, pictures, stories, clothing and food all have cultural meanings which are of interest to semioticians. The chapter then goes on to consider the perspective of structuralism originating in the work of the anthropologist, Claude Lévi-Strauss. Structuralism aims to uncover the underlying structures that determine the cultural formations of a society. Some structuralists have drawn on semiotics, arguing that the meaning of aspects of culture, whether myths in tribal societies or mass media in capitalist societies, must be seen as a manifestation of deeper hidden structures.

The second half of the chapter considers research into the mass media and their audiences. It particularly focuses on research into the way in which audiences actively work to make sense of the messages contained in mass media. This research demonstrates that decoding cultural signs is not a straightforward process, even in the case of what might appear to be relatively trivial and simple media messages like soap operas.

Saussure and semiotics

The Swiss linguist Ferdinand de Saussure (1857–1913) is usually regarded as the founder of **semiotics**, the science of signs. He argued that language is a system of signs which are used to express ideas. Linguistic signs are made up of two elements: the **signifier** and the **signified**. The actual words, either written or spoken, are the signifiers, which represent a particular idea in language. The signified is the concept that the signifier actually represents. A particular signifier comes to be seen in relation to a particular signified in the process of **signification**. Where a signifier and signified are combined in this way they form a **sign**.

For example, objects may be represented by words such as 'table', 'pen' or 'door'. These are all signifiers in the English language for these objects and help us to write or talk about them. However, in other languages the same objects could be spoken about using different words. The signifier 'Tisch' in German signifies the same signified object as the English word 'table'. According to Saussure, the fact that certain signifiers become attached to certain signifieds is purely arbitrary; a table could be called 'Tisch' as in German or 'tavola' as in Italian, but it could just as well be called 'chair' or 'glog'.

Cultural rules and language

Although the original choice of signifiers is arbitrary, in speaking English, or any language, appropriate signifiers must be used. Saussure emphasizes the way in which culture, including language, cannot be made up by individuals but has a structure of its own. By being a part of society, users of a language are forced to use its signifiers to signify particular ideas.

Saussure went on to argue that signs can only be understood from the way in which they are **differentiated** from other signs. Signifiers have a different meaning because they sound or are spelt differently from each other. Moreover, words are defined in relation to one another. In a dictionary, for example, each word is given a definition using other words.

Saussure argued that not only is the choice of signifiers dictated by cultural norms, but the way signifiers are combined to produce meaning also follows grammatical rules. Thus the sentence 'The black man who lives in the white house' has a different meaning from 'The white man who lives in the black house', although both combine the same set of words. Saussure thus distinguishes **parole** – the way in which we use language in everyday life to convey meaning – from **langue** – the underlying grammatical rules that make language possible. This distinction is important in the later development of structuralist theories, since structuralists argue that all aspects of culture reflect underlying rules or structures which need to be understood by social scientists.

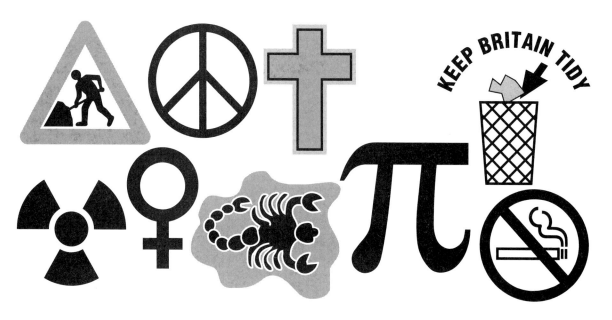

The development of semiotics

The science of semiotics founded by Saussure now extends beyond signs based on words to other kinds of communication. For example, research into the mass media has made considerable use of semiotics. Mass communications researchers argue that media such as television carry messages, or signification, not only in the words used but also in pictures and other symbols.

Icons

In semiotics, pictures and other signifiers which in some way resemble what is signified are described as **iconic**. For example, a photograph or even a cartoon of a famous person is immediately recognizable as representing that person, even though a photograph in a newspaper is only made up of black dots on a white page, while a cartoon may be a very distorted image of the real person. Some icons represent an idea rather than a thing; for example, the sign for a one-way street is a white arrow on a blue background, representing the direction of the flow of traffic. Here the relationship between the signifier and what is signified is less obvious than in a picture – it requires an understanding of the 'codes' or conventions of road signs to decipher the sign.

Paradigms and syntagms

The signifier that is selected to represent what is signified is also important. Different signs carry different **connotations** – they provide a different set of associations. For example, 'Mr Smith', 'David', 'Beergut' and 'our sociology lecturer' could all be signifiers that are applied to a particular person. However, which signifier is selected would carry very different connotations about the person concerned.

Not only is the choice of signs selected significant, but how they are combined is also important. The range of items from which we can choose to communicate a message is called a **paradigm**. This could be the words in a language that can be used to construct a sentence, a selection of images on film to accompany a news report, or the range of items in a person's wardrobe that could be combined in an outfit. The way these elements chosen from a paradigm are combined together according to certain rules is called a **syntagm**.

The semiotics of clothing

Clothing provides a good example of how signs can be combined according to a syntagm to produce a particular message. For example, middle-class students often wear elements of working men's clothes, such as donkey jackets, heavy boots and dungarees, in order to symbolize the fact that they reject middle-class norms of smart dress and materialism – and in the case of women and girls traditional femininity as well. However, by combining these with other elements, such as jeans, an unusual hairstyle or ethnic jewellery, they communicate the fact that they are not really workers but students making a serious intellectual point in their dress.

The meaning of punk

Dick Hebdidge (1979), a member of the CCCS (see pp. 151–5), makes extensive use of semiotic analysis in his work on youth subcultures. For example, he analyses the punk style of the late 1970s, describing their clothing as 'confrontation dressing'. The punk movement aimed to shock respectable people and subvert the establishment. Thus punks deliberately used pegs, razor blades, safety pins and even tampons as jewellery to symbolize their rejection of conventional fashion. Clothes were ripped and torn or included elements of bondage gear, zips, chains and even plastic refuse sacks. Conventional symbols such as the Union Jack or the Nazi swastika were appropriated and used to symbolize the opposite of their traditional signification. Even punks' names (e.g. Sid Vicious and Johnny Rotten of the band the Sex Pistols) were symbolic of the punks' anarchic and anti-establishment stance.

Interpretation and application activity

Take a recent style of dress and analyse it. Consider the following:

1 *What components are used in this style, i.e. what is the paradigm? You could consider hairstyles, jewellery, shoes and make-up as well as clothing in your analysis.*

2 *How are these elements combined together into a syntagm? Are there any rules about this?*

3 *What messages are there in this style, either about the person or group who adopt it, or which they wish to convey to other people?*

The semiotics of food

The idea that all aspects of culture carry codes and have symbolic importance is the basis of semiotics. Even food has been analysed semiotically. Wendy Leeds-Hurwitz (1993) argues that while food is normally associated with the physical and biological processes of nutrition and staying alive and healthy, it also has important cultural meanings in all societies. She quotes the work of the anthropologist Mary Douglas (1979), who pointed out the enormous diversity of human foods and diets despite the fact that human beings all have more or less the same nutritional requirements.

One example of this is the dietary patterns of immigrants. When people migrate to another country they often continue to eat the foods that are part of the culture of the society from which they originated, even if these foods are more expensive than those common in the host country. British Asians, for instance, may prefer to eat rice rather than potatoes, or Italians may prefer pasta.

Food taboos

Certain foods may also be regarded as 'taboo' or forbidden, not because they lack nutritional value but because a culture regards them as inedible. For example, Jews and Muslims are forbidden to eat pork and Hindus do not eat beef – or, in some cases, any kind of meat. While taboos may seem strange, many people in our society operate food taboos. Many British people would not eat frogs' legs, sheep's eyes, horse meat, snakes or insects, even though these are regarded as delicacies in some societies. Other people avoid all meat, alcohol or other 'unhealthy' foods such as those high in fat or sugar. The distinction between 'healthy' and 'unhealthy' food, now quite prevalent in Britain, is one example of the way in which many societies classify foods in opposing categories. Food is thus not neutral but carries messages or codes derived from the culture of society.

Food and identity

Wendy Leeds-Hurwitz (1993) argues that food can be analysed as a signifier that has a relationship to particular social categories (signifieds). People may consciously choose to eat (or not eat) certain foods because they wish to communicate something about their personal identity. The above examples of immigrants illustrate how food may be an important marker of ethnic identity. Food choices may also be linked to religious or political identities. Becoming vegetarian and eating organic foods, for example, may be a protest against factory farming and cruelty to animals and may express a concern about the environment. Certain foods may also be associated with particular classes (wine-drinking and the middle class), regions (Cornish pasties, Lancashire hotpot), events (Christmas pudding, Easter eggs), and social statuses (burgers or fish fingers for children, steamed fish for old people and invalids, Babycham as a woman's drink).

The example of food has been used to illustrate how semiotic analysis can be applied to any aspect of culture. Clothing, art, household objects and cars, as well as aspects of the mass media, have all been subjects of semiotic analysis.

 Interpretation and application activity

The cultural meaning of food and drink

> *Semioticians argue that food and drink have important cultural associations. Examine the picture overleaf and in each case discuss what cultural meanings the food and drink might have. For example, would you associate the food or drink with particular social groups or types of people? Is the food/drink associated with*

significant social occasions? Does the food/drink have any symbolic importance for those who consume it?

Having tried this activity, you could repeat the exercise with some examples of your own.

Lévi-Strauss and structuralism

The ideas of Saussure were influential in the development of **structuralism**, in particular the work of the social anthropologist Claude Lévi-Strauss, who attempted to analyse the underlying rules and structures of the myths and social relationships of people in tribal societies.

Lévi-Strauss argued that members of society make sense of the world around them through their culture. Culture provides individuals with concepts and categories that help them to construct a social reality. Individuals cannot create a purely personal or individual interpretation of reality. Everyone is born into a culture and inevitably learns to use the ways of thinking that are part of that culture to make sense of the world. Therefore, for Lévi-Strauss, the individual alone is unimportant. It is an understanding of the **structure** of society which explains the thinking and behaviour of individuals.

For linguists like Saussure, the surface features of speech could only be understood in terms of the deeper structures of the language that underlie it: for example, the rules of grammar that dictate how individual words should be combined to construct a sentence. Lévi-Strauss developed this type of analysis in his work on social relations. He argued that the interaction between people is based on similar deep structures in society. The job of the social anthropologist was to uncover this hidden 'grammar' of social relations.

Lévi-Strauss (1968) believed that the structures of society reflect universal structures of the human mind. People in both so-called 'primitive' societies and those in advanced industrial societies are responding to the same common structures of thought. Lévi-Strauss thus argued that underlying people's social relations there are hidden structures that determine the outward forms of everyday life. Lévi-Strauss acknowledged that these structures could not be directly observed and studied. However, he argued that such structures could be inferred from the more observable beliefs and social relations in a society.

The structures of kinship

An example of this can be seen in Lévi-Strauss's (1949) work on kinship. He argues that kinship relationships can be seen as a set of 'surface' relations that reflect deeper structures. He identified four elementary kinship relations:

1 marriage (husband–wife);

2 siblings (brother–sister);

3 filiation (parent–child);

4 avuncular (uncle/aunt–nephew/niece).

The way in which these relations are combined reflects an underlying structure. Lévi-Strauss suggests that there is a limited number of possible permutations as to how these relationships can be combined and organized. Moreover, a change in one element in the structure means that other elements will also alter, for example a different kind of father–child relationship will also imply a different kind of uncle–nephew/niece relationship.

In the case of the Trobriand Islands in the Pacific, relations between brothers and sisters are not considered as important as those between husbands and wives (sibling relations have a 'negative value' and marriage is 'positively valued' in Lévi-Strauss's terms). Similarly, because brothers and sisters are not close, children are not as close to their uncles as their fathers in the Trobriands. In Tonga, also in the Pacific, these relations are reversed; brother–sister relationships are more positively valued than marriage and consequently so are uncle–nephew/niece relationships. In such societies boys are often closer to their mothers' brothers than their fathers, with whom they have a respectful rather than familiar relationship. Lévi-Strauss thus argues that by knowing the nature of one element in a structure it is possible to predict the form taken by certain other elements.

Binary oppositions

Lévi-Strauss, like Saussure, saw language as an important component of culture because it allows us to categorize our environment and represent objects and ideas with symbols. Lévi-Strauss argued that the way in which ideas are represented in human thought and language often takes the form of binary oppositions; for example, nature versus culture (what is made by humans), life versus death, light versus darkness, the world of gods (heaven) versus the world of humans (earth). These binary oppositions are often combined to form combinations or **metonyms** in the myths and thought patterns of tribal societies.

The raw and the cooked

One example of this given by Lévi-Strauss (1969) is thinking about food. Food exists in a raw state and can be transformed in two ways, either in a natural way – by rotting – or in a cultural way – by cooking. Thus the binary opposition of nature and culture can be seen in the distinction made in many societies between foods which are cooked and those which are rotted or fermented naturally. The distinction between raw and cooked food is also symbolic of the distinction between nature and culture. Most animals eat raw food, while human food is normally cooked. The transformation of food is representative of the way in which human beings transform a wide range of natural resources into cultural objects.

Figure 7.1 Lévi-Strauss's culinary triangle

Source: based on Lévi-Strauss (1969)

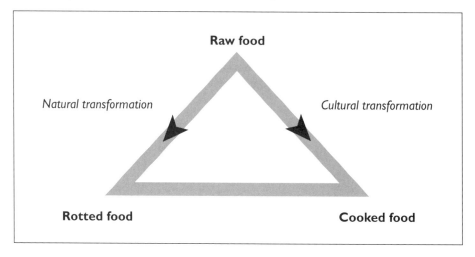

The structure of myths

Much of Lévi-Strauss's work was concerned with analysing the myths and beliefs of so-called 'primitive' societies. Lévi-Strauss tried to show that while the myths of different societies may appear to have little in common, they can be reduced to certain basic elements. When these basic elements are analysed, common structures are revealed. For example, in most myths the kind of binary distinctions and transformations shown above can be seen. For Lévi-Strauss these structures reveal something about the workings of the human mind. He suggests that there is little difference between the thought processes of supposedly 'primitive' people and those of so called 'civilized' societies. In all societies human beings use these kinds of classifications and oppositions to make sense of the world around them. For Lévi-Strauss this is the basis of culture.

Sociology and structuralism

The version of structuralism elaborated by Lévi-Strauss was enormously influential. As a result, cultural theorists began to explore the way in which aspects of the culture of a society might reflect underlying structures. In the case of Lévi-Strauss these were the structures of the human mind itself. For example, Lévi-Strauss argues that myths in different societies contain universal themes that reflect the structures of thought in all human beings.

The structure of Westerns

Contemporary cultural thinkers have applied Lévi-Strauss's structural analysis to the cultural forms of western societies. In an analysis of conventional Western films, such as *Shane*, Will Wright (1994) argues that the same kind of binary oppositions are apparent as in the myths of tribal societies. For example, the opposition between the hero and the villains or the opposition between the hero as an outsider and the established community. Wright claims that most classic Westerns follow a similar structure and reveal similar patterns.

Most classic Westerns demonstrate the same kind of binary oppositions as the myths of tribal societies: hero versus villain; hero as outsider versus the established community.

Structural functionalism

Lévi-Strauss is not the only social scientist to have developed a structural analysis of culture. Elsewhere in this book you have already encountered other structural perspectives. For example, Talcott Parsons (discussed in Chapter 2) developed a structural–functionalist approach to sociology that attempted to show how the social system could be reduced to certain basic structures. Like Lévi-Strauss, Parsons argues that elements of culture are often made up of binary oppositions, for example the opposition between instrumental and expressive pattern variables.

Structural Marxism

Cultural theorists influenced by Marxism have also adopted a structuralist approach, but they emphasize the way in which aspects of culture reflect the economic structures of society. The work of Louis Althusser is a good example of this approach. Althusser (1965) argues that culture is part of the superstructure of society and its role is to assist in the process of social reproduction. For example, the education system has an ideological role in socializing young people to accept their future positions in a capitalist economy. However, Althusser suggests that culture is ultimately determined by the economic base of society. Thus the culture of a capitalist society will reflect its underlying capitalist economic structures.

Feminism and structuralism

Feminists have made use of structural analysis in a similar way. However, their work is concerned with uncovering the structures of gender dominance and subordination rather than those of class. Some feminists have made use of Lévi-Strauss's concept of binary oppositions, but they have pointed out that in such dichotomies or oppositions one side is often constructed as superior to the other. The French feminist writer Hélène Cixous (1975) argues that cultural terms are often gendered, with concepts attributed to masculinity being accorded a superior value to those that have feminine associations. Cixous argues that women are associated with nature and emotions, while men are associated with culture and rationality, the latter often being viewed as superior.

Like Lévi-Strauss, structuralist feminists such as Cixous see deep-rooted binary structures as the basis for our thought patterns and interpretations of the social world. However, unlike Lévi-Strauss, they reject the view that these are inherent in the structure of the human mind. Instead, they see these thought patterns as social constructs open to challenge and alteration. For example, feminists have challenged the view that the female concern with emotion and personal relationships should necessarily be seen as inferior to the rational and logical thinking often associated with masculinity.

Interpretation activity

The following binary oppositions are offered by Cixous as examples of gendered thought. Consider how they are gendered and what women's position is in the dualism.

Where is she?

Activity/passivity

Sun/moon

Culture/nature

Day/night

Father/mother

Head/heart

Intelligible/sensitive

Man/Woman.

Source: Cixous (1975) 'Sorties', quoted in Woodward (1997), p. 36

Like Lévi-Strauss, feminists argue that myths can reveal the unconscious thought processes operating in a culture. A good example of this is feminist analyses of folk tales and fables.

The story of Little Red Riding Hood

Once upon a time there was a little girl, called Little Red Riding Hood on account of the red cape that she always wore. One day, Red Riding Hood's mother asked her to visit her grandmother, who was unwell. Red Riding Hood's mother gave her a basket of food and a bottle of wine for her grandmother and told her not to loiter on the way or speak to strangers.

The grandmother lived deep in the heart of the forest. Red Riding Hood skipped happily along the path, until she was suddenly confronted by a wolf.

'Good morning, Red Riding Hood,' said the wolf.

'Good morning to you, Wolf,' she answered.

'Where are you going this fine morning?' he asked.

'To my grandmother's,' she replied.

'And where does your grandmother live, Little Red Riding Hood?' asked Mr Wolf.

'Oh, she lives in the clearing right in the heart of the forest.'

All this time the wolf was eyeing up Little Red Riding Hood and thinking how tasty she would be to eat. Then it occurred to him that he might have both the little girl and the grandmother for his dinner. The wolf suddenly took his leave and disappeared into the forest.

While Red Riding Hood wandered into the forest to pick some flowers for her grandmother, the wolf ran straight to the grandmother's cottage and knocked on the door. 'Who's there?' asked the old lady.

'It's only your Little Red Riding Hood with some food and wine, Grandmother,' answered the wolf.

'Open the door yourself and come in,' called the grandmother.

The wolf went straight in and without further ado swallowed up the old lady. Then he put on her nightdress and nightcap and got into her bed.

Some time later Red Riding Hood realized it was getting late and, gathering up her flowers, she hurried to her grandmother's cottage. She was surprised to find the door wide open and felt something was wrong, but she wasn't sure what. She went up to her grandmother's bed and exclaimed,

'Oh, grandmother, what great ears you have.'

'All the better to hear you with, dear.'

'Oh, grandma, what great eyes you have.'

'All the better to see you with.'

'What great hands you have got, grandmother.'

'All the better to touch you with.'

'But grandmother, what great teeth you have.'

'All the better to eat you up with,' and, with these words, the wolf jumped out of the bed and gobbled up Little Red Riding Hood.

The wolf was now so full he fell asleep. Soon after a huntsman was passing by and saw the door open. He went in to check on the old lady and found the wolf asleep in her bed. The huntsman was just about to raise his rifle to shoot the wolf when he suddenly realized the old lady might be inside him. Taking his knife the hunter slit open the wolf and found Red Riding Hood and her grandmother inside still in one piece.

The huntsman took the body of the wolf away and Little Red Riding Hood resolved never to go wandering in the wood alone again.

Source: adapted from *Grimms' Fairy Tales*

Research and interpretation activity

Carry out a semiotic analysis of the story of Little Red Riding Hood. You might consider what messages it carries about the roles of men and women. What might the wolf signify? What is the moral of the story?

You could also carry out a semiotic analysis of other folk tales, for example Cinderella or Snow White, using a feminist approach.

There have been a number of attempts at rewriting stories like Red Riding Hood, for example by making Red Riding Hood less helpless or by changing the character of the wolf from an evil predator and male rapist. As an exercise, try rewriting a well-known folk story so that it carries a different message from the original. If possible, compare your version with those of other students.

Barthes and mythologies

Much of the work of Lévi-Strauss is concerned with myths, since they represent one of the main cultural products of tribal societies. The French writer Roland Barthes (1915–80) developed the ideas of structuralism but was more interested in the cultural products of modern capitalist societies. Like other structuralists, Barthes was interested in the meanings attached to aspects of culture, including everyday objects. Barthes's work focuses on aspects of culture such as the mass media and advertising, but in his book *Mythologies* (1973) he also analysed a variety of cultural products, including wrestling, toys, steak and chips, cars and even striptease. For Barthes, these are all part of the 'mythology' of capitalist societies.

Polysemy

Barthes argued that aspects of culture often have more than one meaning – they are **polysemic**. As new meanings are attached to objects or symbols, a process of **layering** occurs whereby a number of meanings are layered one upon another. In a study of the Eiffel Tower, Barthes pointed out how it has had layer upon layer of meaning imposed upon it since it was originally built. He suggests that among its many meanings the Eiffel Tower has been seen as a symbol of Paris, modernity, communication, science, metallurgy, transportation, democracy, tourism, subversion, ascension, lightness, plant, animal, female and male. He concluded that 'the Tower is everything that man puts into it, and that is infinite' (1973, p. 182).

Advertising as mythology

Much of Barthes's work focuses on the significance of advertising in consumer culture. According to Barthes (1967), the product is less important than the image in advertising. Particular products come to be associated with a particular image or selling point. As an example, Barthes points out how very different imagery is used in advertising different cleaning products. Chlorinated cleaning products (e.g. toilet cleaners) use the imagery of burning or purifying – 'killing' dirt or germs in a violent way. By contrast, detergents (e.g. washing powders) are 'separating agents' – the dirt is forced out rather than killed. As Barthes puts it, 'their function is keeping public order not making war' (1973, p. 36).

Interpretation and application activity

Analyse a selection of advertisements using a semiotic approach. Consider the following questions:

1   *What kind of images are being associated with the products advertised?*
2   *How is this used to enhance the appeal of the product to the audience?*
3   *To what extent does the kind of imagery used to sell products vary according to the nature of the audience or the market for the product?*

Mythology as ideology

While Barthes's work draws on semiotics and structuralism, it is also influenced by Marxism. Barthes analysed the way in which what he termed myth helped to sustain the capitalist system. Like Althusser and structuralist Marxists, Barthes sees the cultural myths of modern society as aspects of bourgeois ideology.

Barthes, however, points out that cultural messages can be interpreted in a variety of ways. A text or cultural product may carry an ideological message, but we cannot assume that the reader or member of the audience will interpret it in the way the author intended. Barthes in fact proclaimed the 'death of the author', arguing that readers create their own meanings irrespective of the author's intentions. All texts or cultural messages are unstable and open to different interpretations. This means that what is signified by a particular signifier is not fixed but is constantly shifting according to how the message is 'read' by its audience.

The Romans in films

In Mankiewicz's *Julius Caesar*, all the characters are wearing fringes. Some of them are curly, some straggly, some tufted, some oily, all have them well combed, and the bald are not admitted, although there are plenty to be found in Roman history. Those who have little hair have not been let off for all that, and the hairdresser – the king-pin of the film – has still managed to produce one last lock which duly reaches the top of the forehead, one of those Roman foreheads, whose smallness has at all times indicated a specific mixture of self-righteousness, virtue and conquest.

What then is associated with these insistent fringes? Quite simply the label of Roman-ness. We therefore see here the mainspring of the Spectacle – the sign – operating in the open. The frontal lock overwhelms one with the evidence, no one can doubt that he is in Ancient Rome. And this certainty is permanent: the actors speak, act, torment themselves, debate 'questions of universal import', without losing, thanks to this little flag displayed on their foreheads, any of their historical plausibility.

Source: from Barthes (1973), p. 26

Interpretation and application activity

Barthes suggests that in this film fringes are a sign that signifies Roman-ness. Discuss with other students films you have seen and find examples of similar types of signification.

Often similar signs are used in whole genres of films. For example, James Bond always drives a fast car, wears a smart suit and attracts beautiful women, representing a particular type of suave Englishman. The baddies in Bond movies are usually represented as foreigners or in some way strange or alien (Dr No is Chinese and the Man with the Golden Gun has extra nipples!). See if you can identify any similar examples.

Poststructuralism

Barthes's work has important implications for structuralism and semiotics. It suggests that even the scientific expert cannot assume that he or she knows the 'real' meaning of a text, whether it is a work of literature, an advertisement or the style of dress adopted by a youth subculture. The semiotician is simply adding his or her interpretation to that of many others. In this way, semiology becomes part of the culture which it attempts to study, simply another interpretation of the world it seeks to analyse.

Barthes is thus seen by many as initiating the development of **poststructuralism**. Other writers such as Jacques Derrida (1978) took this further with the notion of **deconstruction**. This involved an attack on the idea that structures have any meaning implicit in them. From this perspective meanings are only created by observers interacting with what they observe. To try to analyse culture in a scientific or rational way is thus impossible. This implies that all interpretations are purely subjective and the kind of rational or objective account of structures sought by earlier structuralists was a hopeless endeavour. Poststructuralism raises interesting questions about semiotics and structuralism. It suggests that in attempting to analyse the meanings of cultural commodities semioticians are guilty of a kind of arrogance in claiming that their interpretations are somehow superior or more scientific than those of the ordinary person.

Poststructuralists also reject the view that people are constrained by structures. Writers such as Derrida and Foucault (see pp. 76–80) argue that our social reality is simply made up of language, writing and discourses that appear to place limits on our freedom of action. Liberation involves challenging the dominant discourses and forms of language and finding our own identities and forms of expression.

Mass-media messages and audiences

Having examined the ideas of structuralism and semiotics, we now turn to the way these approaches to culture have influenced research into the mass media in Britain. In particular, we shall examine how media research has moved from the analysis of representations – for example through content analysis – to a concern with how audiences decode or interpret media representations. Here the influence of poststructuralism can be seen. Media researchers have come to appreciate that a particular set of signifiers may carry multiple meanings, that they do not necessarily signify the same things to all members of the audience. Thus the process of interpretation by the audience may be as important as the structural organization of media messages.

Media effects research

Up until the 1960s research into the mass media had been dominated by two models. In the period up to the 1940s much research had been based on what is often called a '**hypodermic model**'. This implied that audiences were directly influenced by the messages of the media – just as a drug in a hypodermic syringe injected into a vein would take immediate effect.

Mass society theory

An influential version of this model was the **mass society theory** developed by writers of the Frankfurt School, such as Horkheimer, Adorno and Marcuse (see also pp. 64–5). This theory argued that the bonds of community, class and other groupings were breaking down in modern societies, so that people were becoming atomized individuals with only shallow social relationships with others. The consequence was a mass society. Individuals become increasingly dependent on the mass media for information and an understanding of the world around them; as a result, they are easily manipulated by those who control the mass media.

By the 1940s this model was being challenged by American media researchers, who found that the ability of the mass media actually to change people's attitudes and behaviour was quite limited. Moreover, far from being a mass society, individuals still belonged to primary groups such as families, friends and workmates which were often strong influences on attitudes and behaviour.

The two-step flow model

One influential theory developed at this time was the **two-step flow model** (Katz and Lazarfield 1956). This suggested that, rather than the media directly influencing the audience, its message was interpreted by opinion leaders within primary groups. For example, how members of a group might interpret a news item on television would be affected by the opinions of dominant members of their social group. Rather than seeing the mass media as a very powerful agency which could potentially manipulate the opinions of the audience, this model implied that the media could only reinforce existing attitudes and behaviour.

Hall: encoding and decoding

Approaches such as the two-step flow model came under criticism from the late 1960s onwards as sociologists and cultural theorists turned to the ideas of structuralism and semiotics to analyse the media. Stuart Hall was a leading figure in the Centre for Contemporary Cultural Studies (CCCS), a group that did much to develop this type of approach. Hall attacked the idea that communications take place in a direct line between sender and receiver.

Hall (1980) developed the concepts of **encoding** and **decoding**. Encoding describes the way in which a message is constructed from a number of elements before being transmitted. Hall was particularly interested in the way in which the elements were selected and then combined to carry an ideological message. For example, a news programme is constructed from a huge number of potential events that could be reported as 'news'. From these, only a tiny minority actually appear as news items. The way in which these items are selected by news editors and the format in which they are presented is based on the implicit values of those who 'manufacture' the news. Writers influenced by Marxism, like Hall, argue that the way media messages are constructed reflects the dominant ideological assumptions shared by those who work in the media. However, this approach also shows the influence of semiotics with its appreciation of how elements from a particular paradigm are combined in a syntagm (see p. 167).

The audience in its turn decodes these messages to make sense of their meanings. Rather than seeing audiences as passive recipients of media messages, Hall emphasizes the way in which they actively interpret media messages using their cultural knowledge. Newspaper headlines, for example, are written in a kind of shorthand, but experienced newspaper readers are able to decipher this code to understand what the headline refers to. Like Barthes, Hall accepts that media messages may have more than one possible meaning, that they are polysemic. This implies that members of the audience may interpret or 'read' media messages in different ways – we cannot assume that everyone will be affected by what they see/read/hear in the same way.

Reading the media

This is not to say that Hall suggests that media messages are simply open to any interpretation. Much of the work of Hall and his colleagues in the CCCS was concerned to show how media such as television present a **preferred reading** of the message. By this he means that the audience is encouraged to interpret what is happening in a particular way. For example, in a traditional Western the viewer is encouraged to identify with the 'cowboys' and see the 'Indians' as the enemy. It is perfectly possible to sympathize with the Indians and see the cowboys as the 'baddies', but the way events are portrayed does not lead the viewer to this interpretation.

Open and closed texts

A conventional Western is what the Italian semiologist Umberto Eco (1981) would call a **closed text** – it tends to encourage a single interpretation so that most of us agree who are the 'goodies' and the 'baddies'. In news programmes, this interpretation of events is less obvious. News is what Eco would call an **open text** – it invites a multiplicity of possible interpretations. However, even here Hall argues that the construction of news leads the audience towards a particular interpretation of events. Newsreaders are seen as presenting the facts, and film of the events being reported helps to give the impression that these are real events – these are the 'facts'. However, even in news programmes, events are placed in a framework which makes sense of them for the audience. According to Hall, this represents the **dominant–hegemonic position**, the interpretation which those with power choose to put on events. For example, news reporting of strikes often tends to present strikes as the fault of workers and trade unions rather than of the government and employers. Workers involved in the strike are unlikely to accept this version of events, but those who have no reason to question the media version of events are more likely to accept this reading.

Varieties of readings

Hall went on to distinguish three types of **readings** or interpretations of media messages:

1 **Preferred reading**. This is the interpretation of the message implied by the way it has been constructed, for example acceptance that greedy workers are to blame for strikes.

2 **Negotiated reading**. This is the reading taken by the majority, where individuals 'accord a privileged position to the dominant definitions of events while reserving the right to make a negotiated application to local conditions' (Hall 1980, p.137). For example, a worker may agree with the media's view that excessive wage demands by workers create inflation, while maintaining his or her own right to strike for a wage increase. As Hall points out, such negotiated readings are often contradictory.

3 **Oppositional reading**. In this case the member of the audience decodes the media message and reassembles it to construct an alternative version of events. A left-wing trade unionist may hear the news state that strikes are against the national interest because they cause inflation, but reinterpret this to read that strikes are against the interests of the ruling class because they interfere with the profitability of capitalism.

Hall emphasizes that these readings are not discrete or separate; individuals may on some occasions accept some or all of the preferred reading in a message, but on other occasions adopt a more oppositional reading.

While Hall acknowledges that not everyone will accept the preferred reading favourable to the dominant groups in society, he argues that the role of the mass media is to persuade the majority to see the world from this point of view. In Hall's terms the role of the media in capitalist society is the 'manufacture of consent'. In this respect Hall's work is heavily influenced by Gramsci's concept of hegemony (see pp. 61–3). Like Gramsci, Hall argues that the ruling class can only rule by securing the consent of the majority. By encouraging the majority to accept an ideological framework that supports the status quo and inhibits criticism of the existing system, the media play a crucial role in maintaining ruling-class hegemony.

Research activity

Watch and preferably video a television news programme. Select one item and analyse how the story is constructed from a number of elements. For example, how is the item introduced by the newscaster? Is there a report by a specialist correspondent and how is this put into a context by the newscaster's introduction? How much of the story is fact, speculation, comment by journalists, comment by those involved? In what way are film, pictures, graphs, maps or other visual images used to make sense of events? What is the relationship between these visual images and the spoken words?

Using Hall's concept of encoding, write a short report on your news item summarizing the way in which the various elements in the news story are put together to create a meaningful message.

If possible, show a video of your news item to other students and discuss with them whether their reading of the news story is the same as yours.

Morley: the Nationwide *audience*

Hall's ideas were developed in a series of studies of the programme *Nationwide* by David Morley in the 1970s. *Nationwide* was an early-evening current affairs programme that was broadcast after the main news. Charlotte Brunsdon and David Morley (1978) carried out a semiotic analysis of the programme. They argued that *Nationwide* presented itself as speaking for the ordinary man or woman in the street, as sharing the same assumptions and concerns as the average viewer. In this respect the presenters of the programme assumed a consensus and commonality of interests in the audience.

One example of this was the presenters' cosy mode of address to the audience. Phrases such as 'tonight we meet', 'we all of us know that' and '… can happen to any of us', helped to make the audience feel that they shared the same set of assumptions as the presenters, and indeed other viewers. Like Hall, Brunsdon and Morley argue that television presents a preferred reading of events, one which assumes that everyone else shares the same view of the world as that of the broadcasters. This again helps to create the illusion of a society based on consensus and masks the reality of inequalities and conflicts based on class, gender and race.

Reading Nationwide

In a subsequent study of *Nationwide*, Morley (1980) turned his attention to the audience. He attempted to understand how viewers decoded the programme and attempted to use Hall's typology of readings to classify audience responses. Morley played an episode of the programme to twenty-six groups of people varying in class and other social-background characteristics. However, members of each group came from a common background and were interviewed about their response to the programme together. Morley began by asking relatively open questions, but progressed to more focused questions to draw out how audience's interpretations developed through talk and the interchange of views between respondents. Morley argued that in real life people do not watch television in isolation but view in groups and often discuss programmes afterwards, so he attempted to reflect this in his methodology.

At the end of his research Morley suggested that the responses of his groups could to a large extent be categorized into Hall's typology of readings. A group of apprentices felt the programme was simply 'common sense' and approved of its down-to-earth style. This was also reflected in a group of bank managers, though they felt the programme 'talked down' to them somewhat. These groups thus fell in with the preferred reading or dominant decoding of the programme.

The negotiated reading could be seen in the response of a group of full-time trade union officials. They generally approved of the way issues were presented in the programme but were critical specifically of its presentation of trade union issues.

Another group of trade unionists – this time left-wing shop stewards – were much more critical and presented a more oppositional reading. They criticized the presentation of economic issues, stating for example that 'there's no discussion of investment, growth, production, creation of employment'. They also disliked the assumed consensus in the programme, arguing that the programme attempted to side-step real problems and conflicts.

An even more negative response to the programme came from a group of Black further education students. They simply felt the programme was irrelevant to their lives and experience and only suitable for an older, more middle-class audience.

Evaluation activity

Discuss the strengths and weaknesses of the group interview method used by Morley in his research on Nationwide.

Evaluation of Morley

Morley's study represents an important attempt to demonstrate that the responses of audiences to the media cannot be simply read-off from the message itself. Audiences are active participants in the consumption of media messages, and how they interpret television programmes and other media products is likely to be influenced by cultural background factors such as class, occupation, gender and ethnicity.

However, Morley failed to demonstrate exactly how these factors do influence viewers' readings of television. For example, at the end of his study he was unable to demonstrate any clear relationship between factors such as class and the incidence of dominant, negotiated and oppositional readings. Morley's methodology has also been criticized. By interviewing people in groups his respondents tended to achieve a consensus within their groups about how they interpreted the *Nationwide* programme. This may well have masked differences in the reading of the programme between members of the group, or indeed between people from similar social backgrounds in the wider society.

Television and family life

Morley was subsequently critical of his own work. In a later study, *Family Television* (1986), he argues that the way individuals interpret television needs to be studied in the context of family life. Television viewing is part of a wider pattern of leisure activities in most families. For example, many people plan their leisure time around favourite television programmes and record programmes which clash on video. Morley also observed that men are often more dominant in determining what is watched and monopolize the remote control. Morley argues that his earlier research failed to explore these aspects of television viewing because it did not study respondents in family groups, or consider the relationship between television and patterns of leisure or family relationships more generally.

Understanding soap operas

In recent years soap operas have been a popular subject for audience research. Soaps offer an apparently simple storyline and are often portrayed by critics as presenting simplified, stereotyped or over-dramatized images of daily life. However, audience research suggests that the response of viewers to soaps is more complex and sophisticated than this view allows for.

Crossroads

The kind of ethnographic approach (which describes how people use television in everyday life) advocated by Morley is exemplified by a study of the TV programme *Crossroads* by Dorothy Hobson (1982). *Crossroads* was a popular soap opera based on life in a West Midlands motel which ran from the 1960s to the early 1980s. Rather than formally interviewing *Crossroads* viewers, Hobson went into the homes of members of the audience and watched television with them, following this up with long unstructured conversations about the programme.

Hobson points out that viewers do not watch soaps as isolated programmes but build up an expert knowledge of plots and characters which they draw on to make sense of each episode. Other researchers into women and soap operas have made a similar point. Rosalind Coward (1986), in a study of the American soap *Dallas*, points out that the narrative structure of soap operas is very complex; typically, it requires viewers 'to remember back across the years or use deductive skills for missed episodes' (1986, pp. 171–2).

Soap viewing and pleasure

Writers like Hobson are strongly critical of those who denigrate soaps as 'rubbish' or 'trivia'. She argues that not only do audiences use complex skills to decode programmes, but also that this type of television is a source of great pleasure for many people, especially women. Hobson found that many of her respondents felt a kind of ownership of *Crossroads* and its characters and were justifiably aggrieved when the TV company proposed to 'kill off' favourite characters.

Hobson's argument reflects the views of an American writer on day-time soaps, Tania Modelski (1984). She argues that many elements of soaps correspond to aspects of women's own life experience and this explains the pleasure which women derive from them. For example, the viewer often knows more than characters in the story about what is going on. The viewer is invited to care about all the characters but not identify with anyone specifically. The viewer becomes a sort of ideal mother who has more wisdom than any of her children (the soap characters) and watches over all their activities. This fits in with the real-life role of many women.

East Enders

A more recent study of *East Enders* by David Buckingham (1987) shows how children also actively interpret soap operas. As part of his research Buckingham interviewed

sixty young people between seven and eighteen years old in groups organized by age. Buckingham found that much of the pleasure that young viewers gain from *East Enders* lies in the way in which secrets are gradually revealed. Children were well aware of the way in which the programme's writers doled out information, gradually revealing 'secrets' in the plot bit by bit. Buckingham suggests that far from being victims of manipulative television writers, children were fully conscious of this process and took pleasure in the speculation, anticipation and revelation involved. Like Hobson, Buckingham argues that viewers are not stupid. Soap operas require complex skills to make sense of the genre and viewers are able to distinguish fiction from reality.

> **Interpretation and evaluation activity**
> *In a group discuss what you enjoy about a favourite TV soap. To what extent are the studies of TV soaps discussed above applicable in understanding this programme and its audience?*

Evaluation of audience research

The kind of audience research discussed here illustrates how since the 1970s media research has shifted its attention from simply analysing the content and representations within media texts, using techniques such as content analysis and semiotics. Researchers have been increasingly interested in how the audience actively interprets particular messages and why some groups are more likely than others to either accept or resist dominant readings. In this, the influence of poststructuralism can be seen. Media researchers have come to appreciate that in any sign or text there may be a multiplicity of available meanings. It cannot be assumed that all the audience will interpret a particular message in a particular way.

Commonality of audience responses

Recently, however, this kind of research has been criticized (Corner 1991; Seaman 1992). Critics have pointed out that in focusing on the diversity of audience responses researchers may ignore the similarities of interpretation. Jenny Kitzinger (1993), for example, points out how a large proportion of the population accepted stereotypes about AIDS being a disease associated with homosexuals, prostitutes and drug addicts when it was first given extensive coverage by the media in the early 1980s.

Truth and falsity

A second problem is that a poststructuralist approach to culture tends to be based on an extreme relativist position. It becomes impossible to judge the truth or falsity of media messages, since this approach implies that all audience interpretations are equally valid. Some researchers, such as the Glasgow University Media Group (GUMG), argue that sociologists have a role in unmasking the biased and ideological nature of the media. Thus in their work on the Falklands War (1985) they argue that news stories presented as facts were simply falsehoods put across by the Ministry of Defence to improve the government's image. For example, the bombing of Port Stanley airfield was presented as a success, whereas most of the bombs had missed the runway. Whether the audience believed the story or not, the GUMG would argue that it was objectively false.

Media influence?

Finally, Corner (1991) argues that in focusing on the creative response of audiences it becomes more and more difficult to assess what influence the media may have upon them. The danger is in assuming that because different individuals interpret media messages in different ways we may conclude that the media has little or no influence at all relative to other cultural influences.

Conclusion

This chapter has explored some of the ways in which social scientists have attempted to analyse a variety of cultural forms in order to uncover deeper meanings. For these theorists the meaning of words, pictures and other forms of communication is not self-evident. Behind the surface meaning may lie a deeper message. For structuralists this deeper message may be part of a broader pattern or structure, which must be discerned before such cultural messages become meaningful. The problem with such approaches is that they risk imposing meanings on aspects of culture which those who composed the original text may not have intended. Thus the social scientist may read a message into the text which is not really there.

Students of culture have become increasingly aware that aspects of culture may be polysemic or carry multiple meanings. The research into mass-media audiences discussed in the latter part of the chapter shows how it is important not only to decode the meaning of a message as a social scientist, but also to explore how other members of society interpret these messages. The research into media audiences is particularly interesting because it shows how other cultural influences affect the way in which audiences use and interpret the media. For example, gender roles – in themselves a cultural construction – can influence how individuals interpret the media and the use that they make of different types of media.

Coursework suggestion

The approach of semiotics offers many opportunities for coursework. Advertisements, clothing styles, food and even cars are all examples of 'texts' that could be used for semiotic analysis. This is a fascinating area, but it is a fairly difficult research method and you would be advised to do further reading and become familiar with some examples before trying your own analysis.

As with other research methods, you should use some kind of theoretical framework to guide your analysis. For example, you might examine images of femininity from a feminist viewpoint, with a view to analysing how images of women serve to construct ideals of female body type and sexuality.

Semiotic analysis need not be confined to visual images. Texts such as newspaper stories also offer a rich source of data for analysis of the ways in which language can be used to convey hidden messages. Interesting areas to consider might include race and immigration, young people and crime, and the reporting of the private lives of celebrities.

Essay questions

1 *Critically evaluate the contribution of structuralist approaches to the study of culture.*

2 *Assess the contribution of research on audiences to our understanding of the influence of the mass media.*

References and further reading

Althusser, L. (1965) *For Marx*, Harmondsworth: Penguin.

Barthes, R. (1967) *Elements of Semiology*, New York: Hill and Wang.

Barthes, R. (1973) *Mythologies*, St Albans: Granada.

Brunsdon, C. and Morley, D. (1978) *Everyday Television: Nationwide*, London: BFI.

Buckingham, D. (1987) *Public Secrets: East Enders and Its Audience*, London: BFI.

Cixous, H. (1975) 'Sorties', in *La Jeune Née*, Paris: Union Générale d'Editions, 10/12. English translation in Marks, E. and Courtivron, I. (eds) (1980) *New French Feminisms: An Anthology*, Amherst, MA: University of Massachussetts Press.

Corner J. (1991) 'Meaning, genre and context' in J. Curran and M. Gurevitch (eds) *Mass Media and Society* London: Edward Arnold.

Coward, R. (1986) 'Come back Miss Ellie: on character and narrative in soap operas', *Critical Quarterly*, vol. 28, nos 1 and 2.

Derrida, J. (1978 [1967]) *Writing and Difference*, Chicago: University of Chicago Press.

Douglas, M. (1979) 'Accounting for taste', *The Bridge*, 10, 15–16.

Eco, U. (1981) *The Role of the Reader*, London: Hutchinson.

Glasgow University Media Group (1985) *War and Peace News*, Milton Keynes: Open University Press.

Hall, S. (1980) 'Encoding/decoding', in S. Hall, D. Hobson, A. Lowe and P. Willis (eds), Culture, *Media and Language*, London: Hutchinson.

Hebdidge D. (1979) *Subculture: The Meaning of Style* London: Methuen.

Hobson, D. (1982) *Crossroads: The Drama of a Soap Opera*, London: Methuen.

Katz, E. and Lazarfield, P. (1956) *Personal Influence: The Part played by People in the Flow of Mass Communications*, New York: The Free Press.

Kitzinger J. (1993) 'Understanding AIDS: Media messages and what people know' in J. Eldridge (ed) *Getting the Message*, London: Routledge.

Leeds-Hurwitz, W. (1993) *Semiotics and Communication: Signs, Codes, Cultures*, Hillsdale: Laurence Erlbaum Associates.

Lévi-Strauss, C. (1949) *The Elementary Structures of Kinship*, Boston: Beacon Press.

Lévi-Strauss, C. (1968) *Structural Anthropology*, London: Allen Lane.

Lévi-Strauss, C. (1969) *The Raw and the Cooked*, New York: Harper and Row.

Modelski, T. (1984) *Loving with a Vengeance: Mass Produced Fantasies for Women*, London: Methuen.

Morley, D. (1980) *The Nationwide Audience*, London: BFI.

Morley, D. (1986) *Family Television: Cultural Power and Domestic Leisure*, London: Comedia.

Saussure, F. de (1969 [1911]) *Course in General Linguistics*, New York: McGraw-Hill.

Seaman W. (1992) 'Active audience theory: pointless populism' *Media Culture and Society* 14: 310–11.

Woodward, K. (ed.) (1997) *Identity and Difference*, London: Sage in association with The Open University.

Wright, W. (1994) 'The structure of myth and the structure of the Western film', in J. Storey (ed.), *Cultural Theory and Popular Culture: A Reader*, Hemel Hempstead: Harvester Wheatsheaf (originally published as *Sixguns and Society*, Berkeley: California Press, 1975).

8

Interaction, agency and structuration

<table>
<tr><td>

Key ideas
Reflexivity
Meanings
Labelling
Impression management
Stigma
Intersubjectivity
Common sense knowledge
Members' methods
Indexicality
Membership categories
Structuration

</td><td>

Key thinkers
George Herbert Mead
Herbert Blumer
Howard Becker
Erving Goffman
Alfred Schutz
Harold Garfinkel
Anthony Giddens

</td></tr>
</table>

Introduction

Most of the chapters in this book so far have focused on the variety of ways in which our social identities are structured by our position in relation to others in society. For functionalists, like Parsons, the social system comprises a structure made up of institutions, roles, values and norms which guide our personal behaviour and provide us with a place in relation to others. For Marxists, it is our relationship to others in the system of production that is central to our identities; our position as workers or wealth owners is important in creating a sense of class consciousness. We have also examined how gender, sexual orientation, 'race', ethnicity and age are all structural factors influencing our social identity. Finally, the previous chapter examined how structuralists like Saussure and Lévi-Strauss argue that there are deep structures in our systems of language and thought which influence how we see ourselves and the world around us.

The term 'social structure' is problematic in that it is used in rather different ways by different writers. However, in general terms, it is taken by sociologists to mean a relatively stable pattern of social relations that persists over time. Thus we have seen how people who share a common position in the social structure – for example, a common gender or ethnic identity – are likely to share common attitudes and behaviour and to be treated by other people in similar ways to others in their social group.

Interpretation and application activity
Structuralist theories in sociology tend to emphasize the way in which our position
in the social structure can act as a constraint. For example, as a man or a woman
you may be constrained from doing certain things, not because it is physically

impossible but because social pressures encourage you to conform to what is regarded as appropriate to your gender.

Use the following list of prompts to give examples of how in your own life you are constrained by aspects of your social identity. For example, in the box for gender I might write that as a male I feel constrained to dress in trousers rather than skirts, drink beer rather than Babycham in pubs and so on. Try to think of at least one example to put in each box.

Once you have done this, go down the list again filling in the right-hand column. Think of examples of ways in which you have adopted a particular identity or pattern of behaviour out of your own free choice. Thus the clothes I wear tend to reflect my gender – as well as age and occupation – but also reflect something about my personality and give messages to other people about the kind of person I see myself as.

Social identity	As constraint	As free choice
Norms and values of society as a whole		
Social class/occupation		
Gender		
Sexual orientation		
Ethnicity		
Age		
Other examples		

Structure and action

Many sociologists are unhappy with the idea that society simply structures or determines people's behaviour. Taken to its extreme, this would suggest that we are simply puppets blindly following roles laid down by society and taught us through socialization. In reality, few sociologists would adopt such a position. As should be apparent from the activity above, we all exercise a degree of personal choice within the constraints of society. A number of sociological theories stress the importance of individuals' actions in shaping their own identities. These theories emphasize that not only does culture shape the actions of human beings, but also that culture itself is the result of human action. These theories, often described as **interpretivist** or **social action** theories, emphasize the importance of free will in human action and argue that social actors' thoughts and behaviour cannot be seen as determined by forces beyond their control.

This chapter examines a number of theories representing this type of viewpoint, including symbolic interactionism, phenomenology and ethnomethodology. The chapter concludes with a discussion of attempts to bring together structural and social action approaches in sociology, focusing on the work of Anthony Giddens.

The origins of symbolic interactionism

The origins of symbolic interactionism lie in the philosophical approach known as **pragmatism**. Pragmatists such as John Dewey reject the idea that a true reality exists in the real world which can be objectively measured. Instead, our knowledge of the world is based on what works and what we find useful in accomplishing our ends. If a particular way of looking at things or doing things seems to work for us, then we accept it as reality. Dewey emphasized the way in which individuals are constantly engaged in a thinking process, considering alternative ways of interpreting events, choosing alternative courses of action and selecting modes of action which they see as likely to accomplish their goals.

These ideas were a major influence on George Herbert Mead – who is commonly regarded as the founder of symbolic interactionism – in particular, in the development of his concepts of the 'I' and the 'me' (see Chapter 1, pp. 22–3). In this respect, Mead saw human actors as reflexive individuals; in other words, as reflecting on their past experience and alternative courses of action and consciously choosing to act in certain ways. What distinguishes humans from animals, according to Mead, is our ability to select one interpretation of events from an infinite range of possibilities and use it to make sense of a situation. Animals, by contrast, respond to situations on the basis of instinct or are simply conditioned to respond in a certain way to a given stimulus. For example, a dog may learn to sit when it hears a command. Mead thus rejects the view that human behaviour is determined either by biology or by social conditioning.

Blumer and symbolic interactionism

Mead's ideas were subsequently developed and elaborated by his students, notably Herbert Blumer, who invented the name **symbolic interactionism**. Blumer (1969a) summarized symbolic interactionism (hereafter referred to as interactionism) in terms of three main propositions.

1 *Human beings act towards things on the basis of the meanings they have for them.* Blumer argues that things do not have fixed meanings, whether they be physical objects, people or ideas. Different objects have different meanings for different individuals: 'A tree will be a different object to a botanist, a lumberman, a poet and a home gardener' (Blumer 1969b). Thus, like Dewey, Blumer emphasizes that a tree is not simply a physical object that exists but has different meanings according to the purposes of different individuals. Meanings also influence how actors behave towards other people. For example, in Chapter 5 we saw how ideas about 'race' have influenced people's behaviour towards one another in the last three hundred years. While 'race' as a category may have no scientific basis, skin colour has important meanings in many people's minds and affects how they behave towards others.

2 *The meaning of things is derived from, or arises out of, the social interaction that one has with one's fellows.* In this respect, Blumer was critical of other sociological perspectives, such as functionalism. Blumer rejected the view that cultural norms and meanings were simply learned from society. Instead, he emphasizes the way in which individuals are constantly engaged in negotiating social reality. We also saw in Chapter 5 that ideas about race and ethnicity are not fixed and unchanging. Members of groups are constantly interacting and redefining their own identities and those of others. Thus young British Muslim women do not simply accept the role assigned to them by their parents, but develop their own identities through

their interaction with their families and other members of their communities, as well as with the wider society (see pp. 127–8).

3 *Group action takes the form of a fitting together of individual lines of action.* Interactionism is often seen as focusing on the individual rather than the wider society or social structure. However, Blumer argues that individuals do not behave in isolation from one another. As Mead suggests, individuals constantly refer to the 'generalized other' in choosing which actions to perform (see pp. 22–3). In this sense, society is present in all of us when we view our own actions through the eyes of others. Moreover, Blumer argues that actors constantly adjust their own behaviour according to the reactions of others in interaction situations. For example, a teacher and a group of pupils may both approach their first meeting with preconceived ideas about one another; however, in classroom interaction they may redefine their ideas about one another and about the situation as a result of negotiation.

Symbols

In the previous chapter we noted how structuralists such as Lévi-Strauss emphasized the importance of symbols in social life. As their name implies, symbolic interactionists are also concerned with symbols, though they reject the view that symbols are related to any deeper underlying structure. Symbols can be defined as 'social objects used to represent (or "stand in for", "take the place of") whatever people agree they shall represent' (Charon 1985, p. 39). Like Saussure, interactionists recognize that symbols may take the form of words or pictures, but that physical artefacts (e.g. clothing) and actions (e.g. sticking two fingers in the air) can also be symbolic.

Symbolic interactionists regard words as some of the most important symbols, in that it is language which differentiates humans from animals. Symbols allow human beings to name, categorize and remember objects and ideas. For example, I could not communicate these ideas about sociology to you without using symbols which we both interpret in broadly the same way. As human beings we can accomplish a wide variety of complex tasks more effectively by using symbols. In particular, the reflexive aspect of human behaviour, where we consider alternative courses of action, is assisted by our ability to think through symbolically various options before choosing the one we think best. Symbols also allow us to engage in 'role taking'; we are able to put ourselves in imaginary situations or see ourselves from the view of the 'generalized other', as outlined by Mead.

Blumer points out that symbols are necessarily shared, otherwise they would have no meaning. Actors draw on a common stock of symbols (for example, words in their language) each time they act. Actors build up common understandings of how situations are to be defined from experience of previous situations. Thus the symbolic meaning of placing a white rectangular piece of folded paper with a small coloured piece of paper in one corner through a slot into a red cylinder on the pavement is the same for me as it is for the postal worker who collects my letter from the post box. Our shared interpretation of these symbols, as well as the squiggles on the envelope that symbolize the address, enables my letter to be delivered to its destination. This is not to say that symbols and meanings are fixed. Blumer emphasizes the way in which actors continually redefine situations in their interaction with one another.

Interpretation and application activity

Think of examples of ways in which symbols are important in social life. What things do symbols allow us to do which animals are incapable of doing?

Howard Becker and labelling theory

One area where interactionist ideas achieved considerable influence was in the field of deviancy theory. Howard Becker's classic study, *Outsiders* (1963), was one of the earliest studies to apply Mead and Blumer's idea to understanding deviance. Like Blumer, Becker sees meanings as arising out of interaction. This leads him to argue that actions are not intrinsically deviant or socially unacceptable. Instead, he suggests that groups come to define certain forms of behaviour as deviant through interaction and negotiation. As Becker expresses it:

> Social groups create deviance by making rules whose infraction constitutes deviance, and by applying those rules to particular people and labelling them as outsiders. From this point of view, deviance is not a quality of the act the person commits, but rather a consequence of the application of others of rules and sanctions to an 'offender'. The deviant is one to whom that label has been successfully applied; deviant behaviour is behaviour that people so label.
>
> (Becker 1963, p. 9)

Becker suggests that we constantly interpret others' behaviour in interaction situations. In some situations other actors' behaviour comes to be defined as deviant, in other situations very similar behaviour may be tolerated or even praised. Becker uses the example of injecting drugs. For a diabetic to inject herself with insulin prescribed by a doctor would be regarded as acceptable, while a heroin addict injecting himself would be labelled as deviant by most people. Thus it is not the taking of drugs that is deviant; rather it is the reaction of other people to drug taking in certain circumstances that leads to its being defined as deviant. Like many other aspects of social life discussed in this book, Becker sees deviance as something that is socially constructed.

Application activity
Give other examples of ways in which deviance is defined in different ways in different social circumstances.

Becoming a deviant

Like other interactionists, Becker is concerned to understand the motives and meanings of actors. Becker argues that it is important to understand deviance from the point of view of the deviant. One of the studies in *Outsiders* focuses on marijuana users. Becker rejects the view that marijuana users are abnormal individuals who cannot control their behaviour because of their addiction. He points out that marijuana is not a particularly addictive drug and most users learn to enjoy it through participating in smoking with other users.

Becker uses the concept of **career** to point out the similarities between becoming a deviant and pursuing a more conventional occupational career. Thus marijuana smokers must learn the techniques of pot smoking (just as trainee workers learn the job). They must learn to perceive the effects – many users at first do not feel much. Finally, they must learn to enjoy the effects. Becker emphasizes the important role played by the deviant group in transforming the new user's identity. For example, marijuana users come to see the world from the perspective of other users in place of conventional morality.

Edwin Lemert: primary and secondary deviation

Interactionists have also explored the way in which being labelled as an outsider can transform the identity of deviants. Edwin Lemert uses the concepts of **primary** and **secondary deviation** to explain this. Lemert suggests that we all break rules or commit acts of primary deviation at some time or other. It is only when a person is publicly labelled as a deviant that their acts become secondary deviation. This occurs when the deviant is forced to see himself or herself as a deviant because this is how he or she is defined by others.

Lemert uses Mead's concepts of the 'I' and the 'me' to explain this. If a person is continually defined as abnormal or deviant by others, this becomes part of their identity – the 'me'. For example, someone who 'borrows' things from their workplace may not perceive what they are doing as deviant. However, if the person is caught and dismissed from their job for theft, they can no longer avoid the label of thief and it may be difficult for the individual to get another job if they gain a criminal record or a bad reference. For such an individual their self-image is much more likely to be that of a thief than the secret deviant who has escaped labelling. Many deviant labels are described by interactionists as master statuses, since they override all other aspects of a person's identity.

'Borrowing' things from work is officially theft, but unless the person is caught and labelled, this kind of activity may have little effect on the deviant's status and identity.

Interpretation and application activity

Here are some examples of deviant labels. In each case consider how far it might be described as a 'master status'. Consider what effect being labelled in this way might have on the deviant's identity and how it might affect how they are treated by others.

(a) drug addict
(b) child molester
(c) schizophrenic
(d) lesbian
(e) bankrupt

The influence of interactionism

Interactionism had a major influence on the development of deviancy theory from the 1960s onwards and challenged theories of deviance deriving from functionalism, which tended to imply that individuals became deviant because of circumstances beyond their control (see, for example, discussion of Merton on pp. 35–7).

Interactionism and disability identities

Interactionist ideas and the concept of labelling were subsequently applied in a range of other areas of sociology. Steve Taylor cites the following example relating to the sociology of health and disability:

> A striking example of the ways in which societal reaction can shape people's experience of a disabling condition is provided by Scott's (1969) classic study of blindness. According to psychological theory, blindness produces certain personality characteristics, such as passivity and compliance. From his observations of interactions between professionals and blind patients and clients in the United States, Scott provides a different explanation. He argues that the 'blind personality' is the product of a socialization process in which the experts place emphasis on the problems of the client's psychological adjustment to the loss of sight. Thus according to Scott, blindness is a 'learned social role', whereby blind people come to actively accept the experts' view of who they are. In societies such as Sweden, where blindness is viewed less in terms of loss and more as a technical handicap, blind people are more integrated and there is less evidence of the blind personality. Interactionist studies have drawn attention to the importance of social reaction in creating experiences of a variety of other conditions, including epilepsy, physical disability and being HIV positive.
>
> (Taylor 1994, p. 6)

Like the cartoon character Bart Simpson, pupils labelled as 'under-achievers' may come to see themselves as lacking in ability.

 Evaluation activity
'Disability is as much the result of how people are labelled as of their actual physical or mental capacities.' Discuss the arguments for and against this statement, drawing on relevant examples.

Interactionism and classroom identities

Sociologists of education have similarly explored how teachers and pupils negotiate identities in the classroom. Writers such as David Hargreaves (1967) and Stephen Ball (1981) argue that pupils are not simply bright or dull, well-behaved or troublemakers, but come to acquire these kinds of identities as a result of interaction within schools. Thus pupils who are constantly labelled as 'disruptive' or 'underachievers' will come to live up to their labels as this becomes part of their identity.

 Research activity
Using your library, find out more information on any one piece of research which focuses on how actors' identities are affected by their interaction with others. There is a range of interactionist research to illustrate this in areas such as deviancy, education and health. Write a brief summary of the study you have researched and present your findings to the rest of your group.

Interactionism and cultural studies

Since the 1980s the influence of interactionism has waned somewhat. However, many of its concerns have been taken up by other perspectives. Many feminists, for example, have been influenced by the interactionist argument that researchers cannot detach themselves from their subjects but must experience life from the viewpoint of those they wish to study. Similarly, interactionists' concern with the underdog is reflected in feminists' belief that the social scientific study of women's oppression is not incompatible with taking political action to change their situation.

Some sociologists now believe that interactionism can make an important contribution to cultural studies. Norman Denzin (1992) argues that many of the things studied in cultural studies, such as artworks, popular music, popular literature and mass media (see previous chapter), should be of interest to interactionists, and he calls on them to engage in debates with other perspectives on culture such as structuralism, poststructuralism, semiotics and feminist theory.

Erving Goffman

There is some debate over whether Erving Goffman (1922–82) can be described as a symbolic interactionist, but he shares many of their concerns and his work has had considerable influence on interactionist research. Goffman was particularly concerned with understanding the self and how we construct our own identities. Like Mead, Goffman perceived a tension between the 'I', the inner self, and the 'me', representing the social constraints on the individual.

Dramaturgy and the presentation of self

In *The Presentation of Self in Everyday Life* (1959), Goffman uses what he calls the **dramaturgical** approach. In this approach Goffman likens social interaction to a dramatic performance. He suggests that as individuals we create our sense of self by putting on a performance for others. Just as an actor performs for an audience, we try to convince others to accept the view of ourselves that we choose to present. This involves what Goffman calls **impression management**. Thus we may feel nervous or lacking in confidence when me meet other people, but we may try to create the impression that we are confident or knowledgeable in order to create a good impression.

Goffman uses the term **front stage** to talk about the parts of ourselves that we choose to reveal to others, just as on a real stage this is what the audience can see most easily. Front stage may also refer to an actual physical environment. For example, waiters operate 'front stage' in a restaurant when they are serving customers at tables, but they disappear 'back stage' to the kitchen to collect more dishes, wash up and so on. Back-stage actors do not need to be so concerned with managing impressions. For example, in the kitchen a waiter might pick his nose or put his fingers in the soup, but he would not do so in front of the customers. Like real actors, Goffman points to the way in which social actors use props to manage impressions. Thus a police officer's uniform, a doctor's stethoscope and white coat, or a business person's suit and briefcase all help to sustain the role they are playing.

Goffman argues that there is often a discrepancy between the idealized picture that actors try to present of themselves and aspects of their hidden self. For example, doctors make great efforts to present themselves as professional and competent in order to inspire confidence and trust in their patients. However, a doctor may not be as sure of her diagnosis as is suggested to the patient. The doctor may even have aspects of herself which are kept secret; for example, she may be a drug addict or an alcoholic.

Goffman argues that successful performances generally involve a team effort. Thus the patient usually cooperates with the doctor by accepting her in her role. This is not to say that Goffman was not aware that on occasions there may be mistakes in impression management. For example, the patient may notice the alcoholic doctor's hands are shaking and question her capabilities.

Research activity

Carry out observation of any one area of everyday life, for example a classroom, a workplace or a leisure activity. Note down examples of ways in which individuals manage impressions using the concepts provided by Goffman.

Stigma

In another study, *Stigma* (1963), Goffman examines the problems of identity for individuals whose **virtual social identity** (what they ought to be) does not match their **actual social identity** (what they actually are). People who experience a gap between these two identities are, in Goffman's terms, **stigmatized**. Goffman distinguished two types of stigma.

A **discredited stigma** exists where others are aware that the actor is not what he or she should be. For example, someone who is disabled and uses a wheelchair experiences a gap between the expectation that most people can walk and the reality that they themselves cannot. In this situation the problem for the actor is to manage the tension created by the fact that people know of the problem. People who are not disabled may feel uncomfortable or unsure about how to behave with someone in a wheelchair.

A **discreditable stigma** involves a situation where the audience is not aware of the gap between virtual and actual identities; for example, someone who is HIV positive or someone who has a criminal record. In these cases the dramaturgical problem involves keeping the actual identity from the audience and maintaining the virtual identity, for example as an uninfected or honest person.

For Goffman, the stigmatized are only one aspect of stigma. The other aspect is the audience, those who do the stigmatizing. Like Becker, Goffman emphasizes that a stigma is not a quality inherent in the stigmatized but is a label placed on certain individuals by society. Goffman also points out how in reality the 'normal' and the stigmatized overlap. Most of us at some time or other suffer from discreditable stigma, though on other occasions we may be the ones labelling others with a stigma.

Total institutions and identity

While much of Goffman's work is concerned with how we create and sustain identities in daily life, his study *Asylums* (1968) highlights how identities can be rapidly transformed. Goffman's research was based on participant observation as a member of staff in a mental hospital, but he suggests that many of his observations are generalizable to a variety of what he calls **total institutions**. He defines a total institution as 'a place of residence and work where a large number of like-situated individuals cut off from the wider society for an appreciable length of time, together lead an enforced, formally administered, round of life' (1968, p. 11). Mental hospitals, prisons, boarding schools, monasteries and army barracks are all examples of total institutions.

Goffman argues that one of the key characteristics of total institutions is a process of **disculturation**. Individuals have their old identity stripped away so that it can be replaced by a new self moulded to the requirements of the institution. This begins with the process of admission, where inmates are often stripped of personal clothing, property and even their name. For example, prisoners may be forced to wear a uniform and be called by a number rather than a name. This is further reinforced by the **mortification** of the inmate's self (the process of destroying their old identity and replacing it with a new one). Thus inmates may be forced to perform meaningless tasks (e.g. sewing mailbags) and may be subjected to a system of punishments and privileges in order to encourage conformity. This all has the aim of discouraging inmates from returning to their former identities and of enforcing compliance with the new institutional identity.

Goffman also explores a variety of responses by inmates to institutional life. For example, some may respond by 'conversion' (taking on the identity imposed by the institution), while others may respond with 'intransigence' (refusal to cooperate) or simply 'playing it cool' (cooperating just enough to stay out of trouble). In this respect *Asylums* reflects the interactionist view that, even in the most constraining situations, actors have some freedom to manage their own identities. As Mead suggests, actors reflect on their situation and choose the strategy which they feel will be most likely to get them what they want.

Evaluation of Goffman

Some critics have argued that Goffman's view of human nature is a cynical one, which sees individuals as simply pursuing their own ends and manipulating others through impression management. Some writers have also argued that Goffman's dramaturgical analogy is sometimes taken too far and that everyday life cannot simply be reduced to actors and audience in a play. It would seem Goffman himself became aware of this and moved away from the concept of dramaturgy in his later work. Nevertheless, many sociologists see Goffman's work as a major contribution to understanding how identities are formed in everyday life.

Criticisms of interactionism

As noted above, interactionism has had considerable influence on the sociological study of identity. However, it has also been criticized. These criticisms are summarized below.

Lack of scientific rigour

Critics of interactionism see its subjectivity as one of its major weaknesses. Writers such as Mead and Blumer argue that you cannot study human beings in an objective scientific way. Much of the most fascinating interactionist research has been in the form of ethnographic descriptions, often based on participant observation or detailed personal knowledge of its subjects. Critics argue that this very subjectivity means that researchers lose their scientific objectivity and detachment. The concepts used by interactionists, such as Mead's 'I' and 'me', have also been criticized as imprecise and impossible to measure or test in research.

Ignoring structures

One of the major weaknesses of interactionism is its neglect of structures. Interactionists tend to focus on microsociological (small-scale) processes based on the interaction between individuals in small social groups. This ignores the possibility that these personal interactions may be part of a larger pattern or structure. Marxists, for example, would support interactionists in their concern for the underdog, but would argue that interactionists do not really explain why some have power while others are underdogs and consequently are labelled or stigmatized. To understand this one would have to look at society more macrosociologically (on a large scale); for example, how groups with resources such as wealth might mobilize them to ensure that their version of reality dominates the way identities are defined.

Ignoring psychological influences

While interactionists have been criticized for ignoring wider structural influences on personal identity, they have also been attacked for failing to look at psychological influences within the individual. Interactionists tend to portray actors as rational individuals choosing from a number of possible strategies in interaction and constructing identities for themselves. This ignores the extent to which factors such as innate personality traits or subconscious processes over which actors may have little control may act as influences on how they interact with others.

Social action theory

In the nineteenth century most sociologists were influenced by the positivist view, which saw the social life of human beings as subject to the same kind of scientific laws as those found in physics or chemistry. This kind of approach was first challenged by Max Weber, who is usually regarded as the originator of interpretive perspectives in sociology. Weber (1978), like Mead, rejected the idea that it was possible to reduce human behaviour to the operation of scientific laws. He argued that human beings interpret events and give meaning to them in a subjective way. In other words, each individual reflects on their past experiences and makes choices about their own actions according to their own purposes and intentions. It is impossible for sociologists to understand why an individual behaves in a certain way unless we understand what motivates them. Weber advocated the approach of *verstehen* – literally, understanding – in sociology. This involves an attempt to appreciate the viewpoint of actors in order to understand the world through their eyes. Thus in *The Protestant Ethic and the Spirit of Capitalism* (1976), Weber attempts to understand the meaning that capitalistic economic behaviour had for Calvinists in terms of their religious beliefs and attitudes (see pp. 70–2).

Weber's ideas were very influential in the development of later interpretive perspectives in sociology, notably the perspective of phenomenology, which in turn led to the development of the approach known as ethnomethodology.

Phenomenology

The origins of the phenomenological approach to social life lie in the work of the philosopher Edmund Husserl (1859–1938). Alfred Schutz (1899–1959) used Husserl's ideas to criticize and develop Weber's theory of social action and to show how phenomenology might be applied to sociology. Schutz (1972) agreed with Weber's view that individuals interpret and make sense of the social world. However, he argues that Weber places too much emphasis on the individual. Weber recognized that in choosing particular courses of action individuals take into account the behaviour of others. Schutz argues that this ignores the extent to which the meanings of actions are themselves based on shared understandings of the social world. According to Schutz, Weber's theory fails to account for the way in which many individuals all subjectively interpret the world in remarkably similar ways.

Intersubjectivity and common sense knowledge

Schutz uses the concept of **intersubjectivity** to explain this. Like Husserl, Schutz assumes that our experience of reality is a subjective one. We can never be sure that what we actually experience is objectively true or that it will be experienced in the same way by other people. However, in social life we come to share a common view of reality with other members of our society. I cannot be sure that when I see something as red that someone else sees the same colour as me. It is because they describe the same objects as being red as I do that I assume that our experience is the same. Thus the word 'red' has the same intersubjective meaning for us. These kinds of shared assumptions make normal social life possible. Imagine a situation where people constantly disagreed over what colour objects were.

Schutz argues that we all possess a stock of taken-for-granted understandings about the social world, what he calls **common sense knowledge**. This common sense knowledge is what enables us to sort, categorize and make sense of objects and events in daily life. For example, if someone makes a joke, those present will usually laugh. However, we only know what constitutes a joke because of our common sense knowledge. We have heard many jokes before and we identify certain typical characteristics of a joke, for example a punchline. We use these as part of our common sense knowledge to enable us to laugh at the right point and accomplish everyday social interaction. Of course, jokes do not exist as an objective social category; someone from another culture who did not possess the common sense knowledge of our culture might find an English joke incomprehensible. We are only able to perceive the joke because we have acquired the same intersubjective interpretation of events as other members of our social group.

Jokes are one example of what Schutz calls **phenomena**, categories that we use to make sense of reality. Other examples might include 'car', 'riot', 'friend' or 'food'. Phenomenology thus studies the way in which we categorize and make sense of such social phenomena. Schutz points out that we continually reconstitute and reinvent these categories of phenomena. For example, the categories of 'friend' and 'enemy' may change over time as people who were formerly friends become enemies or vice versa. Schutz suggests that we all use common sense knowledge to accomplish what he calls **projects**. A project can simply be defined as the state of affairs an actor wishes to bring about by his or her actions. This might be a long-term goal such as getting on in one's career, but could be something as simple as giving a message to a friend.

Harold Garfinkel and ethnomethodology

Schutz's work was largely theoretical, but it was a major influence on the development of what has been called the 'sociology of everyday life'. This can be seen most clearly in the approach known as **ethnomethodology**. The American sociologist Harold Garfinkel (1967) tried to show how Schutz's ideas could be applied in a practical way to the study of sociology. In a series of studies, Garfinkel showed how ordinary everyday events such as carrying on a conversation were worthy of research by sociologists. Garfinkel rejects the view that we accomplish everyday activities according to some preset rules or procedures laid down by our culture and socialization. He criticizes mainstream sociologists for assuming this, describing them as portraying human beings as 'cultural dopes'. Instead, Garfinkel portrays social actors as highly skilled in accomplishing everyday social activities and creating the appearance of social order.

Garfinkel rejects the view that human actions reflect the influence of wider social structures. He argues that structures are themselves created and sustained by people.

Thus a school only exists as a school because its members share the same intersubjective interpretation of what a school is and how teachers, pupils and other members should behave towards each other. In continuing to behave as teachers, pupils, caretakers, secretaries and so on, members of the school use their common sense knowledge and continually reinforce the reality of the school's existence. However, the social reality of the school depends on all the participants continuing to share this same view of reality. If the pupils decided to hold a party in the school hall instead of attending lessons, or the teachers held a car-boot sale on the playing fields to sell off the classroom equipment, the school would no longer function as a school.

Garfinkel argues that the study of the methods used by members of society to accomplish everyday activities should be the subject matter of sociology. He uses the term ethnomethodology to describe this approach – from *ethno*, to do with social groups, and *methodology*, the study of methods. Garfinkel shows how in everyday life we employ what he calls **members' methods** to make sense of events, to communicate our interpretation of things to others and to confirm that our interpretation of reality corresponds with theirs.

Indexicality

Garfinkel uses the concept of **indexicality** to describe the way in which we make sense of events and categorize them. Indexicality involves using clues from the circumstances or setting in which interaction is taking place, together with our common sense knowledge, in order to arrive at a meaningful interpretation of events. Thus we use indexicality to categorize what people say to us, for example as a question or a statement. We also categorize people themselves, for example as a 'good mate', 'a babe', 'an idiot' and so on. Indexicality enables us to organize and categorize social phenomena to create order out of our experiences.

Sometimes indexicality breaks down on occasions when we misunderstand or are not sure what is going on. However, we quickly engage in **indexical repair** in order to re-establish some kind of order and meaning in social life. For example, if you met a close friend who was unusually rude or insulting this might violate your common sense assumptions about how a friend should behave. If you then realized that the friend was only joking or 'having you on', you would have successfully indexed the situation and would know how to respond. On the other hand, if you interpreted your friend's behaviour as genuinely unpleasant then you might try to find out what had upset him. Realizing that he was having a bad day, or that you had previously said something to upset him, might provide a logical explanation for your friend's behaviour that would fit in with 'common sense'. Garfinkel argues that we are all highly skilled as members of society in using these kinds of methods to accomplish what appear on the surface to be simple and mundane social encounters.

Garfinkel's breaching experiments

In order to reveal the significance of the unquestioned assumptions in common sense knowledge and the importance of members' methods, Garfinkel carried out a series of experiments in which he asked his students to breach or disrupt the normal rules of everyday social behaviour.

In one experiment Garfinkel asked his students to imagine they were boarders in their own homes and to behave towards other family members in a polite formal way. Some students found it impossible, but those who completed the experiment encountered bewilderment, shock, anxiety and hostility from family members. Once students explained what was going on most family members were able to deal with the situation by writing it off as a 'silly sociological experiment'. A satisfactory interpretation could now be provided, allowing the situation to be categorized. Garfinkel used this and similar experiments to demonstrate how much we take for granted in everyday life. It is assumed that parents will behave as parents, children as children, and so on. The breaching experiments show how difficult it is for people to cope with situations where their common sense interpretations of the situation are violated.

Interpretation exercise

The two conversations below were reported by Garfinkel from experiments in which he asked his students to suspend their taken-for-granted common sense understandings when talking to fellow students.

(S = Subject, E = Experimenter)

Conversation 1

(S) Hi, Ray. How is your girlfriend feeling?

(E) What do you mean, 'How is she feeling?' Do you mean physical or mental?

(S) I mean how is she feeling? What's the matter with you? (*He looked peeved.*)

(E) Nothing. Just explain a little clearer, what do you mean?

(S) Skip it. How are your Med School applications coming?

(E) What do you mean, 'How are they?'

(S) You know what I mean.

Conversation 2

The victim waved his hand cheerily.

(S) How are you?

(E) How am I in regard to what? My health, my finances, my school work, my peace of mind, my …?

(S) (*Red in the face and suddenly out of control.*) Look! I was just trying to be polite. Frankly, I don't give a damn how you are.

(Garfinkel 1967, pp. 42–4)

1 What aspects of common sense knowledge were the experimenters failing to demonstrate in this experiment?

2 How can the two conversations above be used to demonstrate the importance of the use of members' methods?

3 How would you explain the reactions of the two subjects in these experiments?

Sex identity: the case of Agnes

Most traditional studies of gender assume that sexual identity is relatively unproblematical. Individuals have a biological sex and are socialized into gender-appropriate behaviour for their sex. Garfinkel uses the case study of Agnes to show how being male or female is a managed accomplishment, part of the repertoire of members' methods which we all use. In the case of Agnes, being female was more problematical than for most women, since she had been born with male genitals and had lived as a boy until she was sixteen, when she adopted a female identity. Agnes had female breasts, a 'perfect' female figure and plucked her eyebrows and wore lipstick. Agnes had a boyfriend and engaged in swimming, dancing and kissing with him. Agnes hoped to have an operation to change her genitals, but in the meantime her sexual identity was a pervasive problem. She had constantly to communicate the fact that she was a woman in her behaviour and appearance, while concealing any evidence of maleness.

While sexual identity was more of a problem for Agnes than for most people, Garfinkel's work illustrates how ethnomethodology can be used to reveal the socially constructed nature of gender. We are male or female not so much because of our biological make-up but because we work at being male or female in the way we interact with others. For example, young men may feel they need to prove their masculine identity by living up to what common sense suggests is 'normal male behaviour'; young women may wear make-up or 'feminine' clothes to emphasize their female sexuality.

Judith Butler: gender as performance

Garfinkel's ideas about gender have been taken up by some feminist writers such as Judith Butler (1990). Butler, like Garfinkel and Goffman, explores the way in which gender is a **performance**. For some men and women the performance simply involves playing the part dictated by the script for their gender. Others, however, may use performance as a means of resisting or challenging conventional gender identities. For example, men who engage in cross-dressing (dressing as women) can be seen to subvert traditional certainties about gender distinctions.

Application activity
Give examples of ways in which we communicate our masculine or feminine identity to other people.

Think of examples of individuals who refuse to live up to what others think of as 'normal' masculine or feminine identities. Why might they choose to do this and how might other people react to such individuals?

Harvey Sacks and conversational analysis

Garfinkel's ideas have generated a range of research into the sociology of everyday life. The method of conversation analysis that he pioneered has been particularly influential. Garfinkel argues that in conversation we employ a variety of skills to interpret what others say and to judge cues – for example, when to speak or when to laugh. The breaching experiments quoted above illustrate what happens when members fail to use common sense knowledge to interpret what is going on in a conversation.

One writer who developed the field of conversation analysis was Harvey Sacks (1936–75). Sacks (1974) argues that in conversation we do not simply talk but produce descriptions. Like Garfinkel, he argues that we use our common sense knowledge to produce descriptions which are meaningful to others and to interpret the descriptions of other people.

Membership categories

One concept used in descriptions, according to Sacks, is identity or **membership category**. For example, I might be described as a sociology lecturer, a father, an author, a driver or a cat owner. Which description is selected in a conversation will depend on the occasion. At college my identity as a lecturer is probably more important, while with my children my identity as a father takes priority. Which category is selected for describing a person may also, in Sacks's terms, constitute the nature of the social occasion in which conversation takes place. Thus referring to Paul Taylor, the lecturer in sociology, provides a different social context to referring to Paul Taylor, father of two children.

Sacks argues that categories or identities such as those above are normally selected from a group or cluster of related categories. He calls this a **membership categorization device** (MCD). MCDs are collections of categories which go together. For example, the category 'lecturer' is part of the MCD 'occupations', while the category 'father' is part of the MCD 'family roles'. Some categories are mutually exclusive. The MCD 'sex' has only two categories, male and female: we assume that if someone is one they cannot be the other.

Sacks argues that MCDs help us not only to identify an individual as belonging to certain categories, but also to make sense of activities or events surrounding that person. Often we associate certain activities with certain membership categories. For example, if someone is arrested we assume it is by the police; if a husband complains of being nagged we assume it is by his wife.

 Application activity
Give five examples of membership categorization devices. In each case find three examples of categories that would fit into this MCD.
　　Example: MCD – Ethnic minority groups
　　Categories – Afro-Caribbean, Punjabi Sikh, Vietnamese

Ethnomethodology and identity

Sacks's work shows how ethnomethodology can be applied to the study of identity. It suggests that many of the identities discussed in earlier chapters of this book are categorizations that we use in everyday life to make sense of the behaviour of others. Moreover, Sacks argues that we often construct common sense understandings of events on the basis of very limited information. Membership categorizations provide important clues as to how we are to interpret people's activities. The following activity on newspaper headlines provides an illustration of this.

PANICKY ARGIES FLEE BAREFOOT

(headline during the Falklands War)

(criticism of council's assistance for gay centres)

CASH FOR 'GAYS' RAP OVER AIDS

(allegations concerning actress Leslie Ash's husband)

TV LESLIE'S HUBBY IN BED WITH A BLONDE

Catholic priest admits fathering love child

BLACK BRIXTON LOOTERS JAILED

Interpretation activity

Newspaper headlines provide good examples of how membership categories are used to create common sense understandings of events.

Take each of the headlines above and identify the membership categories used to describe the people in the story. Why do you think the newspaper editors have chosen these categories? What common sense understandings of the stories are communicated by the way the headlines are constructed?

Try to find other similar examples of headlines from recent newspapers and repeat the exercise using them.

The influence of ethnomethodology

Ethnomethodology has had some influence on mainstream sociology. In particular it has encouraged sociologists to consider the way in which personal identity is never complete. All of us constantly engage in constructing a picture of ourselves which fits in with how we wish to be seen by other people. Ethnomethodology also shows how we use common sense categorizations of other people's membership identities in interpreting their behaviour.

Ethnomethodology has also questioned the view of culture offered by traditional sociology. Culture is not seen as simply a collection of norms, values and beliefs handed down from generation to generation. Instead, culture can be seen as common sense knowledge and skilled methods for dealing with everyday situations. This also has implications for our view of socialization. Matthew Speier (1970) argues that 'socialization is the acquisition of interactional competencies'. Thus we do not simply learn norms in socialization but become competent in using methods such as indexicality to deal with everyday social situations.

Ethnomethodologists also insist that socialization is not simply a one-way process. Children are engaged in an active process of interpreting the messages they receive from parents; they are not simply empty vessels waiting to be filled with the culture of their society. Moreover, children socialize parents as much as parents socialize children.

Phenomenological ideas more generally have also influenced sociologists. In particular the concept of the **social construction of reality** is now widely used by sociologists (see Berger and Luckmann 1967). Thus, elsewhere in this book, you will find discussion of the idea that gender, sexuality, race, ethnicity and age are all socially constructed. In all these areas sociologists have accepted that these categories only have a reality because groups of people share a common subjective understanding. For example, in Chapter 5 we considered the argument that 'races' do not have any objective existence. However, if enough people intersubjectively believe in the existence of 'races' then racial differences come to have a social reality.

Criticisms of ethnomethodology

Ethnomethodology has come under considerable attack from other sociologists, perhaps because it challenges much that is taken for granted by mainstream sociology. The main criticisms can be summarized as follows.

Concern with trivia

Ethnomethodology is in some ways the ultimate in microsociological perspectives. It rejects the study of social structures such as class and power and favours the study of mundane everyday activities such as carrying on conversations or 'passing' as a woman. Mainstream sociologists argue that there is a danger in this that only trivial issues will be considered. In focusing on routine interactions, ethnomethodology may fail to consider broader issues such as social change.

Ignoring structures

Ethnomethodologists argue that social structures only exist in members' minds, since they are social constructs. This ignores the reality of certain structures for those concerned. For example, if a person is Black and experiences discrimination in getting a job or even physical violence because of his or her colour, it is no good claiming that racial differences are simply a social construct. For the person concerned they are very real indeed. Moreover, the treatment experienced by that individual is probably part of a broader pattern or structure across society which cannot be understood simply by looking at the behaviour of individuals in isolation.

Power and conflict

Ethnomethodology assumes that our view of reality is based on shared assumptions or intersubjectivity. However, the origins of these assumptions are not really explored. More importantly, the idea that some individuals may have more power than others in defining reality is not considered. In previous chapters we considered the concept of ideology, which implies that the way reality is perceived reflects the views of powerful groups in society, for example wealthy people, men, heterosexuals or white Europeans. This is not to say that subordinate groups may not develop their own alternative reality. For example, feminism aims to provide women with an alternative view of the world to malestream knowledge. However, the knowledge and ideas of more powerful groups are likely to exert the greatest social influence.

Ethnomethodology and sociological methods

Ethnomethodologists argue that sociologists should not simply study the methods used by members to accomplish everyday social activities, but also the methods they use themselves in their research. Sociology, from this perspective, is simply another form of common sense knowledge which seeks to classify and categorize the social world. This implies that any form of objectivity in studying social life is impossible – sociologists are as subjective as ordinary members of society. Ethnomethodologists even suggest that sociologists should carry out studies of their own research in order to document their own members' methods. Mainstream sociologists object that this is ridiculous – we could have sociologists studying sociologists studying sociologists, and so on, endlessly! Moreover, if sociologists can make no greater claim to objectivity than the ordinary person in the street, where does this leave the theories of ethnomethodologists?

Structuralism and interpretivism

The controversy aroused by ethnomethodology is part of a broader debate in sociology between what can be called structural and interpretive approaches. We will now consider this debate and how it relates to issues of culture and identity.

Interpretivism and agency

The theories discussed so far in this chapter can be broadly termed **interpretivist** or **social action** perspectives. Such theories place the individual human actor at the centre of their analysis. They emphasize the concept of **agency**, which implies that human actors construct their own cultures and identities according to patterns that make sense and work for them. These perspectives all tend to view the social world through the eyes of actors and believe that sociologists can only understand actors' behaviour by understanding the meaning it has for them.

Structuralism and constraint

Running alongside this viewpoint has been a consistent criticism of such theories for ignoring structures. Structuralist sociological perspectives argue that the behaviour and even the thoughts of social actors are constrained by wider social structures which they themselves may have played little part in creating and which they may have little power to change. Many aspects of culture can be seen as examples of structural constraints. The language we speak was not invented by us and we normally have not chosen to speak it. Rather, we use a language because we have been brought up to speak it and need to use it as a medium of communication in our culture. In this sense we are constrained by structures of language most of which evolved before we were born. These patterns of social behaviour over and above individuals are what Durkheim referred to as social facts (see p. 34).

Many sociological perspectives have used the concept of structure to suggest that society is not simply made up of a multitude of individuals. Instead, the way individual actors behave towards one another follows certain patterns and regularities. For

Marxists, it is economic structures that dominate social relationships – the way individuals relate to one another is patterned by their positions in the production system. Feminists similarly emphasize the way in which relations between the sexes are structured by patriarchy or male dominance. Radical feminists argue that while individual men or women may treat one another as equals, women as a sex cannot be emancipated until patriarchal structures are abolished.

Structure and agency

Structuralist theories thus emphasize the way in which human actors are constrained by their identities, for example their class, gender, ethnicity or age. Culture is seen as imposing norms about how particular individuals should behave in given roles. This approach can be most clearly seen in the work of writers such as Durkheim and Parsons (see Chapter 1), but also in structural Marxists like Althusser (see p. 173). Agency or action theories emphasize the way in which we can construct our own cultures and identities – as social actors we can rewrite the script. If identities are socially constructed, it follows that we can reconstruct them to our own choosing. The most extreme version of this is ethnomethodology, but Weber's action theory and interactionism also emphasize this approach.

In reality, few contemporary sociologists totally ignore either approach. Throughout this book you will have encountered studies that emphasize the way in which individuals are constrained by identities based on factors such as class, gender, ethnicity, sexuality, disability and so on; these are all structural influences. However, you will also have encountered evidence that actors are able to fashion their own identities within the constraints of social structures. Thus women, young people, Black people and gay people can all be seen in some ways as disadvantaged by their structural position. All these groups also provide examples of ways in which actors can resist stigmatized or disadvantaged identities and create their own cultures and identities, through feminism, youth subcultures, anti-racism, ethnic identities, gay pride and so on.

Anthony Giddens and structuration

One sociologist who has attempted to overcome this distinction between structure and agency is Anthony Giddens. Giddens (1984) suggests that structure and agency are in fact two sides of the same coin. He uses the concept of **structuration** to describe this duality, the interweaving of structure and agency in social life. Giddens argues that structures only exist because of human agency and are sustained over time because of the actions of individuals. While we may have played no part in creating our language, we all play a part in its development and continued use. Moreover, languages are constantly changing in response to the usage of those who speak and write them. While human agents create social structures, Giddens also emphasizes that social actions are always influenced by structures. In addition, structures are not always constraining but can be enabling. Feminists may criticize man-made language for making women 'invisible', but feminists can use the same language as a weapon of liberation in raising women's consciousness.

Evaluation of Giddens

Giddens's work has been enormously influential and has encouraged many sociologists to explore further the links between social structures and individual agency. The issue of the relationship between the culture of society and personal identity explored in this book is a prime example.

Giddens's work has also received some criticism. Ian Craib (1992) argues that Giddens's concept of structuration tends to stress agency at the expense of structure and fails to get at the structures that underlie the social world. Craib also argues that the real world is too complex and messy to be dealt with by a single overarching theory such as structuration.

Margaret Archer (1982; 1988) has also criticized Giddens. She argues that while structure and agency are intertwined, they remain distinct and cannot be merged into the single concept of structuration. Archer argues that agents are constantly acting to change structures, while changes in structures influence the actions of individuals in a continuous process which she calls **morphogenesis** (literally, giving birth to new bodies). Archer also argues that culture (ideas, values and non-material phenomena) needs to be analytically separated from structure (material phenomena such as ownership of economic resources). Archer argues for more analysis by sociologists of cultural as well as structural influences on human agency.

Case study of structure and agency: **Learning to Labour**

One example that illustrates how it is possible to approach the study of culture and identity with an awareness of both structure and agency is Paul Willis's book, *Learning to Labour* (1977).

Willis studied a group of boys in a single-sex secondary modern school in the West Midlands. The group, which he calls 'the lads', represents an example of what sociologists call a counter-school culture – a group of pupils whose norms and values are directly opposed to those of the school. The boys in the study were opposed to any kind of authority in school and spent much of their time 'dossing, blagging and wagging' – in other words, avoiding working and messing about. Willis describes many of their activities as 'having a laff'. For example, the lads stop second- and third-year pupils and tell them 'Mr Argyll wants to see you, you'm in trouble I think'. As a result, Mr Argyll's room is soon choked with worried kids. For the lads, such events relieved the boredom of school.

Willis describes in detail the attitudes and values of the boys in his study. He notes how they not only show contempt for the usefulness of education, but also how elements of racism and sexism form an important part of their attitudes. For example, the lads were keen to have sex with girls but condemned girls who were too ready to have sex as 'slags'.

Ethnography

The first part of Willis's book is an ethnographic study – it is based on a detailed description of the social life of a group of people. Willis spent months carrying out participant observation, interviews and group discussions in the school in order to build up a detailed picture of the group in question. His study draws heavily on verbatim quotes from interviews and discussions with 'the lads' (see the example on pp. 208–9).

In this sense Willis's work is located in the interpretivist tradition in sociology. He attempts to understand the worldview of a group of people by trying to put himself in their shoes. Like the phenomenologists, Willis suggests that the lads use their common sense ideas to interpret and make sense of their place in the world. While Willis does not use the concept of agency, it is implied in his approach. He portrays the lads as creative social actors who are able to subvert the school system. Their anti-school subculture is influenced by many elements of the working-class culture of their parents, for example disdain for academic learning and pride in physical labour.

However, Willis points to the way in which 'the lads' have adapted this culture to their own situation within the school environment.

Structural analysis

The second part of Willis's book, however, introduces a structural analysis of his case study. This part of the book is strongly influenced by Marxism, particularly the theory that schools are engaged in a process of social reproduction (see the discussion of Bowles and Gintis on pp. 60–1). The subtitle of his book is *How Working-class Kids Get Working-class Jobs*. Willis argues that while it is the lads themselves who choose to reject school and the chance of academic qualifications, in doing so they condemn themselves to unskilled and semi-skilled manual jobs. Willis suggests that the capitalist system needs people like the lads, since they provide the raw material for routine manual work. Because they have rejected school, the system can legitimately label them as failures.

Willis, like many Marxists, argues that the culture of the lads needs to be seen as a reflection of their structural position in the lower working class in a capitalist society. The lads' attitudes are reflective of what Willis terms 'shop-floor culture' – the culture of male manual workers. This culture has developed as both a means of accommodation and resistance by workers to their position in capitalist workplaces. Willis's study thus provides the structural analysis the absence of which is often cited as a weakness in interactionist and phenomenological accounts.

Willis's study predates Giddens's work on structuration and he does not use the concept. However, it represents an example of how it is possible to combine both interpretivist and structuralist approaches. Giddens himself cites Willis's work approvingly in his own discussion of structuration. 'The lads' can be seen both as rational social actors creating their own culture and identities, and as located in a wider social structure that creates constraints and opportunities for them.

Having a laff

In a more general sense, the 'laff' is part of an irreverent marauding misbehaviour. Even strict and well-patrolled formal areas like assembly yield many possibilities.

Joey   The chief occupation when we're all in the hall together is playing with all the little clips what holds the chairs together. You take them off and you clip someone's coat to his chair and just wait until he gets up … and you never really listen … you have to be really discreet, so as Clark [the deputy head] won't see yer, call you out, the other teachers don't matter. (…)

Joey   Even on the hymn … when they mek you sing –

PW   But do they make you sing? I didn't notice many of you singing –

–   I was standing there moving my mouth.

–   When we do sing we make a joke of it.

Fuzz   Sing the wrong verses … So if you're supposed to be singing verse one, you're singing verse three.

During films in the hall they tie the projector leads in impossible knots, make animal figures or obscene shapes on the screen with their fingers, and gratuitously dig and jab the backs of the 'ear'oles' [conformist pupils] in front of them.

The father of one of 'the lads' who works in a car engine factory describes a practical joke. Willis describes these kinds of jokes as 'vigorous, sharp, sometimes cruel, and often hinged around prime tenets of the culture such as the disruption of production or subversion of the boss's authority and status'.

This is a filthy trick, but they do it (...) They asked, the gaffers asked X to make the tea. Well, it's fifteen years he's been there and they say 'go and make the tea'. He goes to the toilet, he wets in the tea pot, then he makes the tea. I mean, you know. He says, you know, this is the truth this is, you know. He says, you know, 'I'll piss in it if I mek it, if they've asked me to mek it' (...) so he goes up, wees in the pot, then he puts the tea bag, then he puts the hot water in (...) Y was bad the next morning, one of the gaffers, 'My stomach isn't half upset this morning'. He told them after and they called him for everything, 'You ain't makin' our tea no more'. He says 'I know I ain't, not now'.

Source: adapted from Willis (1977), pp. 31, 55

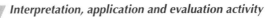

Interpretation, application and evaluation activity

1 Using the first extract, explain how 'the lads' could be seen as actively constructing their own culture rather than as passively accepting their position in the social structure.

2 Using both extracts, identify similarities between the anti-school subculture of 'the lads' and the 'shop-floor culture' of adult male manual workers.

3 In what ways might the attitudes and behaviour of 'the lads' reflect their position in the social structure?

4 What relevance does Giddens's concept of structuration have for Willis's study? Refer to the extracts above in answering this question.

Conclusion

From the 1960s to the 1980s sociology passed through a period of fierce debate between different theoretical approaches. Debates between structuralist and interpretivist perspectives were an important part of this. There are now signs that the work of sociologists such as Giddens and Archer may provide new concepts and theories which allow sociologists to bridge the divide between these two approaches.

There are also signs that in recent years sociological debate has moved on. In particular, sociologists influenced by postmodernism have offered radical and different approaches which to some extent transcend this debate and have thrown up new controversies. We move on to examine some of these debates in the next chapter.

Coursework suggestions

Both interactionist and ethnomethodological approaches offer interesting ideas for coursework. You could draw on Goffman's dramaturgical approach and carry out a study of 'impression management'. This could focus on almost any social setting. A workplace where workers deal with customers would be particularly interesting. A classroom, a student common room or even a nightclub would also provide interesting data. This type of research would almost certainly require participant observation, so you would need to think carefully about how you would blend into the background and how you could systematically record your observations without affecting other actors.

Ethnomethodology could also be used as an approach. If you are interested in conducting 'breaching experiments' like Garfinkel, you should discuss potential ethical and practical problems with your teacher or lecturer. Nevertheless, a suitable experiment could yield some interesting results if carried out in a sensitive way.

You could also consider conversation analysis as a method. This might involve recording and analysing actual conversations, for example to find out what cues participants use in order to know when it is their turn to speak. Alternatively, you could analyse written texts such as newspaper headlines in order to examine how common sense ideas such as 'membership categories' are used in their construction.

DATA RESPONSE QUESTION
Item A

Structures must not be conceptualized as simply placing constraints upon human agency, but as enabling.

(From Giddens 1976, p.60)

Item B

In an article entitled 'Deviance disavowal: the management of strained interaction by the visibly handicapped', Fred Davis examines interaction situations involving people with physical disabilities and able-bodied people. Davis obtained his data from lengthy interviews with people who were blind, facially disfigured wheelchair users. He was concerned with interaction situations that lasted longer than a passing exchange but not long enough for close familiarity to develop. Such situations would include conversation with a fellow passenger, getting to know someone at work and socializing at a party. The person with the disability wishes to present themselves as 'someone who is merely different physically but not socially deviant'. Such people seek to achieve ease and naturalness in their interaction with others since this will symbolize the fact that they have accepted their preferred definition of self, but their disability poses a number of threats to the type of sociability they desire.

(From Haralambos and Holborn 1995, pp. 894–5)

Item C

For Garfinkel every activity, from the most mundane action of daily life to the most arcane practices of science and religion, can be conceived of as having a self-organising character. That is activities are not performed mechanically by participants according to some preset rules or requirements. Rather, participants produce the orderliness of their activities 'locally', that is, in the course of the activity itself. This conception of social order clearly differs from most sociological approaches, which conceive of the orderliness of social activities as the product of 'external' causes or conditions. These external factors are typically referred to as 'the social structure' or 'culture'.

(Adapted from Cuff et al. 1984, pp. 157–8)

1 *Study Item A. Give one example of a social structure and explain how it could be seen as both constraining and enabling. [3 marks]*

2 *Study Item B. Give one example of how a person with a disability might present themselves as 'someone who is merely different physically but not socially deviant'. Give one example of how their disability poses a threat to the type of sociability they desire. [4 marks]*

3 *Identify and explain two advantages of using in-depth interviews for the type of research undertaken by Fred Davis (Item B). [4 marks]*

4 *Study Item C. Explain in your own words what is meant by the phrase 'participants produce the orderliness of their activities "locally", that is, in the course of the activity itself'. [4 marks]*

5 *Assess the usefulness of ethnomethodology to sociologists in understanding culture and identity. [10 marks]*

References and further reading

Archer M. (1982) 'Morphogenesis versus Structuration: on combining structure and action' *British Journal of Sociology,* 33: 455–483.

Archer M. (1988) *Culture and Agency: The Place of Culture in Social Theory* Cambridge: Cambridge University Press.

Ball, S. (1981) *Beachside Comprehensive,* Cambridge: Cambridge University Press.

Becker H. (1963) *Outsiders,* New York: The Free Press

Berger, P. and Luckmann, T. (1967) *The Social Construction of Reality,* London: Allen Lane.

Blumer, H. (1969a) *Symbolic Interaction: Perspective and Method,* Englewood Cliffs, NJ: Prentice Hall.

Blumer, H. (1969b) 'The methodological position of symbolic interactionism', in *Symbolic Interaction: Perspective and Method,* Englewood Cliffs, NJ: Prentice Hall.

Butler, J. (1990) *Gender Trouble: Feminism and the Subversion of Identity,* London: Routledge.

Charon, J.M. (1985) *Symbolic Interactionism: An Introduction, an Interpretation, an Integration,* Englewood Cliffs, NJ: Prentice Hall.

Craib, I. (1992) *Anthony Giddens,* London: Routledge.

Cuff, E.C. and Payne, G.C.F. with Francis, D.W., Hustler, D.E. and Sharrock, W.W. (1984) *Perspectives in Sociology,* London: George Allen and Unwin .

Davis, F. (1975) 'Deviance disavowal: the management of strained interaction by the visually handicapped', in A.R. Lindesmith, A.L. Strauss and N.K. Denzin (eds), *Readings in Social Psychology,* Hinsdale: Dryden.

Denzin, N. (1992) *Symbolic Interactionism and Cultural Studies: The Politics of Interpretation,* Oxford: Blackwell.

Garfinkel, H. (1967) *Studies in Ethnomethodology,* Englewood Cliffs, NJ: Prentice Hall.

Giddens, A. (1976) *New Rules of Sociological Method,* London: Hutchinson.

Giddens, A. (1984) *The Constitution of Society,* Cambridge: Polity Press.

Goffman, E. (1959) *The Presentation of Self in Everyday Life,* Harmondsworth: Penguin.

Goffman, E. (1963) *Stigma: Notes on the Management of Spoiled Identity,* Englewood Cliffs, NJ: Prentice Hall.

Goffman, E. (1968 [1961]) *Asylums: Essays on the Social Situation of Mental Patients and Other Inmates,* Harmondsworth: Penguin.

Haralambos, M. and Holborn, M. (1995) *Sociology: Themes and Perspectives,* London: Collins Educational.

Hargreaves, D. (1967) *Social Relations in a Secondary School,* London: Routledge and Kegan Paul.

Sacks, H. (1974) 'On the analysability of stories by children', in R. Turner (ed.), *Ethnomethodology,* Harmondsworth: Penguin.

Schutz, A. (1972 [1932]) *The Phenomenology of the Social World,* London: Heinemann.

Scott R. (1969) *The Making of Blind Men: A Study of Adult Socialisation* New York: Russel Sage.

Speier, M. (1970) 'The everyday world of the child', in J. Douglas (ed.), *Understanding Everyday Life,* Chicago: Aldine.

Taylor, S. (1994) 'Beyond the medical model: the sociology of health and illness', *Sociology Review,* September.

Weber, M. (1976 [1904]) *The Protestant Ethic and the Spirit of Capitalism,* London: George Allen and Unwin.

Weber, M. (1978 [1921]) *Economy and Society: An Outline of Interpretive Sociology,* 2 vols, Berkeley: University of California Press.

Willis, P. (1977) *Learning to Labour: How Working-class Kids Get Working-class Jobs,* Farnborough: Saxon House.

9

Modernity and postmodernity

Key ideas
Modernity and postmodernity
The Enlightenment project
Globalization
Decentring of subjects
Essentialism and social
    constructionism
Metanarratives
Simulacra
Hyperreality and hyperspace
Fundamentalism
Compression of time and space
Disembedding
Risk society
Instrumental and communicative
    rationality
Lifeworld and system

Key thinkers
Jean-François Lyotard
Jean Baudrillard
Frederic Jameson
Anthony Giddens
Ulrich Beck
Jürgen Habermas

Introduction

Many social theorists believe that in the late twentieth century we are witnessing the emergence of a new kind of society, described as postmodern. This change has important implications for the study of culture and identity. For example, postmodern theorists claim that the boundaries between cultures are becoming blurred. Globalization has meant that western culture and media increasingly influence the cultures of other societies, while members of western societies are keen to incorporate elements of other cultures' music, food, dress, art and so on into their own cultural styles. This has significant implications for our identities. What does it mean to be an English person? Should curries and pasta now be regarded as part of British cuisine? Can we regard the Church of England as the established religion in England when only a tiny minority of the population are practising members? Postmodern theorists would argue that who we are and where we belong have become much less certain because of the rapidity of change and the undermining of stable sources of identity in contemporary societies.

Postmodernity implies something that comes after modernity, so we shall start this chapter by examining what is meant by modernity. The next part of the chapter considers how postmodernity and postmodernism might represent a move away from the societies and cultures of modernity. We shall also examine the work of some of the major social theorists associated with postmodernism. The last part of the chapter considers the work of sociologists who have been critical of postmodern social theory. These writers accept that contemporary societies have witnessed revolutionary changes, but see these as part of modernity rather than as representing a new phase of postmodernity. These modernist theorists also believe that rational and scientific approaches to the study of society, such as sociology, still offer some hope of making sense of the new kinds of societies emerging.

Postmodernism and postmodernity

In Chapter 1 we examined the idea that postmodernity is linked to a disenchantment or loss of faith in the Enlightenment project (see pp. 15–17). The Enlightenment project encouraged the belief that it was possible to organize and control the world on the basis of rational principles, for example by applying scientific theories to control the natural world and by applying rational political and social theories to create a better society.

Postmodern sociologists feel that in the latter part of the twentieth century we have lost confidence in the ability of both the natural and social sciences to provide us with a rational understanding of the world around us. More importantly, this has undermined the belief in progress towards a better society that characterizes most modernist social and political thought.

One example of this is the field of architecture, discussed in Chapter 1 (see pp. 17–18), where the modernist vision of architecture designed on rational principles has come under attack. Critics have argued that modern high-rise housing developments have created more problems than they solved and that modern architecture lacks any soul or sense of style.

In 1989 peaceful revolutions all over Eastern Europe led to the overthrow of communist governments.

The Berlin wall was breached and more than a million citizens of the German Democratic Republic streamed across the open border to West Berlin. Berliners sat for hours on top of the wall and rejoiced at the opening.

Defining postmodernity and postmodernism

The term 'postmodernism' is much debated and is hard to define. George Ritzer (1996) suggests that it is useful to distinguish between 'postmodernity', 'postmodernism' and 'postmodern social theory'.

1 **Postmodernity** refers to an historical epoch. Most postmodern social theorists see postmodernity as a stage in the development of society which is now succeeding modernity.

2 **Postmodernism** is usually taken to refer to a cultural movement. Postmodernist cultural products (for example architecture, works of art, films, television and advertisements) are seen as in some way contrasting with the cultural products of modernity.

3 **Postmodern social theory** represents a new way of thinking. While postmodern social theorists are concerned with examining both postmodernity and postmodernism, their theories also challenge the modernist approach in philosophy and the social sciences which has developed since the Enlightenment.

Modernity to postmodernity

It can be argued that the transition from modernity to postmodernity can be seen in three interrelated sets of institutions: economic, political and cultural.

Economic institutions and postmodernity

A number of writers have suggested that in the late twentieth century we are witnessing a transformation of the world of work and the organization of businesses. This has been described as a move from Fordism to Post-fordism. Fordism represents a system of economic organization based on mass production. Henry Ford's own production system for the Model T was the prototype here. Cars were produced for the first time on assembly lines, with work tasks broken up into small, simple, repetitive tasks that could be performed by comparatively unskilled workers. Ford's production system meant that a large number of cheap cars could be produced quickly, bringing them within the reach of many more consumers. Workers enjoyed relatively high wages, enabling them to buy an increasing range of consumer goods, albeit at the expense of boring and dehumanizing work.

Other writers argue that this kind of production system has been extended to many other types of production. George Ritzer (1993) argues that there has been a 'McDonaldization of society', whereby many products are produced to standardized specifications by workers following a series of pre-programmed tasks. Ritzer argues that this kind of system – used in producing McDonald's hamburgers – has been applied to areas as diverse as banking, car servicing and even childcare.

Writers who use the term Post-fordism (Piore and Sabel 1984; Atkinson 1985) argue that this kind of production system is now becoming obsolete. Firms are organizing themselves on more flexible lines. This often means that production is organized through a network of small firms with parent firms subcontracting work to smaller companies. The clothing firm Benetton has been seen as typifying this approach. Benetton franchises its products to small independent retailers and obtains its clothing from small independent subcontractors in countries like Italy.

Henry Ford's car assembly line and Benetton's flexible network are seen by many sociologists as typical of modern and postmodern work organizations, respectively.

Post-fordist organizations are also seen as flexible in their use of workers, employing a small 'core' workforce who are functionally flexible – able to switch rapidly from one job to another using a range of skills – and a larger 'peripheral' workforce – who provide extra workers as and when needed, for example, part-time, temporary and agency workers. The rise of Post-fordism has been seen as associated with a decline in collective bargaining and trade unionism, and the emergence of systems of reward based on appraisal of workers' performance and motivation through team working and development of a corporate culture.

Political institutions and postmodernity

The emergence of postmodern politics is associated with the alleged decline in class politics (see pp. 74–5), the nation state (see pp. 132–3) and the welfare state. Class-based politics are seen as less significant, since new identities have emerged which cut across class boundaries. This is most clearly evidenced in new social movements such as feminism and environmentalism, and movements demanding equal rights for ethnic groups, religious minorities, gay people and so on.

Nation states are also seen as less significant in postmodern politics as globalization has meant that nations have less influence over economic affairs. Transnational companies operate in a global marketplace linked by rapid electronic communications. In these circumstances the ability of individual nation states to control their own economic affairs is diminished.

Finally, the welfare states that emerged in most industrial societies have encountered a crisis. Welfare states have been seen by many sociologists as an attempt to reconcile the class conflicts associated with modern capitalism. Workers were offered housing, education, healthcare, social security and full employment in return for their acquiescence in their role under capitalism. Increasingly, governments have found it difficult to fund comprehensive welfare services and have turned to commercial, voluntary and informal sources of welfare to supplement the role of the state.

Postmodern culture

Postmodern culture has been seen to have a number of characteristics contrasting with modern culture.

1 Breakdown of the distinction between high culture and mass culture

In modern culture, elite forms of culture such as opera and intellectual art films were produced for the educated elite, while mass cultural products were produced for the masses, for example pop music and Hollywood films. Postmodern cultural forms blur this boundary; for example, Andy Warhol's pictures draw on both popular cultural forms (Coke cans and images of Marilyn Monroe) and high cultural forms (images of the Mona Lisa). In music composers such as Philip Glass draw on both classical and popular musical forms.

2 Breakdown of the barriers between genres and styles

Modern culture was based on distinctive genres, for example romances or detective novels in literature, Westerns or musicals in films, soap operas and situation comedies on television. Similarly, modern culture has developed through distinctive styles, for example, blues, rock and roll and soul in pop music, cubism, surrealism and expressionism in painting. Postmodern culture breaks down these distinctions. Postmodern cultural products draw on different genres and styles and mix and match them, often creating a collage effect. For example, an advertisement for a car may use an image of a Mediterranean landscape with classical music. Postmodern films often combine elements from different genres: *Who Framed Roger Rabbit?* combines elements of the Philip Marlowe detective story as portrayed by Humphrey Bogart with cartoon characters reminiscent of Bugs Bunny and others. Contemporary pop music styles, such as hip-hop, rap and house music, use sampling to create new musical styles from existing recordings, often bringing together sounds originating in quite different genres.

3 Mixing up of time, space and narrative

Modern cultural forms typically tell a story or carry a message. A modern novel or film usually has a plot, which develops over a period of time. Modern artworks often convey a social message. Modern advertisements attempt to persuade the consumer to buy a specific product. Postmodern forms abandon the notion of a consistent narrative. In David Lynch's film *Blue Velvet*, for example, the central character moves between conventional life in a stereotypical small American town and an underworld of drugs, violence and sexual perversion. It seems impossible that the two worlds can exist in the same time and space, and the film's central character moves between them, unsure which is true reality. Similarly, postmodern advertisements may not obviously try to sell anything and often contain very little reference to the product. Guinness advertisements once carried the message that 'Guinness is good for you'; contemporary Guinness advertisements provide no real reason to drink the product.

4 Emphasis on style rather than content

This is linked to the point above. In an advertisement, often the feelings it evokes are what it seeks to associate with the product, rather than telling us much about what the product is or does. Similarly, in supermarkets the packaging becomes as important as the products in selling them. Another example is the 1980s police series *Miami Vice*, which relied as much on its exotic Miami locations, the designer clothes of its leading characters and unusual camera angles as on its storylines to achieve its popularity.

5 The blurring of the distinction between representation and reality

Modern cultural forms are seen to represent the real world in some way. Cultural signs relate to what they signify. The mass media, for example, are traditionally seen as holding up a mirror to or reflecting society. Postmodern theorists argue that contemporary society increasingly reflects the media, that the surface image becomes increasingly difficult to distinguish from the reality. Jean Baudrillard, for example, argues that the Gulf War might never have happened. Baudrillard implies that our view of the Gulf War is so much bound up with the media images of it that were broadcast into homes every night that the reality of the war on the ground is irrelevant, since for most people their experience of the war is the one provided by the media-constructed reality.

Postmodern social theory

Identifying postmodern social theories is not easy. Postmodern writers are a diverse group and many of the most influential ideas have come from philosophers, cultural theorists, literary critics and students of mass media rather than sociologists. Moreover, many writers labelled by others as postmodern reject the term in relation to their own work. In this section we shall examine some key ideas associated with postmodern social theory and consider the work of some of its most influential thinkers. Postmodern social theories can be associated with four interrelated approaches to studying culture and identity.

1 Decentring of the subject

Stuart Hall (1992) argues that the Enlightenment view of the human subject was one which saw every individual as a sovereign agent (see p. 21). In other words, every individual independently works out their own identity and behaves towards others in a rational way. Individuals are seen as having a coherent inner self (the centre of the subject) and a person's actions can be related back to aspects of this self, for example their personality or attitudes.

Postmodern theorists reject this view. They see individuals as fragmented into a variety of selves – different selves may emerge in different social contexts. This means that we can never know the 'real person', since our identities are simply social constructs composed of many differing and sometimes contradictory elements. Some postmodern theorists are also influenced by Freud and psychoanalysis, particularly the concept of the unconscious. If part of our selves exists in the unconscious, this implies that we can never know our real identity – our true self – and that the subconscious will always interfere with rational thinking and behaviour.

The influence of this kind of thinking can be seen in a number of areas in earlier chapters. For example, the discussion of the role of class, gender, ethnicity and age in the formation of identities has emphasized how many writers now argue that none of these alone can explain individuals' identities. These aspects of identity – along with many others – represent multiple facets of our identities, with different aspects coming to the fore in different circumstances. This sense of multiple identities – sometimes resulting in conflicting loyalties and social identifications – is described as the decentring of the subject.

Application activity
Review what you have read in Chapters 3, 4, 5 and 6. Find examples in each chapter of sociological research that shows how individuals may have multiple or fragmented identities.

2 The de-essentialization of the social

Essentialist theories are theories which argue that human behaviour and social life can be explained by reference to some essential feature. For example, sociobiologists argue that ultimately human behaviour is the product of our genetic predispositions, which in turn have been produced by evolution. Marxists argue that ultimately human societies are reducible to the way production is organized and the class relations created by material inequality. Feminists see patriarchy as an essential feature of all societies. Some feminists see this as resulting from an essential difference in the biological and psychological make-up of the sexes which has been exploited by men for their own advantage.

Postmodern social theory rejects the view that human beings can be reduced to any single essence. They develop the idea encountered in many parts of this book that human beings and their social worlds are socially constructed. In this sense, who we are and how we think and behave is not determined by any essential feature. In different times and different places culture and identity will be constructed in different ways. Thus class may have been an important source of conflict in modern societies, but is perhaps being superseded by postmaterialist political issues. New social movements are concerned with political issues such as the environment and the rights of women and minorities rather than material issues such as the distribution of wealth and class inequality.

Gender differentiation and patriarchy may be almost universal features of human societies, but this is an oversimplification. In some societies women have much more freedom than in others and the ways in which women are oppressed or subjugated vary widely among societies described by feminists as patriarchal. For postmodern feminists, it is more useful to examine these sources of difference than to make sweeping statements about the universality of patriarchy.

Interpretation activity
Essentialism versus social constructionism
Essentialist theories argue that human identity and behaviour can be reduced to

some essential feature. Social constructionist theories argue that the social world can be constructed in virtually any way. Things are only as they appear because we agree they are, not because they essentially have to be.

Examine the collection of statements below. In each case decide whether you think the statement is primarily presenting an essentialist or a social constructionist viewpoint and give reasons to support your choice. If you think some statements do not fit neatly into either category, explain why.

Because women get pregnant and have babies they naturally have a more caring instinct than men.

There is no scientific basis for dividing human beings into racial types; however, many people continue to act towards one another on the basis of presumed 'racial' differences.

There can be no hard and fast distinction between homosexuality and heterosexuality because in some societies most men engage in sex with both men and women. In these societies the concept of 'a homosexual' does not exist.

The Japanese are a naturally conformist and deferential people. Japanese workers work harder and show much greater dedication to their companies than do British workers.

The concept of mental illness is very specific to modern western societies. In other cultures people we might define as mentally ill may be seen as possessed by evil spirits and treated by religious rituals or magic rather than psychiatry.

The role of elderly people varies widely in different societies. In Britain elderly people are expected to retire from work, but are often portrayed as a burden on their families or the state. In hunting and gathering societies old people are often seen as a valuable repository of knowledge and experience accumulated over many years.

The mass media serve to perpetuate the ideology of the bourgeoisie and prevent the working class from becoming aware of its true exploited status. Only by achieving true socialist consciousness can it fulfil its historical mission to overthrow capitalism and establish communism.

Racism is a belief system that was developed to justify the dominance of White people over Black people. Thus only White people can be racist and all Black people are in some sense victims of racism.

3 Scepticism towards grand narratives

In traditional societies the world is often described in terms of all-encompassing religious or supernatural explanations. For example, events such as natural disasters may be explained as 'the wrath of God'. Following the Enlightenment, science sought to challenge what were regarded as irrational explanations and provide accounts of the world that could be verified by reference to observable evidence. An important part of the Enlightenment project was to provide a narrative (or account) that would explain everything in the world around us.

Many social scientific theories attempt to provide a **totalizing narrative**. This means a theory that purports to explain everything in the social world. For example, Marxism provides a totalizing narrative in terms of the class struggle explaining the whole of human history. Parsons's structural functionalism attempts to provide a grand theory which is applicable to all human societies. Freud's psychoanalytic theory explains all human behaviour in terms of the conflicts in the psyche between the conscious and the unconscious.

Postmodern theorists reject this kind of grand narrative. Because they reject essentialism, they argue that it is impossible to comprehend all human life in one theory. Instead, they prefer to offer partial or local narratives, which offer an explanation relevant to a particular group of people at a particular time. Thus in Chapter 4 we noted how feminists have moved away from totalizing narratives based on the concept of universal patriarchy to accounts which stress the diversity of women's experience, for example encompassing the voices of Black women, lesbians, older women and so on.

Similarly, many writers on ethnicity reject the view that 'racism explains everything', or that people can be simply divided into White oppressors and Black victims. Instead, there is an emphasis on the diversity of the experience of ethnic groups and indeed, how ethnic groups themselves are hybridized and cut across by divisions of class, gender, age and so on.

4 Emphasis on textuality

In Chapter 7 we saw how in cultural studies almost any aspect of culture can be 'read' as a 'text'. Thus we can analyse the symbolic meaning of a meal, a person's dress or the kind of car they drive in the same way as we might interpret the meaning of a novel or a painting. Postmodern theorists take this idea further by arguing that all reality is constructed from texts, including the reality of sociological theory. Thus the sociologist provides a narrative text that attempts to convince the reader of the reality of his or her story in much the same way as a novelist.

Postmodernists also emphasize that there are many different voices or texts that deserve to be taken into account. This emphasis on **plurivocality** (or many voices) links in with the point above about the diversity of experiences of women or Black people. It is also reflected in the attempt by contemporary sociologists to incorporate into their accounts of the social world the voices of previously marginalized groups such as women, ethnic minorities, elderly people, disabled people and others. In this sense, postmodern theorists reject the idea that sociology can provide some ultimately true account of reality. Instead, reality is seen as socially constructed and different texts seen as constructing reality in different ways. For postmodern thinkers, all voices deserve equal consideration.

Having examined some of the key strands of postmodern social theory, we shall look at the work of three leading postmodern thinkers to illustrate the diversity of their ideas and some of the main influences on postmodern sociology.

Jean-François Lyotard

The French cultural theorist Jean-François Lyotard is one of the leading postmodernist thinkers. Although Lyotard's book *The Postmodern Condition* (1984) focuses on the nature of scientific knowledge in the late twentieth century, it has had considerable influence on debates about postmodernism and culture more generally. Lyotard argues that in primitive societies, what counts as knowledge is based on **narratives**. Narratives are literally stories, but Lyotard uses the term in a wider sense to describe the way in which our knowledge of the world is organized around meaningful accounts. In simple societies narratives may take the form of folk stories, myths and legends, while in modern societies scientific explanations and political ideologies take on the role of narratives. Lyotard sees all narratives as what he calls **language games**. Language games involve attempts by participants to use language to assert the truth of their version of knowledge. Storytellers recounting tribal legends in simple societies, and modern scientists justifying medical research in terms of improving the quality of human life, are both equally engaged in language games.

Lyotard uses the example of the Cashinahua Indians of South America to illustrate the role of narrative in pre-modern societies. Among the Cashinahua, telling stories serves to strengthen social bonds and legitimate the culture of the tribe as a whole. The legitimacy of individual storytellers is established by the narrator first identifying himself by his Cashinahua name – establishing his right to speak – and by telling the story in a ritualized way based on rhythmic chanting – establishing that this is a true Cashinahua story.

According to Lyotard, storytellers in tribal societies and modern scientists are both engaged in providing a narrative that legitimates their own society.

Science as metanarrative

Lyotard suggests that from the eighteenth century onwards modern science has taken over from myths and legends as the dominant structure of authorization. Science relies on argumentation and proof to establish its validity rather than on narratives.

Despite this, Lyotard argues that science has to justify itself and it has done this by appealing to what he calls the **metanarrative** of the Enlightenment project.

Metanarratives are in effect 'big stories' that give meaning to smaller narratives. The metanarrative of modern science has been the project of liberating human beings and extending human knowledge. Thus when scientists make a breakthrough – for example, discovering penicillin or landing astronauts on the moon – these narratives are justified in terms of the metanarrative of human progress. Unlike earlier narratives, which were concerned with rediscovering or returning to original truth – for example, how the world was created – modern narratives are concerned with arriving at a final goal – for example, the liberation of the human race from suffering and oppression. Lyotard points to an apparent paradox here. While science denounces narratives as simply stories that cannot be empirically proved or falsified, it seeks to justify itself in terms of a metanarrative or grand narrative.

Postmodernity and the production of knowledge

Lyotard argues that since the Second World War there has been a growth in incredulity towards metanarratives. Thus people have increasingly questioned the idea that science plays a part in leading us all towards absolute freedom and absolute knowledge. Lyotard argues that scientists themselves resort less and less to the ideals of the Enlightenment project in order to legitimate their work. A group of scientists seeking funding for a project is therefore less likely to justify it in terms of the way it will add to the sum of human knowledge or the common good. Instead, they are more likely to emphasize its practical applications, for example in developing new commercial products and the potential profits to be made from this.

Lyotard, however, is optimistic about the coming of postmodern society. He believes that new technologies, for example computers and electronic communications, will give individuals access to a much greater range of information. As a result, individuals will be able to make imaginative leaps in order to discover new forms of scientific thinking. Lyotard argues that for too long knowledge has been dominated by the narratives of powerful minorities such as white Europeans or men. Scientists have, in his view, too long claimed that their accounts of the world are universally applicable. Lyotard looks forward to a postmodern world where a multitude of incompatible language games can flourish alongside one another. Knowledge will no longer be a tool of power used by those in authority, but other groups will be able to present their own alternative versions of knowledge. This fits in with the postmodern concern with many voices; for example, acceptance that the ideas of other cultures and subordinate groups such as women, ethnic minorities or gay people may be equally valid to mainstream scientific thinking or dominant ideologies.

Some postmodern sociologists, following Lyotard, have pointed to the potential in new technologies such as the Internet for ordinary people to share ideas and information, for example by exchanging ideas on bulletin boards or through network groups. However, sceptics point out that it is mainly the well-off who have access to this kind of information technology and that large commercial organizations are increasingly exploiting new communication systems to market their products.

Evaluation activity
Organize a discussion or write a short evaluation on the following question:
To what extent do new information technologies such as the Internet have the capacity to empower ordinary people with greater knowledge and the means to communicate with others?

Evaluation of Lyotard

Lyotard's ideas have been an important influence on postmodern social theory. In particular, Lyotard represents the postmodern argument that all knowledge is relative; in other words, that there is no such thing as absolute truth, but that all versions of knowledge are socially constructed. This is an argument which many sociologists who are not postmodernists would to some degree accept.

However, Lyotard's argument can also be seen as self-defeating. While he claims to be incredulous about metanarratives, Lyotard himself seems to be developing a metanarrative in his sweeping assertions about modern science and the direction of change with postmodernity. If there is no absolute truth, why should we accept what Lyotard himself says?

Lyotard also claims that scientists and indeed people in general are increasingly critical of metanarratives. However, the evidence for this is not clear. While science has become more commercialized, so that scientists have to be concerned with how their ideas can be used to generate profits, this has arguably been the case ever since the Enlightenment. Capitalist economies have always sought to harness science to profit accumulation. Moreover, scientists have not abandoned the notions of rationality developed in the Enlightenment. Scientists still have to demonstrate empirically the proof of their theories, otherwise it is unlikely that investors would be prepared to invest as heavily as they do in scientific research. In this sense, the continuities between early modern societies and contemporary societies are perhaps more significant than the term postmodernity implies.

a) The aftermath of the meltdown at Chernobyl nuclear power station.

b) The side-effects of Thalidomide used to treat morning sickness in pregnancy.

c) Modern transport is fast and comfortable.

d) A heart transplant operation.

Evaluation activity

Evaluate Lyotard's argument that we have lost faith in science as the means of achieving human progress. Using the pictures above and any other examples, try to think of arguments and evidence both for and against.

Jean Baudrillard

Jean Baudrillard has been particularly influential on sociology for his work on consumption. Sociologists influenced by Marx have emphasized the idea that the way production is organized determines how culture and the sphere of consumption develops. For example, Marxists see the mass media and its messages as shaped by the requirements of capitalist ideology. This in turn reflects the fact that most of the means of media production are owned by big business organizations. Baudrillard rejects this emphasis on production. He argues that we now live in a **society of signs**, where cultural commodities such as television programmes, pop music and computer programmes have assumed as much economic importance as food, beer, cars or washing machines. Even these products are as important for their symbolic value as for their practical use. For example, we may drink a certain lager or drive a certain car as much because of the message it conveys about the kind of person we wish to be as because it tastes good or gets us from A to B efficiently.

Unlike structuralist thinkers and semiologists, Baudrillard does not see signs as having any underlying meaning. In the past, the car a person drove, the kind of music they listened to or the beer they drank could be seen as signifying something about their social position. However, Baudrillard sees signs as having become detached from what they originally signified. As he himself puts it:

> The signifier and the referent are now abolished to the sole profit of the play of signifiers of a generalized formation in which the code no longer refers back to any subjective or objective 'reality', but to its own logic.
>
> (Baudrillard 1975, p. 127)

Like Marxists, Baudrillard sees signs and symbols as a form of domination, but while Marxists see cultural symbols as part of an ideology that masks an underlying exploitative production system, Baudrillard seems to see the system of signs itself as the system of domination. Thus Baudrillard, like Lyotard, rejects the Marxist view that culture simply reflects the system of production and sees the sphere of culture as assuming major importance in its own right.

Media representations

One example of this is Baudrillard's (1981) analysis of the mass media. Baudrillard rejects the Marxist view that the media are simply used by the ruling class as a mouthpiece for its own ideology. He also rejects the alternative view that the media are potentially liberating, allowing many groups to express their views. Instead, he argues that the system of communication embodied in mass media is essentially one-way. Broadcasters talk to the audience but the audience has little opportunity to respond directly. Baudrillard claims that the media 'fabricate non-communication'. Even when dissent or criticism is expressed in the media, it is neutralized because it becomes simply another viewpoint, another sign, with no greater signification than any other. Thus the reporting of a bomb in the news can be equally interpreted as a terrorist outrage, the heroic struggle of a group of freedom fighters, or an attempt by the authorities to discredit political extremism. All these interpretations are equally available in a situation where distinctions between truth and falsity, reality and simulation, become blurred or, to use Baudrillard's terminology, 'imploded'.

This echoes the argument of Dick Hebdidge (1988), who points to the way subversive messages, such as punk in the 1970s, are incorporated or made safe by the media. Thus punk ceased to have a critical or anti-establishment message but became simply another fashion or style. Baudrillard argues that instead of passively consuming media products, people should aim to achieve free exchange of communication along the lines of discussion on street corners or the slogans painted on the walls of Paris by revolutionary students in 1968.

The development of signs

Baudrillard (1983) argues that signs and representations have developed through four historical stages:

1 *The sign is the reflection of a basic reality.* For example, scientific knowledge may represent something in the real world.

2 *The sign masks or perverts the basic reality.* The image is a distortion of the truth it purports to represent, for example capitalist ideology.

3 *The sign masks the absence of a basic reality.* For example, a religious image of a god may mask the fact that the god does not exist.

4 *The sign bears no relation to any reality whatsoever: it is its own pure simulacrum.*

Baudrillard points out that he is not claiming that each type of representation simply succeeds historically the one before. However, he does argue that the final stage is what dominates in contemporary culture, where images cease to have any reference to reality. Baudrillard describes this situation where images cease to be rooted in reality as **hyperreality**.

Simulacra

To illustrate his concept of a simulacrum Baudrillard uses the example of the Tasaday Indians, an isolated stone-age people found living in the jungle in the Philippines. In 1971 the Philippine government decided to return the Tasaday to the jungle to protect them from the corrupting influence of civilization. Baudrillard points out that from then on the Tasaday could never be a real primitive people but became a simulation or simulacrum of everything western science imagines as typical of primitive peoples.

Baudrillard argues that Disneyland also provides an example of a simulacrum. Disneyland presents an image of what America should be like. For example,

Disneyland: an example of hyperreality?

Mainstreet USA is an image of a typical smalltown American street and shops, although of course no real American street is like that. In the Epcot Centre (in the Florida Disneyworld), a variety of pavilions provide simulations of what we imagine Mexico, Japan or Italy to be like. These images are not the real country and turn out to be a series of rides and shopping opportunities. Baudrillard goes on to suggest that it is not simply Disneyland that is hyperreal, but Los Angeles and indeed the whole of America. As Baudrillard puts it: 'It is no longer a question of a false representation of reality (ideology), but of concealing the fact that the real is no longer real and thus saving the reality principle' (1983, p. 25).

Baudrillard is pessimistic about the prospects for political change or escape from the endless procession of signs. Since he implies that simulation and reality are now indistinguishable it is difficult to see how anyone could achieve any real power. Baudrillard is also critical of the social sciences and sees them as simply another simulation. Thus social theories are in his view simply simulacra which purport to represent the societies they are studying but which have no real link with reality. Baudrillard is therefore pessimistic about the capacity of social theory to act critically or change society.

Evaluation of Baudrillard

Baudrillard's work has been important in encouraging sociologists to focus on the sphere of consumption rather than production. This has resulted in some interesting studies of the symbolic importance of consumption (see, for example, Hides's study on ethnicity and material culture on p. 126). Baudrillard's work also points to the way in which signs and symbols are endlessly recycled by the contemporary mass media. Advertisements, for example, use landscapes, styles of music or genres from other media to sell products to which they have little relevance.

Many sociologists have some sympathy with Baudrillard's view that we live in a media-saturated society, where life and its representations in the media merge into one. For example, newspapers report on the activities of soap-opera characters as if they were real people. The tourist industry is increasingly based on the presentation of traditional culture and 'heritage' in theme parks, museums and historical sites, but it is difficult to know how far these represent an 'authentic' version of life in the past or traditional culture, and how far they are simply a simulation designed to entertain tourists like any other form of entertainment.

However, Baudrillard's work can be criticized for similar reasons to that of Lyotard. Like Lyotard, Baudrillard implies that social science has lost its capacity to look at society critically and that it provides no more than a simulacrum of society. However, Baudrillard could be criticized for the same reasons. It could be argued that his own ideas are, after all, simply another simulation of reality. Many sociologists argue that writers such as Lyotard and Baudrillard have taken postmodern theory to its extreme, to the extent that sociologists can no longer say anything meaningful about the social world without its authority being undermined as simply another metanarrative or simulation.

Baudrillard also seems to have a very cynical view of the mass of ordinary people. He portrays them as a 'black hole' absorbing media images and passively resistant to change. Studies of television audiences (see pp. 178–84) show that viewers are far from passive and actively interpret messages for themselves. Thus soap-opera viewers are perfectly able to distinguish soaps from reality and are often quite perceptive about the strategies used by scriptwriters. Baudrillard's view that signs such as media messages have become meaningless and detached from any reference to reality ignores the extent to which media audiences create their own meanings and are capable of comparing media images with their own lived experiences.

Application activity

In the advertisements above the signs and images used to sell the product have little or no relevance to the product itself. Find other examples from contemporary advertisements to illustrate Baudrillard's idea that cultural symbols have become detached from the reality they purport to represent.

Frederic Jameson

Writers such as Lyotard and Baudrillard have been referred to as 'extreme' postmodern theorists. Their work implies a radical move from modern society to postmodern society. Moreover, their argument and style of writing moves away from conventional sociological approaches. Baudrillard, for instance, makes little attempt to back up his ideas with sociological evidence and his style of writing is often playful, ironic and reliant on sweeping statements rather than conventional social scientific logic.

Frederic Jameson's (1984; 1991) work is more conventionally sociological and has been described as 'moderate' postmodern theory. Rather than seeing a break or disjunction between modernity and postmodernity, Jameson sees postmodernism and postmodernity as simply a feature of advanced capitalist society. Jameson's work draws heavily on Marxism; he argues that the underlying economic system in most contemporary societies remains capitalist and therefore what drives the system is still the search for profits by capitalist business.

Capitalist development and the commodification of culture

Jameson draws on the ideas of the Marxist economist Ernest Mandel (1975) to argue that capitalist societies have passed through three stages:

1 **Market capitalism**. This resulted in the emergence of unified national markets. Thus goods and services were not simply produced and sold locally, but organized on a national basis.

2 **Monopoly capitalism**. Imperialist countries developed colonial empires to provide raw materials and markets for their own products. A world economy began to develop.

3 **Late capitalism**. International corporations become more economically dominant and national boundaries are less economically significant. New areas are opened up to commodification (as things that can be bought and sold).

Jameson sees the emergence of postmodern culture as the 'cultural logic' of late capitalism; in other words, the direction of economic development in the third stage of capitalism encourages the development of new cultural forms. Jameson particularly emphasizes the commodification of culture in late capitalism. Orthodox Marxists tend to see cultural forms such as art, mass media or religion as simply a form of ideology masking the exploitative nature of the production system. Jameson argues that cultural forms are increasingly a central part of the economic system in late capitalism. A large amount of business activity is geared to selling images, lifestyles and representations as much as actual products themselves.

Postmodern theorists argue that advertisements such as this are as much about selling a lifestyle as a specific product.

The characteristics of postmodern culture

Jameson argues that the consequence of this is the emergence of a postmodern culture which has the following characteristics.

1 *Superficiality and lack of depth or emotion*. For example, pop music videos often present a series of easily consumable images which have little apparent link to the song or to any real message.

2 *It is ahistorical and immediate*. Cultural forms do not provide any real links to the past or references to human suffering or struggle. Increasingly, writers, musicians,

film makers and other artists simply plunder the cultural forms of the past but lose the message of the original form. One example of this is the use of collage (images made up of many pieces taken from other sources), as in the use of sampling in house and hip-hop music. Another characteristic form is pastiche, where artists simply copy or parody earlier styles, for example an office block in the style of an eighteenth-century mansion or an advertisement using the style of a 1950s newsreel.

3   *It is timeless.* For example, pop music videos may provide no obvious plot or narrative and do not seem to be set in a specific time or place. Similarly, the novel *Ragtime* by E.L. Doctorow contains what appear to be real historical characters such as Harry Houdini, but sets them in a story which is not based on historical fact.

4   *New technology.* Postmodern culture results from new technologies such as television, computers and electronic communications. These result in what Jameson calls a 'flattening' of images; we see what is superficial or on the surface. TV news, for example, brings us immediate events but no real sense of the background causes or the social or economic context of stories. Jameson contrasts postmodern technologies based on reproductive systems (for example, television and computers) with modern technologies where the emphasis was on production (for example, steel plants and assembly lines).

Application activity

Frederic Jameson uses these two pictures to contrast modern and postmodern art. The Scream *expresses in painting the feelings of anomie and alienation described by modern social theorists such as Durkheim and Marx. Warhol's painting of Marilyn Monroe deliberately lacks depth and feeling and has the appearance of a photograph. Find other examples from your own experience of modern and postmodern cultural forms that might illustrate this contrast. These could come from television, film and video, music, literature, art, architecture or any other cultural forms.*

Hyperspace and identity

Jameson sees postmodern culture as having important implications for our identity and sense of place. He argues that people are now adrift in a world where traditional landmarks which helped them to establish their place in the world have disappeared. Individuals are unable to comprehend the immensity of the global capitalist system and are confused by the exploding cultural messages with which they are bombarded.

Jameson gives the example of the Hotel Bonaventure in Los Angeles, designed by the postmodernist architect John Portman. The hotel lobby is surrounded by four symmetrical towers containing the rooms. The design makes it extremely difficult for guests to orient themselves, since all four directions appear identical. Eventually, the hotel had to introduce colour coding and direction signs to help guests find their way.

The Hotel Bonaventure is an example of what Jameson calls **hyperspace**, that is, an area where modern conceptions of space are useless. He suggests that we all increasingly live in hyperspace. We have already encountered evidence elsewhere in this book that traditional conceptions of identity appear to be weakening or even disintegrating in contemporary societies. For example, people's consciousness of belonging to a class, an ethnic group or a nation state can be seen to be eroded or fragmented. Jameson argues that we need new mental maps to find our way in this postmodern society. These might be provided by social theorists, novelists or even ordinary people who create their own mental maps. However, the difficult nature of many of the ideas discussed in this chapter illustrates the very real problems for sociologists who wish to produce some kind of map of postmodernity.

Evaluation of Jameson

Many sociologists see Jameson's attempt to combine a Marxist analysis with postmodern social theory as a particular strength in his work. In this way Jameson is able to point both to continuities and changes in contemporary societies. There is continuity in Jameson's assertion that society is still essentially capitalist – postmodern cultural forms are simply another set of commodities to be exploited for profit by big business. However, Jameson also points to the emergence of a different kind of culture in late capitalism and a blurring of the division between the economic and cultural spheres. In this respect he shares some of the concerns of writers such as Baudrillard about the lack of meaning and depth in contemporary culture.

What some see as Jameson's strength has also been a source of criticism from other writers. Marxists have criticized him for moving away from orthodox Marxist theory and placing too much emphasis on postmodern culture at the expense of analysis of production relations. Conversely, postmodern thinkers accuse him of attempting to provide the kind of grand narrative (based on Marxism) rejected by writers like Lyotard.

Debates about postmodernity

While Lyotard, Baudrillard and Jameson differ in their theoretical arguments, they all to some degree share the view that we are moving into a postmodern society. Many other sociologists argue that there are important continuities between contemporary societies and the modern societies of recent history. In this section we shall focus on three interrelated problems with the concept of postmodernity:

1   To what extent have grand narratives or metanarratives ceased to have any relevance in contemporary societies?

2   To what extent do production relations still influence consumption patterns?

3   To what extent are contemporary societies simply a continuation of modernity rather than characterized by postmodernity?

The end of metanarratives?

Postmodern social theorists such as Lyotard have argued that the modernist certainties in progress, whether through science or political change, have been called into question in the twentieth century. For example, the fall of communism in Eastern Europe has meant that many commentators feel that Marxism can no longer present itself as a credible alternative metanarrative to capitalism. Similarly, for Baudrillard, political differences have become 'imploded', so that differences between right and left become meaningless. Individuals in postmodern societies are portrayed as cynical, shallow, nihilistic consumers who have no clear-cut identity, but simply drift from one immediate experience to another.

Despite these claims by postmodern theorists, there is much evidence that strongly held beliefs – whether political or religious – are an important feature of the culture and identity of many social groups in the late twentieth century. Consider the following examples.

● In the United States fundamentalist Christians campaign against abortion, homosexuality and single-parent families. In some US states there are campaigns under way to force schools to teach the Christian story of creation alongside Darwin's theory of evolution.

● In Iran a revolution inspired by the Islamic teachings of Ayatollah Khomeini overthrew the pro-western government of the Shah in 1979. The government – led by religious leaders – enforced traditional Islamic Sharia law and adopted a hostile attitude to westernization.

● In Afghanistan Muslim nationalists, the Mujahaddin, fought a bitter guerrilla war against the Soviet-backed government, so that Soviet troops were eventually withdrawn. The civil war continues with a fundamentalist Islamic group called the Taliban in control of much of the country by 1996. The Taliban imposed traditional Muslim laws, including forcing men to wear beards and women to wear veils. Traditional punishments, such as loss of a hand for theft and stoning to death for adultery, have been reintroduced.

● In Bosnia civil war erupted after the break-up of communist Yugoslavia. The main parties are the three main ethnic groups in the area: Muslims, Croats (mainly Catholics) and Serbs (mainly Orthodox). The war has been accompanied by 'ethnic cleansing' as areas are occupied by one of the armies in the conflict. Members of other ethnic groups have been forced from their homes and in some cases imprisoned in internment camps or even murdered in order to create areas which are 'ethnically pure', i.e. occupied by only one group.

● After the fall of communism in the former Soviet Union the USSR broke up into smaller nation states. Some smaller states which remain part of the new Russian nation have attempted to break away and achieve autonomy or full independence, notably in Chechnya, where rebels have fought a war of independence against government troops. In the 1996 Russian presidential election a candidate favouring extreme nationalist views and old-style communism came second to the liberal reformer, Boris Yeltsin.

Fundamentalisms

Some sociologists have seen the emergence of these movements as a sign of the resurgence of what is often called religious and political **fundamentalism**. As Grace Davie (1995) points out, there are dangers in lumping together what are very diverse social movements under the category of fundamentalism. Nevertheless, such movements do share some broad areas of similarity. Fundamentalisms tend to occur where traditional cultures are challenged from outside, whether by 'westernization', outside invasion or a perceived threat by rival groups. Such movements typically seek to defend and conserve traditional values and often call on traditional sources of authority, for example a sacred book such as the Bible or the Koran, or traditional legends such as those of Christian Serbs defending the Balkans against Muslim invasion in the Middle Ages.

For postmodern theorists fundamentalisms represent a reaction to the postmodern condition. The dislocation, decentring of the self and uncertainty about identities regarded as characteristic of postmodernity can be seen as encouraging individuals to look to the past for traditional certainties. However, critics of postmodernism argue that such movements can also be seen as a reaction to modernity rather than postmodernity. Modernity is represented by scientific rationality and secular belief systems such as communism. Fundamentalisms can be seen as an attempt to reassert pre-modern values based on religion, nationalism or ethnicity. The spread of fundamentalisms, and indeed more radical social movements such as environmentalism, may indicate that some of the metanarratives of modernity have been undermined or weakened, but these new belief systems may represent the rise of new metanarratives rather than the decline of all metanarratives.

Evaluation activity

'The emergence of many competing belief systems undermines the idea that there is any fundamental truth.'

'Contemporary societies are characterized not so much by a loss of belief as by a proliferation of very powerful belief systems.'

Evaluate the two statements above and state which perspective you feel comes closest to your own views.

Production and consumption

Postmodern social theorists have placed considerable emphasis on consumption. Writers such as Baudrillard argue that increasingly we consume signs, symbols, images and lifestyles as much as actual products. Some sociologists have seen the shopping mall as a metaphor for postmodern society. We are all like consumers strolling from shop to shop, picking and choosing products (or identities and lifestyles) as the mood takes us.

The problem with this type of approach is that it gives little attention to how the products or lifestyles come to be available to consumers in the first place. Marxist critics of postmodern theory argue that it fails to deal adequately with production. Nicholas Garnham (1990) argues that cultural commodities are no different from any other products. Capitalist business organizations will invest in developing and producing products like new pop groups, computer games or films because they believe that they are likely to provide them with a good return on their investments.

Cultural production and the Virgin Corporation

Paul Manning (1993) gives the example of the Virgin Corporation. In 1992 the Virgin Group had four multinational divisions with interests in music production, retail distribution, video, hotels, leisure, games and air travel. Virgin has since expanded its retailing chain of Megastores and has branched out into the insurance and personal finance markets. This enables the Virgin organization to achieve a high degree of what is called vertical integration. This means that research and development, production, marketing, distribution and retailing can all be carried out by different arms of the same corporation. As Richard Branson, the head of Virgin, explained:

> You start with artists. They need the best recording studios, so you build them. They need videos, so you set up a video company. They also need overseas companies to promote them. Ditto. They need more outlets to expand the market for their products, so you open more shops and so on.

(*Guardian*, 11 October 1991, quoted in Manning 1993, p. 21)

The point being made by Manning is that the cultural products we consume are powerfully shaped by the investment decisions of huge business organizations. For example, the endless recycling of old music may not be a symptom of the postmodern mixing of musical styles but of the conservatism of big music corporations. New and innovative bands represent a risk that may not result in profits for sponsoring companies. Songs that have already been a hit are a safer bet, albeit repackaged for a new generation of consumers.

Writers like Manning thus point to the continuing relevance of Marx's concern with production relations and to the tendency of postmodern theorists to ignore them and focus instead on the process of consumption. It can be argued that consumers do not freely choose lifestyles or consumption patterns but are all too often constrained by what is currently promoted by big business interests. Thus the shift from listening to music on records to CDs may be due as much to the marketing of CDs and the lack of availability of records and equipment to play them on as to the demand from music consumers for a new format.

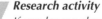

Research activity

If you have a shopping mall in your town or city, visit it and make notes on the following points:

- *What lifestyles, images and identities are offered to consumers?*
- *Is there really a choice or is this limited by what retailers have on offer?*
- *Which retail organizations are represented in the mall?*
- *What proportion of them are part of large national or multinational chains?*
- *What implications does this have for consumer choice?*

Report your findings and compare them with other students in your group.

Postmodernity or higher modernity?

Sociology in the twentieth century has been dominated by the work of classical social theorists such as Marx, Durkheim and Weber. They were all concerned in different ways with the consequences of living in a modern industrial society. As we approach the end of the twentieth century some sociologists argue that these modern social theories are no longer adequate to understand the very different societies that are emerging. Postmodern theories are seen as offering a radical alternative which is more relevant to the contemporary postmodern age.

A number of other writers have sought to defend modern (as opposed to postmodern) sociology. They have argued that while classical sociological theories certainly need reformulating in the light of contemporary developments, there is no reason why we should abandon the attempt to understand society in a social scientific way. These writers have also pointed out that in many respects current human societies are better viewed as a further development of modernity, rather than the radical break with the past indicated by the concept of postmodernity. In the next section we shall examine the work of three influential sociologists, who argue that the contemporary world can be seen as a higher stage of modernity rather than as postmodern.

Anthony Giddens

Anthony Giddens's theory of structuration has already been introduced in the previous chapter (pp. 206–7). Structuration implies that society is created and influenced by human action, but that we are also constrained as individuals by society. This argument is implicit in Giddens's view of the modern world. He likens the modern world which has developed since the seventeenth century to a juggernaut. He describes this as 'a runaway engine of enormous power which, collectively as human beings, we can drive to some extent but which also threatens to rush out of control and which could rend itself asunder' (Giddens 1990, p. 139).

Giddens thus sees the development of modern societies as unpredictable and difficult to control, though some critics like Ian Craib (1992) have pointed out that this seems difficult to reconcile with his emphasis on the power of human agency. Nevertheless, Giddens is not wholly pessimistic about the ability of ordinary people to influence the direction of social change. He points to the success of new social movements such as environmentalism (in encouraging governments to exert some control over the global risks to the planet) and feminism (in encouraging more egalitarian and caring personal relationships).

Giddens argues that modernity has four main characteristics:

1 **Capitalism**. This is based on commodity production, private ownership of capital, propertyless wage labour and a class system based on these characteristics.

2 **Industrialism**. This involves the use of inanimate power sources and machinery to produce goods and also to facilitate transportation, communication and domestic life.

3 **Surveillance capacities**. Here Giddens draws on the work of Foucault (see pp. 76–80). Giddens argues that in modernity populations are subject to much more effective supervision. For example, governments can keep detailed computerized records on their citizens and companies can monitor the productivity of their workers.

4   **Control of the means of violence**. Unlike pre-modern societies ordinary people may not legitimately use violence to settle disputes. The use of violence is centralized in the hands of the state, notably in the military. War itself becomes increasingly industrialized.

Modern technology means that human beings have a much greater capacity to kill one another than in societies of the past.

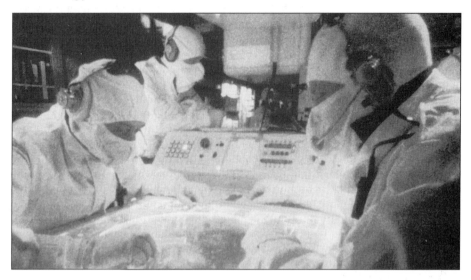

Time and space

Giddens argues that modernity has important consequences for our sense of time and space. In modern societies time has become standardized by the use of clocks, uniform calendars, international time zones and so on. The linkage between time and space is also broken. In the past, distances were measured by how long they took to walk and time was measured by the movement of the sun and the changing of the seasons. Today, time and space are compressed; for example, a person can travel from London to New York on Concorde and return the same day. Electronic communications are virtually instantaneous, enabling live television coverage of events on the other side of the world.

Modern communications allow people who are physically very distant from one another to engage in social relations. These dealers on the London stock exchange may be making investment decisions in the Tokyo, New York or Hong Kong stock markets via their computer screens.

Application activity
Give your own examples of ways in which our perceptions of time and space in the modern world are different from those of traditional or pre-modern societies.

Disembedding

Giddens argues that this has had the consequence of **disembedding** social relations from local contexts and restructuring them across indefinite spans of time and space. One important disembedding mechanism is **money**. In early modern societies money provided a symbolic token of wealth allowing a wider range of business transactions. In contemporary modern societies this has been taken further. Financial transactions can now take place via electronic communication, allowing financiers to make investment decisions affecting the stock markets of distant countries.

Like some postmodernists, Giddens sees this as having important consequences for our identity and sense of place. As individuals we no longer feel rooted in a particular place or community. Giddens see this change as having its origins in the beginnings of modernity, rather than as something novel to the twentieth century. Voyages of discovery from the fifteenth century onwards began to change Europeans' sense of space, while industrialization demanded standardized timekeeping so that hours of work could be measured by employers. Modern transport and communications have only extended and accelerated the compression of time and space and thus do not represent a radical break with modernity.

Money also illustrates another aspect of modernity: trust. Because we are involved in relations with many people we have never met, we increasingly have to rely on trust. Thus we trust our banks to look after our money and pay our bills for us; we trust insurance companies to pay up if we have an accident; and we trust the government or our pension scheme to pay us a pension when we retire. The whole economic and legal system of modern societies relies on this kind of trust to operate.

Reflexivity and self-identity

In *Modernity and Self-Identity* (1991) Giddens goes on to explore the consequences of modernity for the self. He argues that in the modern world the self has become a **reflexive project**. By this he means that we increasingly reflect upon ourselves and our place in the world. The exploration, creation and maintenance of the self is, in Giddens's view, a continuous and all-pervasive project for individuals in modern societies. Like Goffman (see pp. 194–6), Giddens sees us as constantly concerned with our image and how we present ourselves to others. He suggests that this is particularly apparent in our concern with the body, for example the obsession with diet, exercise, health, make-up, clothing and so on. In pre-modern societies, what a person ate or how they dressed were taken for granted and were often prescribed by the traditional rules of society. In modern societies they are much more questions of personal choice requiring careful consideration. The proliferation of books, magazines, TV programmes and videos devoted to advice and information about lifestyles, health and fitness gives some support to Giddens's argument.

The body and identity

The body is now a major area of interest for sociologists. Many sociologists observe how in modern societies the body has come to be something that is worked on and manipulated. Feminist writers like Susie Orbach (1993) point to the fact that eating disorders such as anorexia nervosa (starving oneself) and bulimia (bingeing and then vomiting) are overwhelmingly female problems. For feminists, this reflects the images of slimness and femininity projected in the media, and also the fact that, for many young women, determining what they eat may be one of the few ways in which they feel they can assert power and control in their lives. Other studies (Dutton 1995) have described how men may seek to manipulate their bodies in different ways, for example through the cult of body building. (For a useful discussion of this area see Benson 1997.)

Giddens argues that there is a threat of **personal meaninglessness** in modern life: serious issues such as sickness and death tend to be hidden away from everyday life so that we do not have to think about them. The concern with our bodies may be one of the ways in which we try to find meaning in our lives by pursuing projects with a view to becoming slim, muscular, healthy or beautiful. Despite the threat of meaninglessness, Giddens is optimistic that the increasing reflexivity of individuals will lead them to ponder important moral and philosophical questions, ultimately leading to a **remoralization** of society.

Interpretation activity

How can Giddens's ideas about reflexivity and self-identity be applied to the magazine articles illustrated above?

Collect a selection of teenage/women's/men's magazines and analyse how far it is true that a concern with lifestyle, identities and the body is characteristic of these media.

Modernity and intimate relationships

Giddens's optimism about modernity is also reflected in his book, *The Transformation of Intimacy* (1992). Here he focuses on the nature of personal relationships in the modern world. Giddens argues that these have been transformed into something closer to what he calls a **pure relationship**. By this he means a relationship which individuals enter into purely for its own sake and which continues only because both parties derive satisfaction from it. Thus in pre-modern societies marriage was often more an economic relationship between two families than a personal or sexual relationship between two individuals. In modern societies marriage is seen more in terms of the satisfaction each partner can gain from the relationship. High divorce rates are no doubt a consequence of this, as most people see little point in continuing a relationship when it no longer satisfies one or both parties. Moreover, people have greater choice in the kinds of intimate relationship they can engage in, with more tolerance of cohabitation, homosexual relationships and other kinds of relationship not based on conventional marriage.

While many conservative critics see this trend as symptomatic of a decline in morality in modern society, Giddens sees as it as the basis of a new kind of morality. He points to the democratization of personal relationships brought about by feminism, where women increasingly expect to be treated as equals and are less likely to tolerate subjugation and abuse by men.

 Evaluation activity
Evaluate Giddens's claim that intimate relationships in modern societies tend to have the characteristics of a 'pure relationship'.
Consider arguments and evidence both for and against the proposition before reaching your own conclusion.

Evaluation of Giddens

Giddens's work has had an enormous influence on sociologists' ideas about modernity: some have gone so far as to describe him as the greatest living British sociologist. Certainly, Giddens's work has played an important role in pointing out how a variety of existing sociological theories can be synthesized or fused together. His work thus draws on the work of writers such as Goffman and Garfinkel in understanding the nature of social action in everyday life, but also draws on the classical theories of Marx and Weber in analysing the transition from traditional societies to modernity and the role of wider social systems.

Giddens's theories, however, go beyond classical sociology. His work highlights many of the momentous changes affecting modern societies today, for example the acceleration of globalization, the compression of time and space, the rise of new social movements and the development of new kinds of intimate relationships. Giddens has been at the forefront of those sociologists who have argued that we cannot understand these changes solely by relying on concepts and theories developed in the nineteenth century. At the same time, Giddens has rejected the postmodernist argument that we should abandon any attempt at a rational understanding of what is going on in the social world. Giddens, like other modernist sociologists, seems to believe that the Enlightenment project of attaining a rational understanding of social life is still worth pursuing.

Some of the criticisms of Giddens's work have already been explored in the previous chapter (see pp. 206–7), in particular the problematical relationship between structure and action. This leads Derek Layder (1994) to criticize aspects of Giddens's analysis of modernity. Giddens tends to represent structures as simply the outcome of human actions. This ignores the extent to which structures assume a life of their own and become difficult for human beings to control. For example, the process of globalization and the development of massive transnational business organizations is the result of human action, but this is a process which it would now appear difficult for individuals to change. Giddens himself, however, does acknowledge this tendency of structures to achieve a life of their own with his metaphor of modernity as a 'juggernaut out of control'. There is perhaps a shift in Giddens's thinking, from his emphasis on human agency in his work on structuration to an emphasis in his more recent work on the degree to which the structures of modernity are out of control.

A related problem for Layder is that Giddens tends to 'flatten out social reality' (Layder 1994, p. 142). By this he means that Giddens fails to distinguish between those aspects of social reality which are directly and immediately controllable by individuals and those which are more distant in terms of how they impinge on daily experience. Thus how we conduct ourselves in everyday encounters – for example, cashing a cheque at the bank – represents a different level of analysis from the place that bank has in the global economy, which is rather more distant from our daily experience, even though it may well affect aspects of our lives, such as interest rates on loans. Layder thus suggests that in combining structure and action in his concept of structuration, Giddens has failed to build in an element of 'depth' into his theory that would capture the difference between the more immediate and more distant aspects of social reality.

Ulrich Beck

Like Giddens, the German sociologist Ulrich Beck views contemporary societies as moving, not into postmodernity but into a higher stage of modernity. Beck argues that while early modern society was an **industrial society**, we are now developing into a **risk society**. He, too, sees modern societies as increasingly reflexive. By this he means that individuals reflect more on their possible courses of action, which are not determined so much by structural constraints such as class. This means that individuals' social relationships and social networks are more freely chosen.

Risk society

According to Beck, the transition from industrial society to risk society means that the issue of the distribution of wealth becomes less important socially, while the issue of how risk can be prevented or minimized becomes of major importance. As Beck puts it, the ideal of equality has been replaced by the ideal of safety. Ironically, it is the very processes involved in the production of wealth which produce the major risks of the risk society. Pollution, nuclear accidents, diseases caused by contaminated food and the unforeseen side-effects of drugs, all provide examples of the kind of risks associated with modern life with which Beck is concerned.

BSE linked to new strain of CJD in humans

Application activity

What relevance does Beck's concept of a risk society have to the issue illustrated above?

Like some postmodern theorists such as Lyotard, Beck is critical of modern science and points out that 'it is no exaggeration to say that in the way they deal with risks in many areas, the sciences have squandered until further notice their historical reputation for rationality' (1992, p. 70). However, unlike Lyotard, Beck sees the risks associated with scientific progress as evidence that we still inhabit a modern society. Modern science has always generated these risks; what characterizes the new stage of modernity is the scale of these risks, which are now vastly greater in both time and space.

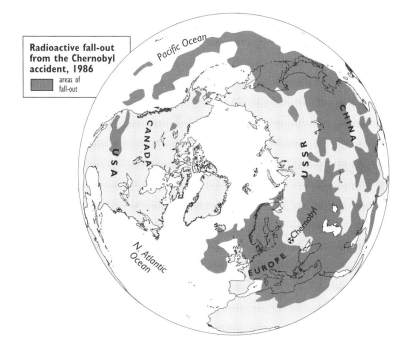

Radioactive fall-out from the Chernobyl accident, 1986
areas of fall-out

Application activity

1 *Using the map above, explain why Beck argues that many of the risks affecting the world today are global in scale.*
2 *Why might risks such as nuclear fallout extend across time as well as space?*
3 *Give examples of other global risks similar to those associated with nuclear power. How might the existence of such risks affect the way people live their lives at the end of the twentieth century?*

Evaluation of Beck

Much of Beck's argument echoes aspects of Giddens's work, in particular his view that as we move into higher modernity the scale on which human societies operate becomes ever larger. As we have noted, there is obviously much evidence to support his view that this is associated with ever-increasing risks.

Beck argues that these risks tend to affect everyone equally and that we all therefore have a vested interest in working to reduce risks, for example by supporting safer environmental policies. His critics have pointed out that risks are not in fact equal, but fall most heavily on disadvantaged groups. Thus western countries may relocate dangerous industrial processes in the third world, where health and safety legislation or controls on pollution are weaker. People in those regions may therefore be at greater risk of industrial accidents and diseases. Similarly, in advanced industrial societies the poorest citizens are likely to be those most exposed to hazards to health in the workplace, in the environment and in cheaper foodstuffs.

Jürgen Habermas

Jürgen Habermas is often regarded as one of the leading defenders of modernity in sociology and has also strongly criticized postmodern social theorists. Habermas's criticisms of postmodern theory have been summarized by Robert Holub (1991) as follows.

1 *It is not clear if postmodernists are engaged in producing serious social theories or literature.* If they are producing social theories, then their failure to make use of the normal rules of evidence and ways of expressing oneself in the social sciences means that their work is incomprehensible. If they are simply producing literature then their work cannot be taken seriously as social science.

2 *Postmodernists are animated by normative sentiments.* Postmodernists tend to deny that they have any normative position; in other words, they refuse to support any one political or ideological position over another. However, Habermas suggests they have merely hidden their normative sentiments. Moreover, by failing to state their own normative position they fail to offer any solutions as to how we might create a better or more meaningful society.

3 *Postmodernism fails to differentiate phenomena and practices that occur in modern society.* In other words, postmodernists engage in broad generalizations. For example, they see the world as dominated by power and surveillance but do not look in detail at specific sources of oppression in the modern world, such as those based on class, gender, ethnicity or rich versus poor nations.

4 *Postmodernists ignore everyday life and its practices.* The concerns of interactionists and ethnomethodologists with how individuals make sense of the world around them in a rational way are central to Habermas's work. He suggests that it is the ability of humans to communicate rationally with each other that gives hope for a better understanding of the social world and the construction of a better society. He accuses postmodernists of failing to address how ordinary people make sense of the world. Thus, for Baudrillard, the masses are 'a black hole' and he makes little attempt to discover how ordinary people interpret media images, signs and simulacra.

Modernity: an incomplete project

For postmodernists, the Enlightenment project of modernity has failed. Science has failed to offer a more rational understanding of the world and political ideologies aimed at liberating human beings have simply resulted in new forms of oppression. Habermas, however, rejects this analysis and believes that modernity is 'an unfinished project' rather than a failure.

Habermas's early work was strongly influenced by the Frankfurt School of critical theory (see pp. 64–5). Members of the Frankfurt School argued that in modern capitalist society science and technology had not been used to liberate human beings, but had instead been used to create a system of exploitation and domination. The Frankfurt writers argued that, because of this, science (including social science) was not a neutral form of knowledge but was inextricably linked to the technical requirements of a capitalist system of domination. Habermas has some sympathy with this, but he argues that the Enlightenment project – which aimed to establish a more rational understanding of the world – should not be completely abandoned.

Instrumental and communicative rationality

Habermas argues that thinkers since the Enlightenment have been too concerned with 'instrumental rationality' at the expense of what he calls 'communicative rationality'. **Instrumental rationality** involves applying technical means to achieve specific ends, using whatever means are deemed to be most rational or efficient to achieve the end. Max Weber especially emphasized this kind of rationality in his work on bureaucracy. Weber argued that the spread of bureaucracy in modern life was due to its technical superiority. Henry Ford's car assembly line or McDonald's standardization of burger production represent successful attempts to apply bureaucratic systems in order to maximize production of specific products.

Habermas argues that in stressing this kind of rationality we ignore communicative rationality. **Communicative rationality** involves the way in which people attempt to reach understandings in interactive situations. This is the type of rationality emphasized by writers such as Mead and symbolic interactionists. Habermas argues that in the case of instrumental action individuals are persuaded to cooperate because of 'sanctions, gratifications, force or money'. Thus workers in car factories or McDonald's restaurants cooperate with the system because they want to earn money and keep their jobs, not necessarily because they believe the production system is how they would like work to be organized. In communicative action people are persuaded to cooperate because they can see the reasoning behind the arguments of others. The aim is to reach a mutual understanding rather than for one party to force or bribe others to do what they want.

Validity claims

Habermas argues that in communicative action people put forward validity claims in order to convince others of the rightness of their arguments; these are of three types:

1 Claims based on the objective, external and factual world about the best way of achieving a desired state of affairs.

3 Claims based on the world of interpersonal relations arguing about the normative rightness of what is being claimed.

4 Claims drawing on the world of subjective experience based on the sincerity of one person's advice to another.

Application activity

Derek Layder gives the following example of action based on communicative rationality. Consider the claims made by each party in this dispute and how they might provide examples of Habermas's three types of validity claims.

> For instance a daughter may take it upon herself to convince her aged, widowed mother, who lives on her own in what has become a red light district in the city centre, to move out of this neighbourhood ... The daughter may suggest a number of things to back this up which draw upon the three worlds and types of claim Habermas identifies. For example, she may suggest that it is a dangerous area for an aged person to live and that her mother therefore runs a greater risk of being attacked or burgled ... Secondly, she may suggest that a senior citizen cannot lead a dignified existence in such an area because people who live there are 'looked down upon' by others living in more respectable neighbourhoods ... Finally, the daughter may try to convince her aged parent by saying that she feels unhappy about the situation and that this could be considerably alleviated if her mother moves to a safer and more respectable area.
>
> Now the mother may counter these arguments with her own (it's not really dangerous, other people are snobs, your feelings are not my problem) and win the argument against moving. On the other hand, the parent may be convinced and ask her daughter to help her to move away. In either case, shared understanding and eventual agreement has been reached through the mutual give and take of discussions involving various claims to validity. Habermas feels that in such instances of communicative action there is a natural push towards a shared understanding based on the free exchange of arguments founded upon genuine information (rather than on deceit, lies or manipulation – that is being economical with the truth).

(Layder 1994, p. 191)

Now think of some examples of your own to illustrate the three types of validity claims.

Lifeworld and system

Habermas sees the kind of validity claims described above as taking place against the background of a set of assumptions: for example social experience, cultural knowledge and language forms. These assumptions provide us with recipes for dealing with social situations and help us to make sense of the social world. Habermas describes this world of competing validity claims and cultural assumptions as the **lifeworld**. In this respect, Habermas's work has some parallels with the phenomenologists' concept of common sense knowledge (see p. 198).

Alongside the concept of lifeworld Habermas has developed the concept of **system**. Habermas's concept of social system has some similarities to that of Parsons (see pp. 44–8). Like Parsons, he sees the system as the means by which actions are organized and coordinated in relations of functional interdependence in order to allow a society to survive and adapt itself to its environment. Thus Habermas draws on both action theorists like Mead and structural or systems theorists like Parsons.

Habermas argues that in simple societies lifeworld and system are virtually indistinguishable. For example, in hunting and gathering societies social organization is typically based on kinship. Social relations are typically linked to religious or magical beliefs. Economic activities such as hunting (part of the system) may be imbued with spiritual significance or accompanied by religious rituals (part of the lifeworld).

The development of modern societies

Habermas argues that the emergence of modern societies has been accompanied by a growing specialization of systems such as economic and political systems. These systems have tended to develop their own rules of action (for example, market forces in the economy), which have less and less relation to the lifeworld. In these circumstances, Habermas argues that communicative action becomes more and more difficult. Areas such as law, science, politics and economics are increasingly the province of technical experts and ordinary people have difficulty in sorting through the competing validity claims made in these areas. In these circumstances, money and power have become more important as means of deciding between competing validity claims and as the major influences on the running of the social system.

For example, whether or not to shut a factory and make hundreds of workers unemployed is no longer a question to be decided by communicative action, perhaps by the workers and employers rationally debating the issue. Rather, it is the money and power of the employer that decides the issue. Employers are likely to decide on the basis of instrumental rationality that the factory is no longer profitable or that they can make a bigger profit elsewhere. Therefore the workers' claims that their jobs and their community are important need not be considered.

Application activity
Think of other examples of situations in modern society where issues are decided on the basis of instrumental rationality (e.g. market forces, profitability, the needs of those with power) rather than communicative rationality (e.g. through shared discussion of the needs of all those involved).

Modernity and the lifeworld

In these circumstances Habermas, like Giddens, sees individuals as feeling that modern society is out of control. In Habermas's terms the system has become detached from the lifeworld. However, Habermas argues that the system is now also colonizing the lifeworld. Thus in making decisions in everyday life we are increasingly influenced by issues of money and power and less able to engage in communicative rationality. For example, the environment we live in is threatened by economic exploitation. This has an impact on our lifeworld through such things as higher levels of pollution, loss of unspoilt natural scenery, possible global warming and so on.

Unlike earlier members of the Frankfurt School and postmodern theorists, Habermas is not pessimistic about our ability to counter this sort of threat. He points to a variety of forms of resistance to the colonizing tendencies of the system towards the lifeworld: most notably, new social movements such as environmentalism, feminism and the peace movement. Such movements have called for a free and open debate about the future direction of social development. They have questioned the view that society should necessarily be run on the basis of market forces or in the interests of the rich and powerful. New social movements also emphasize the value of personal relationships and the moral and spiritual aspects of life which Habermas believes have been relegated in importance in comparison with technical and utilitarian values.

Evaluation activity
Habermas suggests that new social movements offer the possibility of claiming back the lifeworld from the instrumental rationality of the economic system. Using the example illustrated above and any examples of your own, evaluate this claim.

Modernity: an incomplete project?

Habermas argues that modernity is an incomplete project. Since the Enlightenment we have succeeded in developing a social system that delivers an unparalleled standard of living. Habermas does not wish to jettison this benefit, but he points out that it has been gained at the expense of the lifeworld. He calls for a greater emphasis on communicative rationality in everyday life, whereby the viewpoints of all actors in a situation are considered on their merits, rather than simply questions of economic utility and efficiency predominating at the expense of quality of life. Habermas rejects the nihilism of postmodernists, who seem to see little prospect of changing anything. He also rejects the relativism of postmodern theory. Habermas clearly believes it is possible to arbitrate between competing claims about truth, but this must be based on communicative rationality, whereby those involved come to some agreement on what is true or correct.

Evaluation of Habermas

Habermas has been portrayed as the main champion of modernist sociology in the face of the criticisms of postmodernists. In particular, Habermas has encouraged those sociologists who believe in the Enlightenment project of using the social sciences to make rational sense of the social world and in the long run to create a better society. Habermas's ideas offer a programme not only for sociologists but also for political change. Habermas clearly believes that political and economic institutions (what he calls the system) need to be made more responsive to the needs of individuals and their personal lives (the lifeworld). He points to the new social movements as offering hope of a new kind of politics based on human needs rather than economic calculation.

Critics of Habermas see his work as over-optimistic and even utopian. Postmodernists like Baudrillard are sceptical about political action achieving anything, since they believe that political protests disappear into the black hole of the media and fail to have any real impact on the ideas of ordinary people. Marxist critics by contrast have criticized Habermas for his emphasis on communicative action as the means of achieving political change. They argue that simply sitting around talking to one another will not necessarily change the world and that sometimes more violent and revolutionary action is required to accomplish change.

Writers such as Zygmunt Bauman have suggested that modernity is inevitably repressive and destructive. Bauman (1989) points out that the Holocaust relied on the same bureaucratic system to put to death six million Jews as is used to deliver social security or run a hamburger restaurant. Bauman argues that the Nazis simply used modern technology (in the form of railways and gas chambers), together with bureaucratic organization, and applied them to the horrific goal of the 'final solution'. While bureaucracy might appear to be a neutral tool that can be used for good or evil aims, Bauman believes that it has a tendency to favour inhuman processes. He suggests that there is no guarantee that in the future bureaucratic systems could not be used for even more terrible purposes than the Holocaust.

Evaluation activity
Organize a class debate on the following statement: 'Contemporary human societies have become so vast and complex that the organization of social life is beyond the control of individuals'.

Conclusion

Although some sociologists appear pessimistic about the future of modern societies, it would be a mistake to dismiss Habermas's more optimistic arguments. It is only by taking control of our own destinies that we can achieve our full potential as human beings. Social sciences can play a part in understanding how social systems can be organized to serve the needs of people rather than to dominate their lives.

Coursework suggestions
Postmodern culture offers a number of exciting possibilities for coursework, but as this is a vast and complex area it is important to keep your research aims clear, simple and small in scale. For example, you might be interested in investigating the impact of postmodernity on cultural forms. However, you should restrict yourself to a fairly specific area, perhaps advertisements, films or music. You would need to operationalize the term postmodern to define what aspects of culture might be counted as showing postmodern influences. You would also need to consider how you would assess the impact of postmodernity, for example by using methods such as content analysis and semiotics. In terms of evaluation, you might also want to consider how far 'modern' influences continue to determine cultural forms. For example, what impact do systems of production and the ownership and control of culture industries have on the cultural forms you have investigated?

Giddens's work also offers some interesting coursework possibilities, particularly his idea that people are more reflexive and pursue life projects. This could be illustrated by a case study on a small group of people such as body builders, sports enthusiasts, or people dedicated to any hobby or leisure activity. Suitable methods for investigation might include in-depth interviews with a small sample of participants in order to uncover the meanings that their activities have for them and how far this affects their sense of identity. You could also include some participant observation if you have the opportunity to join such a group yourself.

Essay questions

1 'Theories of postmodernity have ignored the extent to which contemporary forms of cultural consumption are dominated by the requirements of the means of cultural production.' Discuss.

2 Assess the view that postmodernity has resulted in an increasing 'incredulity towards metanarratives'.

References and further reading

Atkinson, J. (1985) 'The changing corporation', in D. Clutterbuck (ed.), *New Patterns of Work*, Aldershot: Gower.

Baudrillard, J. (1975) *The Mirror of Production*, St Louis: Telos Press.

Baudrillard, J. (1981) 'Requiem for the media', in *For a Critique of the Political Economy of the Sign*, St Louis: Telos Press.

Baudrillard, J. (1983) *Simulations*, New York: Semiotext(e).

Bauman, Z. (1989) *Modernity and the Holocaust*, Cambridge: Polity Press.

Beck, U. (1992 [1986]) *Risk Society: Towards a New Modernity*, London: Sage.

Benson, S. (1997) 'The body, health and eating disorders', in K. Woodward (ed.), *Identity and Difference*, London: Sage in association with the Open University.

Craib, I. (1992) *Anthony Giddens*, London: Routledge.

Davie, G. (1995) 'Competing fundamentalisms', *Sociology Review*, April.

Dutton, K.R. (1995) *The Perfectible Body: The Western Idea of Physical Development*, London: Cassell.

Garnham, N. (1990) *Capitalism and Communication*, London: Sage.

Giddens, A. (1990) *The Consequences of Modernity*, Cambridge: Polity Press.

Giddens, A. (1991) *Modernity and Self-Identity*, Cambridge: Polity Press.

Giddens, A. (1992) *The Transformation of Intimacy*, Cambridge: Polity Press.

Hall, S. (1992) 'The question of identity', in S. Hall et al. (eds), *Modernity and Its Futures*, Cambridge: Polity Press.

Hebdidge, D. (1988) *Subculture: The Meaning of Style*, London: Routledge.

Holub, R. (1991) *Jürgen Habermas: Critic in the Public Sphere*, London: Routledge.

Jameson, F. (1984) 'Postmodernism, or the cultural logic of late capitalism', *New Left Review*, 146 (July/August), pp. 53–92.

Jameson, F. (1991) *Postmodernism or The Cultural Logic of Late Capitalism*, Durham, NC: Duke University Press.

Layder, D. (1994) *Understanding Social Theory*, London: Sage.

Lyotard, J.F. (1984 [1979]) *The Postmodern Condition: A Report on Knowledge*, Manchester: Manchester University Press.

Mandel, E. (1975) *Late Capitalism*, London: New Left Books.

Manning, P. (1993) 'Consumption, production and popular culture', *Sociology Review*, February.

Orbach, S. (1993) *Hunger Strike: The Anorectic's Struggle as a Metaphor of our Age*, Harmondsworth: Penguin.

Piore, M. and Sabel, C. (1984) *The Second Industrial Divide: Prospects for Prosperity*, New York: Basic Books.

Ritzer, G. (1993) *The McDonaldization of Society*, Thousand Oaks, CA: Pine Forge Press.

Ritzer, G. (1996) *Modern Sociological Theory*, London: McGraw-Hill.

Index

media *see* mass media
medical knowledge 77
members' methods 199
membership categories 202
membership categorization devices (MCD)
	202
Merton, R. 35–7
metanarratives 221–3, 231–2
Mies, M. 87
migrant labour 118–21
Miles, R. 113–14, 116–17, 121
Millett, K. 87
mode of production 55, 56, 224
Modelski, T. 183
modern society 244
modernism 212–47
modernity 15–18, 128–9, 234, 241–2, 244–5
Modood, T. 123–5
money 236, 244
monopoly capitalism 228
moral panic 155–7, 158
Morgan 101
Morley, D. 181–2
morphogenesis 207
mortification 196
Moss, H. 90
multiculturalism 19, 24, 124
multiple ideologies 73
multiracism 121–2
Murray, C. 120
mythology 174–6

names 111–13, 168, 196
narratives 221
National Association for the Advancement
	of Colored People (NAACP) 113
National Curriculum 12, 61, 91–2
national identity 130–1
national markets 130
nationalism 111, 128–30, 132–3, 137
	post-colonial nationalism 132
nationality 136
neo-Marxism 54
neo-Weberianism 72–4
neutrality 46
new man 101
new racism 119–20
New Right 105
new social movements 59, 215, 244, 245
normalization 77
norms 27, 31, 33, 44–5, 47, 50, 203
Northern Ireland 133–4

Oakley, A. 89–90, 91
O'Connell Davidson, J. 98
O'Donnell, M. 124
Oedipus complex 84
open texts 179–80
oral stage 84
Orbach, S. 236
orientalism 113–14
orientation 46
'other' 113–14

oversocialization 98

Pahl, R. 71
Pakulski, J. 74–5
paradigms 167
parenting 28–9, 33, 86, 88–90, 189–90,
	199–200
parole 166
Parsons, T. 7, 44–8, 72, 85–6, 187
	agency 206
	social system 243–4
	structural functionalism 50, 219–20
particularism 46–7
patriarchy 87–8, 97, 99–100, 206, 218, 220
pattern variables 46–7
peer groups 31–2
penis envy 84
performance 201
personal meaningless 237
phallic stage 84
phenomenology 50, 188, 197–8, 204
pleasure principle 6
plurivocality 220
political institutions 215
political society 62
politics 105, 244, 246
polymorphous perversity 85
polysemy 176, 179
populism 64
Postman, N. 145
postmodernism 25, 73, 75, 79, 212–47, 214
	feminism 97–8
	identity 126–7
	nationalism 137
	youth subculture 162
postmodernity 17–20
poststructuralism 76, 177, 194
poverty 65, 73
power 51, 54–81, 204–5, 222, 244
	blocs 63
	disciplinary 79
	knowledge 76–7
pragmatism 189
printing 129, 130
prisons 77–8, 79, 195, 196
production 55–6, 224, 232–3
projects 198
proletariat 59, 65
Protestant ethic 70–2
psychoanalytic theory 6–8, 84–5, 218, 220
psychology 197
punishment 77–8
pure relationships 237–8

race 111, 114–18, 121–2, 136, 158–60, 189
	terminological problems 113
racial dualism 123
racialization 121
racism 115–22, 158–60, 207, 219–20
Ranger, T. 131–2, 133
Rastafarianism 159, 160
rationality 242
rationalization 71

rave subculture 155–6, 160–2
reality principle 7
reciprocity 43
Redfield, R. 10
Redhead, S. 155
reflexivity 189, 236
regulative institutions 45
relationships 237–8
relativism 14–15
religion 32, 39–40, 48
remoralization 237
representations 224–5
research
	audience 183–4
	ethnicity 122
	gender 97–102
resistance 105, 126, 152
resocialization 33–4
revolutionary consciousness 59
Rich, A. 106
rituals 40, 131, 244
	national 130
	resistance 152
Ritzer, G. 214
Roethlisberger, F.J. 32
roles 22, 33, 44–5, 83, 85–6, 190
romantic fiction 97
romantic individualism 95
Rubin, L. 104
rules 166, 191
Rushdie, S. 123–4

Sacks, H. 201–2
Said, E. 113
Saunders, P. 74
Saussure, F. de 165–7, 187, 190
Savage, M. 73–4
schools 30–1, 60–1
	see also education
Schudson, M. 130–1
Schutz, A. 197–8
science 92, 221–2, 223, 240
Scotland 133–4, 136
secularization 71
Segal, L. 101–2
Self 90
'self' 113, 194–5
	identity 236
	mortification 34
	orientation 46
semiotics 96, 151, 153, 165–70, 177, 181
	structuration 194
	structures 183
sex identity 200–1
sexuality 79, 82, 84–5, 88–90, 104–5
Sharpe, S. 93
Shils, E. 129, 131
signified 165–6
signifiers 165–6, 176, 224
signs 165–85, 224, 225–6, 232, 241
Simmel, G. 11
simulacra 225–6, 241
slavery 115–16